Belfast punk and the Troubles

Manchester University Press

Belfast punk and the Troubles

An oral history

Fearghus Roulston

MANCHESTER UNIVERSITY PRESS

Copyright © Fearghus Roulston 2022

The right of Fearghus Roulston to be identified as the author of this work has been asserted by them in accordance with the Copyright, Designs and Patents Act 1988.

Published by Manchester University Press
Oxford Road, Manchester M13 9PL

www.manchesteruniversitypress.co.uk

British Library Cataloguing-in-Publication Data
A catalogue record for this book is available from the British Library

ISBN 978 1 5261 5223 7 hardback
ISBN 978 1 5261 8246 3 paperback

First published 2022
Paperback published 2024

The publisher has no responsibility for the persistence or accuracy of URLs for any external or third-party internet websites referred to in this book, and does not guarantee that any content on such websites is, or will remain, accurate or appropriate.

Typeset
by New Best-set Typesetters Ltd

Well, what the fuck is it about? Like I said, I did it to stand up for Airdrie. I did it because of Memorial Device. I did it because, for a moment, everybody was doing everything, reading, listening, writing, creating, sticking up posters, taking notes, passing out, throwing up, rehearsing, rehearsing, rehearsing in dark windowless rooms at 2pm like the future was just up ahead and we better be ready for it. And now already it's the rotten past. That's why I did it, if you want to know the truth.

David Keenan, This is Memorial Device

To my parents

Contents

Acknowledgements	viii
Note on transcription and notation	x
Introduction	1
1 Alternative Ulster? Sectarianism, segregation and the punk scene	11
2 The Belfast punk scene in cultural memory	36
3 Epiphany, transgression and movement	65
4 Making affective and political spaces	91
5 Gender, respectability and emigration	116
6 Collecting, storytelling and memory	141
Conclusion	167
Appendix: Bands	173
Select bibliography	179
Index	191

Acknowledgements

It has been a little strange drafting a book about friendship, sociality, collectivity and the pleasure of live music during a period where all of these things have been harder to find in the context of a global pandemic. But it continues to be true that no writing is individual, and the work here would not have been possible without the help of many people. Firstly, thanks to Graham, Leila and Catherine, who were crucial in the development of the research presented here; thanks especially to Graham, for his enthusiastic help with the production of the book itself.

Much of the writing here was done while working at the University of Brighton, and my friends and colleagues there have been a constant support. Thanks to Afxentis, Becca, Louise, Emma, Eugene, Gab, Gio, James, Joel, Kristin, Lars, Lorenza, Marina, Meg, Melayna, Sam and Viktoria for their help. The Complex Temporalities reading group – Áine, Andrea, Gari, Ian, Jessica, Kasia, Melina, Struan, Sophie, Vansch – provided both inspiration and relief. Thanks also to the Centre for Memory, Narrative and Histories at Brighton; to Joel and the Institute for Historical Research's oral history seminar series, where one chapter here got a helpful early airing; and to colleagues at the Oral History journal, particularly Isabel. Anna and Paul also offered helpful comments on an early draft of the manuscript. Tom Dark and Manchester University Press have been invaluable in bringing the book to print. Finally, Kate has been the ideal reader of all of my drafts and remains an irreplaceable co-writer and ally.

Outside of the university, my thanks go to my friends in London and Ireland, with a special mention to David for his helpful reading of Chapter 6; to my partner Carla, whose thoughtful and generative reading has been important throughout; to Titus the cat; to Lucy, who made the posters and helped make the book possible; to Imogen and Sophie in the writing group; to Debbie at the British Library; to Marc for some very patient driving lessons; to comrades in Brighton Solidarity Federation (and to all the non-competitive footballers). My family (Caitlin, Marie, Patrick, Stephen) have provided care, patience, amusement and unhelpful suggestions that I should interview Van Morrison throughout – love and thanks to them. Finally, my deepest gratitude goes to all of my interviewees, whose warmth, wit and passion form the best part of the book. I hope I have captured something of that energy here.

Note on transcription and notation

Wherever possible I have retained the original ordering and style of the speaker, which extends to an attempt to render informal language precisely ('gonna' for 'going to', for instance). An ellipsis (…) in the transcript signifies a pause in the formulation of a sentence, and a dash (–) signifies a shorter pause. An ellipsis in square brackets […] signifies an excision made by me after transcription, generally for reasons of clarity. Square brackets are sometimes used within transcripts to include non-verbal cues [such as laughter], contextual information or clarifications. And occasionally, when my question or statement cuts across an interviewee, the question is included in square brackets within the text: in general, questions by me are signified by a paragraph break and the initial 'F'.

Introduction

This book is an oral history of the punk scene in Belfast from the mid-1970s to the mid-1980s. It reads a series of interviews with former participants in the scene to consider what they think about punk and about their experiences of growing up in Northern Ireland during the Troubles. As with other music scenes around the world, the Belfast punk scene was essentially something around and within which groups of young people congregated. Because the method used here is oral history, I am interested in two things about these congregations.

Firstly, I am interested in what they were. Or, to put that slightly differently, I am interested in what the constellation of places, institutions (record labels, venues), bands and quotidian practices that constituted the punk scene were in the specific context of Belfast during the Troubles, and in how this constellation was related to the wider social and cultural conditions of Northern Ireland. What does the specifically Northern Irish manifestation of punk tell us about the material, social and cultural world of the North in this period? How did the scene relate to the conditions of sectarianism, segregation and violence that everyone growing up in the North experienced in various ways? How should we make sense of the practices of sociality, friendship, intimacy and care that constituted the everyday life of the scene in relation to their wider social contexts?

Secondly, I am interested in how the congregations of the punk scene are remembered by former participants telling their stories in the present. Oral history, as Alessandro Portelli reminds us, 'tells us less about events than about their meaning'.[1] This suggests that when analysing oral sources we need to bear in mind that 'what is really important is that memory is not a passive depository of facts, but an active process of creation of meanings'.² How people create and narrate their memories can tell us something about the construction of subjectivity and about the residue of the past made visible in that construction. It can also tell us something about how social discourses about the past, or cultural memories, mediate and shape the formation and expression of individual memories. In addition to considering what the punk scene was, and analysing its relationship to Northern Irish society during the conflict, I will draw on the particular insights offered by oral history to connect individual memories of the punk scene to Northern Irish cultural memory. The book asks what it means to *have been* a punk – that is, how punkness unravels as a thread through the life course of my interviewees, and how they relate their subjectivity in the present to their experiences in the past. Alongside this, it will consider how the shared memory of the punk scene is connected to contestations around wider memory culture in Northern Ireland, where 'memories of the war – concerning, for example, what is at stake in the conflict, the justification of organised violence, what has been perpetrated and suffered, and by whom – structure the identities of participants and underpin their broader political aspirations in respect of a settlement'.³

The introduction will begin with a brief history of the punk scene in the city before suggesting some of the specific insights generated through using an oral history approach.

'Kids in funny clothes': a history of punk in Belfast

It is impossible to isolate a moment that you could call the start of the punk scene in Belfast, but the protests that followed The Clash's cancelled gig at the Ulster Hall on 20 October 1977 suggest one possible beginning. This could be described as the moment where the nascent punk scene saw itself for the first time, as teenagers from across Northern Ireland gathered on Bedford Street in central Belfast and swapped rumours about what was going to happen. Brian Young of Rudi wrote their song 'Cops' – which begins and ends with chants of 'SS, RUC' – in response to the heavy-handed tactics of the police (the Royal Ulster Constabulary) – who attempted to disperse the young crowd gathered outside the venue.⁴ He told me: 'It wasn't a Belfast, it wasn't a proper Belfast riot, it was like kids in funny clothes, you know what I mean, a few windows were broken and people sat in the road, it wasn't like a proper riot you know. But the police just went in as if it was. It was just stupid.'[5] Brian was also at pains to point out to me that Rudi's song should not be taken as an expression of anti-RUC or anti-state politics as such, and that it was inspired by the specific events of the Bedford Street riot rather than by any wider view on Northern Ireland or the Troubles. Another interviewee, Hector Heathwood, jocularly described the local news coverage of the scuffle as his first TV appearance: 'There's a bit of footage with me with a cop on each corner you know, and I'm trying to get my ma and da to look at something else.'[6]

Why the gig was actually cancelled remains unclear. The city council attributed it to issues with the venue's insurance, but both at the time and since many punks preferred to understand it as an expression of a diffuse anti-punk sentiment among elements of the Belfast establishment. In his memoir, the promoter, record shop owner and impresario Terri Hooley describes the subsequent events as perhaps 'the only riot of the Troubles where Catholics and Protestants were fighting on the same side', with a typical flair for fanning the flames of punk's mythology. For him, it emphasised that 'to be a punk was to be a pariah'.[7]

Caroline Coon, the artist and activist who was working as The Clash's manager in 1977, wrote an article about the night's events, published a week later in the weekly music magazine *Sounds*. Entitled 'Clash in the City of the Dead', it evokes an uncanny landscape that is at once familiar and exotic, normal and militarised. 'Belfast is one long nervously obsessive security check. You can't cross a road, drive down the street, walk into a shop or hotel without passing through an elaborate system of flashing lights, concrete and steel barricades, high barbed wire fences or road blocks.'[8] These markers of conflict sit in contrast with the crowd that turn up for the gig – 'within minutes of arriving in town, The Clash are surrounded by fans. Heavy punks. Safety pins through their cheeks. Dog collars. Bondage straps. The lot. They are feverishly excited' – who adhere reassuringly to the transnational signifiers of punkness as visible in London, Leeds or Manchester. But the comprehensibility of the young gig-goers only heightens the incomprehensibility of the city and the conflict, in Coon's account – in a particularly telling metaphor in terms of the construction of Northern Ireland as a place apart from the rest of the United Kingdom, 'The Clash are examined as if they are visitors bringing a magic interlude from another planet'.[9]

The band's bass player, Paul Simonon, speaks to a teenage laboratory assistant, George, and asks him if both Protestants and Catholics will attend the gig. George, presumably somewhat starstruck, says: 'Oh yes. We all mix and we get on together. Everybody's bored with the fighting. Only a minority are fighting. It's music we want to hear — not religion.'[10] But the crowd and the band are left disappointed when they're told the gig cannot go ahead. 'Slowly the fact that there's nothing anybody can do to save the gig sinks in. Go home everybody.'[11]

Between the laconic recollections of Brian and Hector, Terri Hooley's more bombastic account, and Caroline Coon's story about The Clash's abortive visit to the city, an image of Northern Irish punk is visible, projected against a second, backdrop image of Northern Irish society. Coon and Hooley represent punk as an oasis of non-sectarian sociality and interconnection in the midst of a violent conflict predicated on sectarian animosity; Brian and Hector, working in a lower key, represent punk as a site of youthful bravado and experimentation, still taking place in the context of the Troubles but perhaps sidestepping it rather than engaging it directly – 'it was like kids in funny clothes, you know what I mean', says Brian.[12] In that sense, the cancelled gig is a good beginning for thinking about punk and its situatedness in the context of the conflict.

But really the history of punk in Belfast started somewhere before this, with a handful of young people forming bands and buying records, avidly reading the music press to keep track of the scene's development in London and elsewhere, listening to John Peel and watching Top of the Pops and The Old Grey Whistle Test. Bars like the Viking in Belfast and the Trident in Bangor were attracting a punky crowd by 1976, and by 1977 Rudi had started playing gigs at the Glenmachan Hotel in the north-east of the city. The Undertones, in Derry, were beginning to play gigs around the same time.

In the same period in England, punk was entering a period of notoriety after the Sex Pistols' famous appearance on Bill Grundy's *Today* programme, on 1 December 1976. This incident (in which the band, goaded by Grundy, uttered a few obscenities on live, teatime television) had an impact in Northern Ireland, as did the media furore that surrounded it. Brian Young told me:

> Once 'God Save the Queen' came out sorta '77, people forget, the press, the Pistols were on that Bill Grundy show ... the press hyped it up something rotten ... Punk had sort of ... once it got popular like that and it got popular very quick through late '76 right into '77 ... there were a lot of, it actually lost it, it became more of a – I mean it was still, don't get me wrong, it was still brilliant, it was still really exciting, it was still the really early days over here – but it sort of in a way, in England certainly, it had lost its innocence.[13]

So just as punk was losing its innocence in England – becoming a media-driven spectacle rather than a do-it-yourself (DIY) movement, in Brian's account – it was hitting its stride in Northern Ireland. Terri Hooley, a former participant in the attenuated but persistent countercultural life of 1960s Belfast, opened the Good Vibrations record store in mid-1977, taking the lease on a derelict building on Great Victoria Street. Along with other record stores like Caroline Music and Rocky Mongo's, Good Vibrations became an important site for the Belfast punk scene, partly as somewhere to meet and hang out, and partly as somewhere to buy hard-to-find records from England and the USA. Just Books, an anarchist bookstore managed by Dave Hyndman and a rotating cast of comrades, opened up shop above Good Vibrations and became another gathering place, one that had a formative influence on the more politically minded participants in the scene. New bands began to form. Again, Brian's account of the early history of the scene is informative here. 'I mean I was at [the] first Stiffs gig and the first Outcasts gig and they were within a week of each other in late '77 in Paddy Lamb's in Ballyhackamore [a suburb of east Belfast]', he told me.[14] Stiff Little Fingers (the Stiffs) and The Outcasts were followed by a host of new bands in Belfast and in other towns around the country, as detailed in the comprehensive 2004 encyclopedia of this period in Belfast, *It Makes You Want to Spit*.[15] The Belfast punk fanzine *Alternative Ulster* also published its first issue in 1977.[16]

After The Clash's famous almost-gig in October 1977 was cancelled they returned to play the McMordie Hall, a student venue associated with Queen's University Belfast and now called the Mandela Hall, in December of the same year. Early in 1978 the Harp Bar and the Pound both started putting on regular gigs with local punk bands – the Harp even formed a small organising committee to arrange its punk nights featuring, among others, Terri Hooley and Hector Heathwood.[17] In February, two Rudi tracks – 'Big Time' and 'No. 1' – were recorded at Hydepark Studios in Templepatrick for Hooley's new record label, also called Good Vibrations; these went on sale in Terri's shop in April 1978, making them the first punk records cut in Northern Ireland. Three thousand copies were re-pressed by EMI in Dublin and the BBC DJ John Peel played the single on its release. In June, a Battle of the Bands concert was organised at the McMordie Hall featuring seven local punks bands, and in September the Ramones made their first of several visits to Belfast, a formative experience for many of the people I talked to about the scene. In the next six months or so Good Vibrations pressed several more records – 'Justa Nother Teenage Rebel' by The Outcasts, 'Teenage Kicks' by The Undertones, and other singles by Protex, the Xdreamysts, The Idiots and Spider. In 1979, John T. Davis' *Shellshock Rock*, a documentary about punk in Belfast, premiered in Cork, although it was withdrawn from the Cork Film Festival for dubious reasons at the last minute, in an echo of the cancelled Clash gig in 1977.[18]

Throughout the 1980s the punk scene fragmented and shrank, much as it did in England a couple of years earlier. Of most interest to this project is the small anarcho-punk scene that emerged in Belfast from the early 1980s. The first flashes of this came from the A Centre, a social centre organised by Dave Hyndman and others, who had previously been involved in the Just Books collective mentioned above. The A Centre opened on November 1981, remaining open for just six months or so before closing down following the end of its lease and some issues with the RUC. The anarcho-punk bands Crass, Poison Girls and Conflict all played there in this period, in a set of gigs that proved formative for another one of my interviewees, Petesy Burns.[19] In 1986 Petesy, along with Rab Wallace and some others, opened the Warzone Collective in a building near The John Hewitt pub in what has become the Cathedral Quarter. This was the most visible remainder from the ashes of the original punk scene throughout the 1980s, although many of the participants were different and the music and fashion changed a great deal.[20]

Oral history and memory

I will engage with this rich history throughout the book using an interpretative or a post-positivist oral history method inspired by Luisa Passerini, Penny Summerfield, Alistair Thomson, Graham Dawson and Alessandro Portelli, among others. Rather than fragmenting the interviews into thematic chunks, or using them to illustrate a chronological re-narration of the events described in the previous section, I have written about a small number of interviews in some detail, analysing only one or two in each chapter. The decision to do this was partly driven by the strong impression each interview made on me after I had transcribed it, and by a desire to convey something of that impression in the analysis. Giving each interview a relatively large amount of space helps to keep the interviewees' voices a little louder in the mix, and to insist on their capacity to order, make sense of and narrate their own experiences and memories rather than to position either me or the reader as the sole carriers of that capacity. It also emphasises the intersubjective, constructed nature of the interview as an encounter, or as a moment in time – it is this moment and this interaction the text of the interview gives us access to, and any analysis needs to bear this intersubjectivity in mind.

These general methodological imperatives were reinforced by three specific facets of the history the interviews are engaged with. Firstly, because I am interested in everyday life (both as a way of thinking about what it was like to be a punk and as a way of thinking about what it was like to grow up in Northern Ireland), engaging with the interview material in granular details makes it easier to bring the quotidian and the everyday into view, in a way that a thematic approach (for instance) might not. Rather than thinking about the punk scene as separate from the social worlds of the North, I want to see what happens when we think about it as imbricated in those worlds. The use of oral history in this project is driven by my intuition that listening to these narratives is a way of writing about the daily actions and performances that made Belfast's social world.[21] In his oral history of the Fosse Ardeatine massacre during the German occupation of Rome in 1944, Alessandro Portelli argues that the history of everyday life and the memory of everyday life is particularly potent in this context because 'history wears a capital H, and its burden seems to frustrate and annihilate the work of memory or to make it seem irrelevant. Too often, history is a faraway sphere, distant from the daily lives of its people or a crushing, annihilating weight upon them.'[22] The role of history with a capital H is similarly potent in Northern Ireland, meaning the history and memory of everyday life has a similar resonance.[23]

Secondly, the relationship between sectarianism, segregation and subjectivity in Northern Ireland is relatively understudied, and focusing on how people narrate their memories of punk is a way to think about this relationship, particularly in terms of its impact on people's subjectivities, or their sense of who they are and how that relates to their social world. A central contention of the existing literature on the punk scene in the North is that it was non-sectarian, meaning that young Protestants and Catholics took part in it on friendly terms. My analysis does not seek to challenge this claim, exactly, but it does try to complicate what sectarianism and non-sectarianism really meant in the context of 1970s and 1980s Northern Ireland, and to consider carefully how sectarianism appears as a presence across the interviews. Reading a small number of interviews closely helps to think about how people understand the function of sectarianism in the North and in their own lives.

Thirdly, I am particularly interested in what Graham Dawson calls 'composure' – that is, the twofold way people 'compose' their memories, both in terms of the various strategies of telling and expression they use to describe their experience of the past to an interviewee, by making them comprehensible within dominant cultural forms, and in terms of the way these strategies help to tamp down the difficult or complicated elements of that past experience, smoothing off its more jagged edges into a 'composed' narrative.[24] Composure makes sense of the staggered or striated texture of a remembered life by connecting the disparate aspects of subjectivity into a straight line, from who you were to who you became to who you are at the moment of telling the story. Dealing with the interviews in the way I have done allows for a more nuanced sense of how this process works in oral history work, and particularly of the fluid movements between different selves, possibilities and temporalities that are apparent across each discussion.

The structure of the book

The remainder of the book is separated into six chapters. The first two offer two different frames for the brief history of punk offered above. Chapter 1 places it in the context of the historical production of sectarianism and segregation in Ireland and then in Northern Ireland. In doing so it suggests we understand punk as constituting what Raymond Williams calls a 'structure of feeling'. Chapter 2 develops this idea to trace the structure of feeling (and the cultural memory) of punk through various texts and through the built environment of the city of Belfast itself. The following four chapters read a series of interviews with former participants in the punk scene, conducted in 2016 and 2017, as expressions of punk as a structure of feeling in the context of Northern Ireland during the Troubles.

Notes

1 Alessandro Portelli, 'What Makes Oral History Different', in Rob Perks and Alistair Thomson (eds), *The Oral History Reader* (London: Routledge, 2003), p. 67.
2 Ibid., p. 69.
3 Graham Dawson, 'Trauma, Place and the Politics of Memory: Bloody Sunday, Derry, 1972–2004', *History Workshop Journal* 59:1 (2005), p. 153.
4 Interview with Brian Young, conducted by Fearghus Roulston, 2016.
5 *Ibid.*
6 Interview with Hector Heathwood, conducted by Fearghus Roulston, 2016.
7 Terri Hooley and Richard Sullivan, *Hooleygan: Music, Mayhem, Good Vibrations* (Belfast: Blackstaff Press, 2010), p. 60.
8 Caroline Coon and Giovanni Dadomo, 'Clash in the City of the Dead', *Sounds*, 29 October 1977.
9 *Ibid.*
10 *Ibid.*

11 *Ibid.*
12 BY, 2016.
13 *Ibid.*
14 *Ibid.*
15 Sean O'Neill and Guy Trelford (eds), *It Makes You Want to Spit: The Definitive Guide to Punk in Northern Ireland* (Dublin: Reekus Music, 2003).
16 *Ibid.*, p. 18.
17 HH, 2016.
18 Interview with John T. Davis, conducted by Fearghus Roulston, 2015.
19 Interview with Petesy Burns, conducted by Fearghus Roulston, 2016.
20 *Ibid.*
21 William Kelleher, *The Troubles in Ballybogoin: Memory and Identity in Northern Ireland* (Ann Arbour, MI: University of Michigan Press, 2003), p. 13.
22 Alessandro Portelli, *The Order has Been Carried Out: History, Memory and Meaning of a Nazi Massacre in Rome* (Basingstoke: Palgrave MacMillan, 2003), p. 9.
23 Brian Graham and Yvonne Whelan, 'The Legacies of the Dead: Commemorating the Troubles in Northern Ireland', *Environment and Planning D: Society and Space* 25:3 (2007), pp. 476–95; see also Karen Lane, '"Not-The-Troubles": An Anthropological Analysis of Stories of Quotidian Life in Belfast' (unpublished PhD thesis, University of St Andrews, April 2017).
24 Graham Dawson, *Soldier Heroes: British Adventure, Empire and the Imagining of Masculinities* (London: Routledge, 1994); Alistair Thomson, *Anzac Memories: Living With the Legend* (Oxford: Oxford University Press, 1994); Penny Summerfield, *Reconstructing Women's Wartime Lives: Discourse and Subjectivity in Oral Histories of the Second World War* (Manchester: Manchester University Press, 1998).

1

Alternative Ulster? Sectarianism, segregation and the punk scene

'It is nearly a year since the first copy of *A.U.* came out and what has happened in this time? "Nothing" say the cynical, "Everything" say the foolish, but the truth is probably somewhere between these two statements.'[1] This opening salvo from issue 34 of *Alternative Ulster* (or *A.U.*), one of the first punk zines to come out of Northern Ireland, adopts a nicely ecumenical tone in assessing the fledgling scene's impact. Where the foolish might be inclined to hyperbolic pronouncements about the revolutionary potential of young Protestants and Catholics joining together through the transformative power of music, and the cynical might be inclined to dismiss these claims as idealistic, romantic or naive, the editorial – written by someone working under the mononym of Ziggy – proposes a compromise. What the punks have actually done, in Ziggy's assessment, is twofold. Firstly, they have claimed or created some space for themselves in the city, mainly through the establishment of a regular weekend slot for gigs at the Harp Bar – although it also notes, acerbically, 'now that owners are beginning to realise that there is a demand for this "despicable" punk music they are falling over themselves to book bands'.[2] Secondly, they have ensured that this space is interdenominational and non-sectarian, or shared by both Protestants and Catholics. The bands that constitute the musical elements of the scene, the writer says with the fastidious tone of a budding music journalist, cater for every taste and range 'from the sublime to the ridiculous'.[3] But what they have in common is:

> A great degree of determination and dedication to a cause which has brought new hope to this godforsaken place. For the first time in my life I had the pleasure to be part of audiences which are made up of people of all religious creeds and denominations and no one gave a

damn. This is something for which all the bands should be congratulated. They have done something politicians have not been able to or not wanted to do in endless years of trouble. It was done and is being done by a mutual understanding of and love for rock 'n' roll – yes, rock 'n' roll. It may sound pretentious but it is not.[4]

Handwritten in a slanting script, in fading photocopy on cheap paper, the brio and enthusiasm of this text still jump off the page some forty years later. The final disclaimer – 'It may sound pretentious but it is not' – reprises the ecumenical tone of the opening lines, but with a sharper, fiercer edge, and a more defiant expression of punk's meaningfulness in the context of the Troubles and of Northern Irish society.

This opening chapter takes this *A.U.* editorial as starting point for thinking about the distinctive context of the punk scene in Northern Ireland. What is emphasised in the *A.U.* piece is segregation, or the physical separation of Protestants and Catholics through material, social and psychic structures embedded in the everyday lives and spaces of the North, and in this context particularly in the city of Belfast. Sectarianism, not mentioned directly by Ziggy, is a critical element in this architecture of segregation – although exactly what sectarianism is and how it works in Northern Ireland is more complicated than any simple account of interpersonal animosity between different religious denominations would suggest, not least because of the central role of the post-partition state in the formulation and maintenance of sectarian division.[5] And the nature of punk's intervention in the structures of sectarianism and segregation is – as my interviewees suggest throughout the book – complicated in itself. How did punk claim space in the city? What did this mean in the context of the segregation of Catholics and Protestants? And how did it relate to sectarianism and to politics in the North more broadly?

That young Protestants and young Catholics both took part in the punk scene is undoubted, as the documentary record as well as the interviews I conducted for the book show.[6] But what this actually meant in the context of the Troubles is less clear. An inkling of this difficulty leaks into the otherwise bravura performance of the *A.U.* editorial when it praises punk's capacity for doing 'something politicians have not been able to or not wanted to do in endless years of trouble' – that is, its capacity for establishing a non- or un- or anti-sectarian collectivity in Northern Ireland. The phrase itself – 'have not been able to or not wanted to do' – is ambivalent, in that some analyses of the conflict and its long-term causes would suggest that the post-partition Northern Irish state was both the product and the producer of sectarian division, and that despite its occasional funding of cross-community summer camps and its occasional disavowals of discrimination it depended on the existence of this division for its continued viability.[7] If 'the establishment of the state was thus the first and overarching sectarian act from which the other sectarian institutions, relations and practices flowed', how should we make sense of punk's intervention in this confluence?[8] The tension between punk as entailing an antinomian form of resistance to the state, or as deconstructive of sectarian identity, and punk as entailing a kind of management of or mediation of sectarian identities, is one of the tensions that will animate the interviews I analyse in the following chapters. The remainder of this chapter will contextualise the *A.U.* editorial as an historical introduction to the punk scene and to the interviews analysed throughout the book.

Sectarianism, religion and identity

Why did it matter that, as Ziggy says, 'people of all religious creeds and denominations' made up the audience at punk shows in the North? The answer lies in the history of colonial Ireland, firstly, then in the partition of the island in 1921 and in the formation of a Unionist state in the six counties of the North, and finally in the outbreak of the Troubles in the late 1960s. The early modern period and the seventeenth-century plantation of Ulster by the English Crown embedded an unequal relationship between Catholicism and Protestantism in the structure of Irish society, via a complex intersection with the pre-existing Gaelic society of the island; as John Brewer puts it, 'colonisation proceeded on the basis of neutering the remnants of Gaelic and Catholic wealth and power by the ascendancy of Protestantism, linking this form of theology forever after with political loyalty, economic privilege and cultural superiority'.[9] In 1641, some 12,000 Protestant settlers in Ulster were killed in an attempted uprising by the native Irish, when 'popular indiscipline gave rise to localised vendettas' and led to a particularly brutal iteration of the rebellion in the north-east; less is known about retaliatory attacks on Ulster Catholics by the settlers, but several are recorded, including the death of five hundred people, mostly women and children, in an attack in the Mourne Mountains in County Down.[10] The events of 1641 became a central part of the narrative of Reformation-era anti-Catholic propaganda in Britain, portraying Catholicism in graphic terms as a violent and authoritarian force bent on the extirpation of Protestants and Protestantism.[11] This was also part of the historical backdrop for the passing of the penal laws between 1695 and 1709, which placed various prohibitions on Catholics (and Protestant dissenters) in Ireland around land, voting rights and so on, although the practicing of the Catholic religion was not in actuality made impossible; while revisionist historians have pointed out that the application of this legislation was piecemeal and that the traditional or nationalist view of the period as unremitting repression is inaccurate, Marianne Elliott argues that 'the penal laws were products of and enshrined a frame of mind about Catholics which continued long after their effectiveness had passed'.[12] Like 1641, they passed into popular memory in a way that helped to politicise religious identification in Ireland, as would the Siege of Derry in 1689, the Battle of the Boyne in 1690 and the victory of Williamite forces against King James II subsequent to those events.

A dynamic of politicised religious identification remained important (although not immutable or unchanged in its expression) to Irish politics and society through to the nineteenth century, contributing both to the 1798 Rebellion and to the experience of the famine, which was slightly less devastating in Ulster than in the rest of the island, but still consequential.[13] As the nineteenth century progressed and demands for Home Rule – a limited form of independence from Britain – increased, religious identification continued to map onto political or ideological identification, with most Protestants in the north-east of the country anxious to retain the British connection, and the Gaelic revival creating an increasingly confident form of Catholic Irish nationalism.[14] Eventually, after the First World War and the Easter Rising in 1916, the Government of Ireland Act was passed in 1920. This entailed the partition of Ireland between the six counties in the north-east and the twenty-six counties in the south, both of which were initially intended to remain under some form of British rule. After the War of Independence and the Irish

Civil War between 1920 and 1922, the remaining twenty-six counties established their own parliament outside of the Westminster system, leaving the six counties of Northern Ireland with a devolved parliament and an ongoing link to, and dependency upon, Britain.

Joe Cleary helpfully defines partition as 'an attempt to engineer, usually in an extremely compressed period [of time], nation-states with clear and decisive ethnic majorities'.[15] This process entails 'a reorganisation of political space', but one in which the legacies of the previous state structure are central; so in the Northern Irish case, Protestants were constructed as 'loyal' citizens of the new state and Catholics as 'disloyal' by definition, whether their political sympathies were republican, nationalist or apathetic.[16] The main thrust of Cleary's argument is that it is not the innate strength of ethnic or sectarian animosity that produces partition but rather a mixture of colonial or imperial institutions and structures, transnational and global concerns, and political expediency. Because partition takes 'virulent ethno-national conflict as an absolute given', it 'is designed to restructure political space to accommodate such conflict rather than to tackle or transform the wider conditions that generated it in the first instance'.[17] In other words, sectarianism should be seen as the consequence of Irish history – particularly of colonial structures of power – and not as its hidden engine. The early modern history of religion in Ireland (and of religion's entanglement with politics) did not lead ineluctably to partition as a means of containing anti-Protestantism or anti-Catholicism within acceptable bounds; partition created a reorganised political space in which those identities existed and mattered in new ways, not without traces of the older past, but equally not with an umbilical connection to it.

This analysis is particularly important when thinking about the fifty-year period between the formation of the new state and the start of the Troubles, within which Protestantism and Catholicism took on a new salience. From partition in 1921, Northern Ireland was a society predicated on segregation in which the hegemonic political culture was Unionist and thus Protestant. The vast majority of the Protestant population voted for the Ulster Unionist Party (UUP), which would rule the state for some fifty years before the imposition of direct rule from London in 1972; the vast majority of the Catholic population considered themselves to be Irish and were at the very least discomfited by this new geographical arrangement, imposed by the dictat of the British state. This discomfort was quickly heightened by the fact that 'the Unionist establishment … actively discriminated against Catholics in the allocation of jobs and housing, over political rights and in other areas'.[18] The post-partition state orchestrated a formidable sectarian apparatus of direct and indirect discrimination against the minority Catholic population, particularly in the westerly counties of Tyrone, Fermanagh and Derry, where local government made extensive use of gerrymandering practices to maintain Unionist domination of the political system.[19]

Some forms of discrimination were subtle, indirect and simply condoned rather than organised by national or local executives (practices like employers only advertising job vacancies in newspapers read largely or exclusively by Protestants, for instance); others, such as the gerrymandering of electoral boundaries and the use of the 1922 Special Powers Act (SPA) to ban publications, public assembly, the flying of flags and so on, were directly and undeniably driven by the post-partition legislature. While the SPA and its attendant laws were formally neutral (in that they do not explictly name either community in laying out their provisions) they were exclusively levied against Catholics in this period – so tricolour flags referring to the Republic of Ireland were banned but not Union Jacks referring to Britain or to England, for instance.[20]

This sectarian state architecture shaped segregation between Protestants and Catholics, both by disadvantaging Catholics in various ways and by creating a symbolic political and spatial landscape that was overwhelmingly British and Protestant, encompassing 'the union flag; royal toasts; the British national anthem played on formal occasions'.[21] It also worked to manufacture a conditional consent from the Protestant working class, staving off fears of cross-community, class-based alliances against capital or the state, particularly at moments of high unemployment.[22]

By the 1960s the conditions allowing for this half-decade of uneasy domination were shifting. High rates of unemployment and some of the worst housing conditions in the UK (for working-class people of both religious communities) were making the UUP's electoral monopoly harder to justify or maintain.[23] The long decolonial moment of the 1950s and 1960s – including the civil rights movement in the United States, a tactical and symbolic inspiration for the civil rights movement against anti-Catholic discrimination in Northern Ireland – was tangible in protests such as those against housing policy.[24] Simon Prince encapsulates this transnational dynamic nicely, describing the activism of the Homeless Citizens League in Dungannon against the local Unionist council: 'When young Catholic mothers from the town of Dungannon protested at the lack of public housing in May 1963, they carried placards bearing slogans like "Racial Discrimination In Alabama Hits Dungannon".'[25] The Northern Ireland Labour Party (NILP), which was in favour of the union with Britain but attracted some cross-sectarian support and attacked the UUP from the centre-left, posed a further threat to the long-standing political order in the North – they won 26 per cent of the total vote in the 1962 election which brought Terence O'Neill to power.[26] Additionally, O'Neill's reformist ambitions – including a heavily publicised meeting with Seán Lemass, the Irish Taoiseach – attracted the ire of some loyalists on the far right of the Unionist coalition, coalescing around the figure and oratory of the Reverend Ian Paisley.

Influenced by modernist and technocratic currents in British politics and elsewhere, O'Neill's explicit overtures to middle-class Catholicism and his faith in the interventionist capacities of the state were different in tone from the 'hunting-and-fishing' country gentleman style of his predecessor Basil Brooke or Lord Brookeborough. Of particular interest here (because of its relevance to segregation and to the urban landscape that punk was part of) is his promotion of spatial modernisation along the lines suggested by the Matthew Plan, a report on infrastructure in Northern Ireland actually published in the last days of Lord Brookeborough's reign. Infrastructural investment was understood by O'Neill and his advisors as a means to develop the Northern Irish economy and improve what was euphemistically referred to as 'community relations' – that is, as a means to bring both Protestants and Catholics into a broadened tent pegged into newly prosperous land, as a means of preserving the post-partition state. It is also part of a wider history of post-war spatial interventions in Britain intended to create new types of political subject.[27]

But it is clear that two fundamental ambivalences characterised high-profile modernising projects like the Belfast Urban Motorway, the 'new town' of Craigavon, and the demolition of 'slum' housing in Belfast alongside the construction of Divis flats, Rathcoole, and other, smaller housing schemes.[28] Firstly, there was O'Neill's stated policy on the sectarian divide, which baldly reasserts the logics of sectarianism and segregation despite its apparent desire to critique or deconstruct them:

> It is frightfully hard to explain to a Protestant that if you give Roman Catholics a good job and a good house they will live like Protestants, because they will see neighbours with cars and TV sets. They [that is, the fictional Protestant being ventriloquised] will refuse to have eighteen children, but if the Roman Catholic is jobless and lives in a most ghastly hovel he will rear eighteen children on national assistance. It is impossible to explain this to a militant Protestant ... He cannot understand, in fact, that if you treat Roman Catholics with due consideration and kindness they will live like Protestants, in spite of the authoritarian nature of their church.[29]

It is notable that the prime minister displaces the responsibility for sectarianism and segregation here onto a putative (and putatively male) 'militant Protestant' rather than onto the state itself. The evocation of housing and employment as solutions to Catholic unhappiness in the post-partition state refers to O'Neill's plans to address discriminatory practices in these areas, as demanded by the increasingly influential civil rights movement; but it is notable that economic prosperity is supposed to encourage Catholics to 'live like Protestants' in the Unionist-dominated state, rather than work towards the reunification of Ireland. The tone here is similar to that of the debate around assimilation, immigration and race in post-war Britain; economic prosperity is figured as a solvent that will enable the minority population to melt into the majority population, transcending their backwardness, their recalcitrant adherence to an Irish national identity and 'authoritarian' Catholicism, their inherent lack of work ethic, their irrational fecundity, or whatever.[30] O'Neill's technocratic approach was partially intended to appeal to the emergent Catholic middle-classes to shore up the Unionist base against the NILP – as well as mediating between internal divisions within Unionism – but it rested on a fundamentally sectarian logic in its construction of the two communities, as the quote above makes unavoidably clear.[31] It was also, as Brendan O'Leary suggests, predicated on the adherence to capitalist developmentalism that characterised O'Neill's politics – '[the prime minister] sought to improve cross-community relations as a byproduct of his determination to ramp up economic development.'[32] In any event, while his attempts at economic reform did attract some international investment, his reforms failed to meet the demands of the Catholic minority while also splintering his Unionist base of support beyond repair.

In January 1969, a group of protestors mostly under the aegis of People's Democracy (a largely student-led offshoot of the civil rights movement) marched to Burntollet Bridge and were ambushed and attacked by loyalist counterprotestors, with the Royal Ulster Constabulary (RUC) accused of facilitating rather than preventing this ambush. Despite his rhetorical commitment to reform, O'Neill's response to this alteration was unequivocally critical of the marchers, concluding his speech by saying that 'we have heard sufficient for now about civil rights; let us hear a little about civic responsbility'; his solution to the increasingly febrile situation was to call a snap general election intended to bolster Unionist power in the state and his personal power within the party.[33] The upheaval this campaign generated – including, notably, the election of the socialist and People's Democracy activist Bernadette Devlin in the Mid-Ulster constituency – only made his situation more precarious.

O'Neill resigned and was replaced by James Chichester-Clark; in August 1969, in the wake of violence in Belfast and Derry that saw eight people killed, five by state forces, the British Army sent military troops to the North to supplement the local police force. A brief impasse followed before increasingly widespread fighting, leading to a profound intensification of segregation in Belfast and Derry through the displacement of thousands of families from 'mixed' areas, and the imposition of a curfew and house-to-house searches of the (majority-Catholic) Lower Falls in the summer of 1970, in which four people were killed, none of whom had any connections with the Irish Republican Army (IRA) despite the alleged counter-insurgent intention of the raids – 'the sense that the army was being deployed against the general Catholic population was compounded when troops brought in two Unionist ministers to tour the area in armoured cars'.[34] Along with the introduction of internment without trial in 1971, and state atrocities such as the Ballymurphy killings of 1971 and the Bloody Sunday killings of 1972, this period sharpened support for the republican movement against the British state. In 1972, 'direct rule' was imposed and the Northern Irish parliament at Stormont was suspended. Marianne Elliott summarises the atmosphere of the time in a way that emphasises its relevance to the interviews I will analyse throughout the book:

> The vacuum created after 1972 … produced some of the bleakest moments of the Troubles. Random and brutal sectarian murders made ghost towns of city centres after dark. Places of amusement closed down, and mass fear trapped people (particularly those young men most likely to be both the recruits and the victims of the paramilitaries) in their own areas.[35]

The next thirty years would entail further conflict between loyalist and republican paramilitaries, the police and the British Army. Some 3,500 people died over this period, with over 50,000 injured – 'assassinations and assassination attempts, sniper attacks, bombings, bomb scares, street riots, civilian searches, and vehicle checkpoints had become part and parcel of life in Northern Ireland'.[36] Of the deaths, 1,533 were of people under the age of 25 and 257 under 18. Over 2,000 deaths were caused by republican paramiltaries groupings; over 1,000 by loyalist paramilitary groupings; and the remainder by state forces – although it is important to bear in mind that collusion between state forces and loyalist paramilitaries makes the connection between the latter two figures somewhat unclear.[37]

This history, both the longer history of the poltical valence forcibly attached to religious identities and the shorter one of the emergence of the Troubles in the North, explains Ziggy and A.U.'s excitement at the punk scene's capacity to bring young Protestants and Catholics together in the zine editorial quoted at the start of the chapter. I want to make three points about these histories in relation to the interviews discussed later in the book.

Firstly, the tendency of schematic narrative history to simplify complicated dynamics should not elide the complexity of sectarianism on local and personal levels. As Alan Ford puts it in referring to the early modern period in Ulster, 'attempts to study the emergence of sectarianism, or to trace its continuity across the centuries are continually questioned, contradicted and undermined by the evidence of peaceful coexistence and the ability of Protestants and Catholics to live together', and the strange proximity of peace and violence was an often-remarked-upon feature of the Troubles.[38] The account given above is intended to 'denaturalise' sectarianism, or insist upon its material, historical construction and reconstruction via structures of power; but it is not intended to suggest that these structures were immutable, omnipotent or one-dimensional. Affordances, gaps and exceptions within the infrastructure of segregation and sectarianism always existed, of course, even at the height of the Troubles, from surreptitious romantic relationships and neighbourhood friendships to more formal arrangements (for instance the NILP and later the civil rights movement were both determinedly non-sectarian, at least on a formal level, as was the Northern Ireland Gay Rights Association, founded in 1975). And equally, as the analysis of the interviews will make clear, sectarianism was a structure that worked in intersection with various others, with class, gender and sexuality the critical ones to bear in mind for understanding the punk scene.

Secondly, the account given here emphasises that sectarianism is not the product of interpersonal animosity or of atavistic, tribal or pre-modern feuding. It should be theorised and understood as a structure of discrimination first and foremost, and as a structure that is inextricable from the post-partition Northern Irish state, as well as from the British state that the newly partitioned North was entangled with. Desmond Bell, in his 1990 ethnography of loyalist youth culture, makes a similar argument, noting that in much of the discourse about young people in Northern Ireland 'the issue of sectarianism has been reduced to one of personal prejudice and aberrant cognitions', occluding the 'penetration of sectarian modes of experience into the routinized practice of everyday life in Ulster.'[39] What this also means is that any account of the conflict that sees the British state as a neutral arbiter between two competing factions is fundamentally misguided. In stressing the structural nature of sectarianism, my analysis will follow on from the important work of Robert McVeigh, Bill Rolston and Chris Gilligan, all of whom have made this point in sociological work on the still-undertheorised and under-historicised problematic of sectarian structures in the North, arguing that sectarianism should be understood as a form of racism and as such as a structure. [40] Listening to the interviews as, in part, accounts of what it was like to encounter these structures (rather than as accounts of conversion narratives from individual sectarianism to individual non-sectarianism, for instance), opens up a space to understand the complicated dynamics being described by the interviewees.

Thirdly, it is critical, particularly for oral history work, not to lose sight of the fact that sectarianism, like all structures, is a lived experience defined by relationships of power. Structures do things in the world, to people's imaginations, subjectivities and identities, as much as to their material or physical conditions.[41] This dimension is perhaps underemphasised in the literature cited above on sectarianism as a structure. The anthropologist Frank Burton, in his mid-1970s study of 'Anro' or the Ardoyne area of Belfast, gives a good example of one of the manifestations of this process, which he calls telling. He says that telling – ascertaining whether an interlocutor is Protestant or Catholic based on verbal and non-verbal cues – 'furnishes an insight into the nature and depth of a riven society by illuminating the centrality of difference as a typical mode of thought'.[42] So, for example, the way your pronounce the letter 'H', or the length or colour of your hair, or what football team you support, could mean you are read as Protestant or Catholic in certain situations. The use made of these 'semiological clues' does not mean that the differences they rely on are factual – they are not – but that a series of historical and material conditions have marked the social constructions of self and other with what Burton calls, in a nice phrase, 'the sediment of history'.[43] Claire Mitchell, whose sensitive ethnographic work on religion and identity is an exception in the literature for its engagement with people's lived experience of these structures, argues that 'religion often plays a much more significant role in social relationships than just providing group labels. In societies with significant religious presence or history, it can form a kind of cultural reservoir from which categorizations of self and other may be derived.'[44] This 'cultural reservoir', in her suggestive phrase, is joined to the structures described in this section but not reducible to them. Again, the lived experience of these structures is one of the lenses through which the oral history interviews of the following chapters are read.

Segregation and sectarianised space

Sectarianism, in short, is complicated. That is not meant as a facile point; the problem with it being mobilised in an uncomplicated way is that it conceals the social and political relationships it is supposed to explain.⁴⁵ One site where this complication is highly apparent, and a critical one for the punk scene, was segregation, or the material division of Protestants and Catholics, which functions in part through the sectarianisation of space, or the production of certain spaces as belonging to one or the other community, and as thus being safe or unsafe, comfortable or uncomfortable, and so on. To return to the *A.U.* editorial, one thing the punk scene attempted to do was to claim space in the city – this space, shared between Protestants and Catholics, clearly needs to be understood as formed in response to the segregated conditions of life in Belfast in the 1970s.

Some residential segregation between Protestants and Catholics was already a feature of mid-nineteenth century industrial Belfast, as the city was reaching its economic heyday as an important part of the British imperial nexus.⁴⁶ Initially this was often to do with employment – people living near to where they were able to find work – and the persistence of pre-urban familial and social ties. As the nineteenth century wore on spatial division and boundary-making was increasingly reinforced by violence and the threat of violence.⁴⁷ This violence reached its apogee in the early 1920s; in 1920, during the fraught build-up to partition, over 20,000 Catholics, a quarter of the city's Catholic residents, were expelled from their homes, and Catholic workers as well as some Protestant trade unionists were expelled from the shipyards.⁴⁸ Five hundred Catholic businesses were also destroyed in this period. Jim McDermott suggests that 'the shipyard expulsions and the manner in which they happened divided Belfast even more permanently on religious grounds'.⁴⁹

Throughout the period of Unionist rule from 1921 described in the previous section, residential segregation continued to be a feature of the city. Other mechanisms of segregation, such as the segregated education system, were further embedded in society throughout this period, with Catholics attending schools run by the Church and Protestants schools run by the state; workplaces were also often divided along religious lines.⁵⁰

The outbreak of violence in 1969 contributed to the segregation of space in the city, particularly in terms of housing. Between August 1969 and February 1973 some 60,000 people, 12 per cent of the population of the city, left their homes because of direct intimidation or the risk of violence; the majority of these were Catholic families living in majority-Protestant areas, as well as some Protestants living in majority-Catholic areas.[51] This period also saw the increasing centrality of paramilitary groups to the conflict, particularly in the wake of heavy-handed British counterinsurgency tactics in the early 1970s.[52]

In addition to the Provisional IRA's resurgence, other paramilitary groups emerged in the wake of the rioting that marked the start of the decade. The Official IRA retained a presence in the city throughout this period, and from 1975 the Irish National Liberation Army also took part in acts of violence in Belfast. In terms of loyalist violence, the Ulster Volunteer Force and the Ulster Defence Association were the most significant organisations for Belfast in the 1970s, with the Red Hand Commandos also formed in around 1972.[53] Along with the increased segregation described above, and the violence and intimidation of the state forces, these organisations played an important role in generating and maintaining spatial divisions between Catholic and Protestant communities in the city, through 'informal' policing tactics including punishment beatings and shootings.[54]

This generated a spatial framework within the city whereby working-class areas became almost exclusively Catholic or Protestant, following the pattern laid out in the nineteenth century but to a more extreme degree; it also led to the creation of militarised boundaries between segregated spaces, in what are now known as 'interface areas', where a great deal of the violence in Belfast was enacted throughout the years of the conflict. Many of these areas were divided with literal walls – 'peace lines', as they are somewhat strangely known – which continue to shape patterns of segregation in the city.[55]

Segregation was also produced and maintained through urban redevelopment and securitisation. Research based on declassified planning documents has shed light on the contentious issue of to what extent urban planning in Belfast was led by state security agencies. According to Tim Cunningham, these unsealed documents suggest that 'the planning system in Northern Ireland was very much "steered" in the direction of securing (literally) the maximum degree of segregation possible between contentious areas of the city and ensuring the delivery of "defensive planning"'.[56] This influence ranged from the macrocosmic to the microcosmic – so security input was offered on turning the route taken by the Belfast Urban Motorway into (in the words of the military liason group) a *cordon sanitaire*, forcibly dividing the west and north of the city from the centre, but also on the material used for pavements – flagstones, which provided ideal ammunition for rioters, were discouraged. The motorway, in particular, entrenched sectarian division in the built environment of Belfast and separated working-class parts of the city from the more affluent or commercial areas in the centre and the south.[57]

This process of redevelopment was also facilitated by a concerted attempt to police space in the centre of the city. On 21 July 1972, 9 people died and a further 130 were injured over the course of 'Bloody Friday', when the Provisional IRA detonated 22 bombs across Belfast, many in bus stations and other transport hubs. Following this attack and the launch of Operation Motorman, which brought about the deployment of 40,000 further British troops in Belfast and Derry, Belfast became 'a laboratory for radical experiments on the fortification of urban space', where defensive planning and architecture worked along with the police and the army to create a heavily securitised and surveilled urban environment.[58] A cornerstone of this policy, mentioned by many of my interviewees as part of the experience of going in and out of the city, was the 'ring of steel', a means of separating the commercial centre of the city from the areas outside of it via walls, gates, chicanes and guards. A similar model was used to separate the City of London from the rest of central London in the wake of Provisional IRA bombings in the early 1990s.

Initially, the Belfast ring of steel was split into four zones; by March 1976 it had been amalgamated to form one zone, meaning only one search was required when entering this part of the city rather than several as the shopper or walker moved between each area. The 'ring' consisted of 'one large security sector ringed by 17 ten to 12-foot-high steel gates'; this reduced the number of personnel needed to maintain the cordon, although many shops employed their own teams of security staff to carry out further searches.[59] Working in tandem with a concerted effort on the part of the military to control and contain working-class estates, this strategy of insulation and normalisation – while largely functioning as a technique for keeping violence to the residential areas outside of the city centre – gave the area 'the appearance of a besieged citadel'.[60]

As well as exporting violence to the working-class interface areas of the city, this policy contributed to the somewhat dismal aspect presented by the centre of town. In a 1978 attempt to ameliorate this atmosphere (and its fiscal consequences), the then Secretary of State for Northern Ireland, Roy Mason, set up a working group 'to make the centre of Belfast a lively centre of social entertainment for citizens and visitors'.[61] However, in 1980 the *Belfast Telegraph* reported that the group's ambitious proposals, which included a ballroom, a family entertainment centre, an ice rink and an indoor sports stadium, would not be met with any additional state funding. With admirable understatement, a spokesperson for the Department of the Environment told the paper that 'there are ... many other pressing demands on public funds', suggesting that the private sector should be encouraged to cover the costs of any potential developments.[62] But as the punk scene attests to, shops and bars continued to operate in the city centre all the way through the conflict.

In summary, residential segregation and the sectarianisation of space in Belfast has a historical basis in the conflicts of the nineteenth and early twentieth century, although the way in which this segregation was articulated and marked out changed following the violence of 1969. It is unevenly dispersed across the city, particularly pronounced in some parts and less pronounced in others. Residential segregation went along with social segregation, because residents understood certain spaces as safe and certain spaces as unsafe, although again this was never totalising. The former punks I interviewed all had different experiences of segregation, depending on where in the city they grew up in, or where they lived after that, and whether their families were Catholic or Protestant; however, they were all conscious of it in some way.

They generally grew up in areas that were predominantly Protestant or Catholic, although some of them remembered having friends from both communities in their childhood and adolescence.[63] If they went to church, as the vast majority of families did in Northern Ireland in the 1970s, their churches were segregated along religious lines.[64] When they started attending school, their schools were also segregated along religious lines – the first integrated school in Northern Ireland, Lagan College, opened in 1981.[65] If they played a sport or engaged in any kind of formal extracurricular activity, they probably played it mostly with people of the same religious denomination as them; if they engaged in any of the more informal kinds of sociality and pleasure enjoyed by young people – illicit drinking, drugs, sex and so on – this was probably also done with people of the same religious denomination as them, not least because of the difficulty of finding spaces where people from different communities could mix safely.

For those of them who left school to get a job, starting work would generally have meant entering into a workforce composed mostly of Protestants or mostly of Catholics.[66] Higher education and university were not segregated in the same way as schools, and so could sometimes represent a chance to mix across the religious divide, although this was limited by various factors of habit, choice and politics. Because many Belfast-based students continued to live with their parents, residential segregation would have continued to play an important factor in their lives; the civil rights leader Bernadette Devlin, expressing her initial disappointment at not finding a radical, bohemian counterculture at Queen's, writes in her memoir that 'everyone went to bed early in Belfast: at midnight we all turned into pumpkins'.[67]

Punk as a structure of feeling

Segregation, like sectarianism, had a long history in Belfast by the 1970s. By the period of punk's emergence, the Troubles had further entrenched segregation and generated new conditions for the expression of sectarian identities. So how should we understand the punk scene in Belfast in relation to these histories? How should we make sense of what what Ziggy and *A.U.* describe as 'a cause which has brought new hope to this godforsaken place?' Firstly by defining of what 'the punk scene' actually means. Throughout the book this term will be used as shorthand for venues, institutions (record labels, record shops) and bands, and also for the constellation of spatialised, quotidian practices that make up the everyday life of its participants – buying and modifying clothes, going to gigs, gathering together in pubs and public spaces, listening to the radio and so on. These together constitute and will be read as something like what the Marxist cultural theorist Raymond Williams calls a structure of feeling – 'social experience in solution', the liquid and felt sense of connectivity between a group of people – often constituting a generation or a shared temporal moment, in Williams's case, although not always.[68] In thinking of the punk scene as a structure of feeling I am interested in considering its relationship to social conditions, or structures; and I am interested in how people made sense of their emotional lives and feelings within that context. Reading the punk scene as a structure of feeling makes it possible to tease out its complicated relationship with Northern Irish culture (and with sectarianism), to recognise its capacity to generate relational moments in which my interviewees encountered aspects of their everyday lives differently, and to apprehend its affective dimensions and political possibilities, without extricating these hopes and feelings from the conditions out of which they emerged.

In adopting this approach – that is, in interrogating the nature of punk as a structure of feeling in the cultures of 1970s Northern Ireland – my analysis will draw on historical work on the British punk scene by David Wilkinson and Matt Worley, who both mobilise the concept of structure of feeling to think about punk scenes in Manchester and in Britain respectively.[69] Both Wilkinson and Worley want to historicise punk, place it in a social and political context, and take it seriously as a cultural response to that context. In a 2017 review article with John Street, they call for a historical practice informed by Williams's cultural materialism that entails 'the combination of empirical and archival research with a theoretical method that allows for the complexities, contradictions and contentious nature of punk's cultural practice to be embraced'.[70] While broadly sympathetic to this approach, I would add that an oral history methodology suggests some further complexities. How was the punk scene experienced as an everyday as well as an exceptional set of practices? How does the meaning ascribed to punkness change when described by someone who was a punk for a few years as a teenager, forty years ago? What does this shifting semiotic and subjective content tell us about political and social changes in that forty-year period?

In posing these questions, my approach will differ somewhat from that of Worley, Wilkinson and Street, given their focus on the archival and documentary record of the punk scene. I share Worley's sense that 'not only did punk engender creativity, it also forged cultures that challenged prevailing social (and socioeconomic) norms in irreverent and provocative ways', and agree with his suggestion that it 'both reflected lives being lived and uncovered portals to other worlds and ideas'.[71] But what I want to argue for is a slightly broadened sense of the structure of feeling, one that is not simply applied to what we can trace through the residue of the past (zines, records, newspaper interviews and so on) but also to people's memories of the past – memories that are formed relationally within and against these cultural representations, but not reducible to them in their full expressiveness and complexity. My intention here is to consider the way in which memories of the punk scene are marked by the institutional conditions and discourses circulating at the time as well as by the conditions of the contemporary moment, but not to argue that these memories are exclusively expressions of domination, institutional power or sectarianism. This approach follows the argument of the Popular Memory Group that 'memories of the past are, like all common-sense forms, strangely composite constructions, resembling a kind of geology, the selective sedimentation of past traces'; these are traces of sectarian structures but also traces of disputation and discomfort within those structures, in this context.[72]

David Wilkinson – whose conceptualisation of the post-punk scene in Manchester I am especially indebted to – argues that 'freedom and pleasure are surely among the most deeply, personally "felt" experiences within an encompassing hegemonic process. They are irreducible to purely abstract and conceptual understandings if their varied expressions – dominant, alternative, or oppositional – are to have any genuine hold.'[73] This emphasis on felt experience as 'the means by which people encountered and remade the world around them, often in relation with others' will be echoed in my interview analysis in the subsequent five chapters.[74] Apprehending the structure of feeling of the punk scene in Belfast through oral histories both makes it possible to ask different questions about these felt experiences and to access different bits of them – so the felt experiences of those whose band never left their friends' garage, or whose zine never progressed beyond a doodle on a school jotter, or whose position or subjectivity leads them to think that their narrative exists on the margins of the scene and so outside of its historicisation. In this sense, the ambit of the structure of feeling is widened in the analysis that follows.

Conclusion

Sectarianism – the structures of discrimination that characterised the Northern Irish state, and the lived experience of those structures – and segregation – the the physical separation of Protestants and

Catholics through material, social and psychic means –were the twin contexts for the *A.U.* editorial that opened the chapter. Its defiant tone, as well as its twinge of uncertainty with regards to the intentions of Northern Ireland's political class, are initial examples of the structue of feeling the rest of the book will be pursuing. The following chapter picks up this thread through an analysis of the cultural memory of the punk scene, charting its different articulations from the 1970s through to the present day to consider how they relate to events and political feelings in the North more broadly.

Notes

1. Ziggy, 'The Story So Far', *Alternative Ulster* (34) (Belfast: Just Books, 1977), p. 24. It is worth noting that *A.U.*'s deliberately anarchic and non-linear numbering scheme means this was most likely not the thirty-fourth issue they published.
2. *Ibid.*
3. *Ibid.*
4. *Ibid.*
5. Robbie McVeigh and Bill Rolston, 'From Good Friday to Good Relations: Sectarianism, Racism and the Northern Ireland State', *Race & Class* 48:4 (2007), pp. 1–23.
6. O'Neill and Trelford, *It Makes You Want to Spit.*
7. McVeigh and Rolston, 'From Good Friday'; see also Chris Gilligan, *Northern Ireland and the Crisis of Anti-Racism: Rethinking Racism and Sectarianism* (Manchester: Manchester University Press, 2017).
8. McVeigh and Rolston, 'From Good Friday', p. 6.
9. John Brewer and Gareth I. Higgins, *Anti-Catholicism in Northern Ireland, 1600–1988: The Mote and the Beam* (London: Macmillan, 1998), p. 15.
10. Marianne Elliott, *The Catholics of Ulster: A History* (London: Penguin, 2001), pp. 101–02.
11. Ethan Howard Shagan, 'Constructing Discord: Ideology, Propaganda, and English Responses to the Irish Rebellion of 1641', *Journal of British Studies* 36:1 (1997), pp. 4–34.
12. Elliott, *Catholics of Ulster,* p. 164. For an example of the kind of revisionist approach she is referring to which deals narrowly with inheritance and the 'gavelling clause' but contains a good overview of the historiography on the laws, see Richard Fitzpatrick, 'Catholic

Inheritance under the Penal Laws in Ireland', *Irish Historical Studies* 44:166 (2020), pp. 224–47.
13 Trevor Parkhill, 'Emigration & The Great Famine: The Ulster Experience', *Folk Life* 37:1 (1998), pp. 80–91.
14 Alan Parkinson, *Friends in High Places: Ulster's Resistance to Irish Home Rule, 1912–14* (Belfast: Ulster Historical Foundation, 2012).
15 Joe Cleary, *Literature, Partition and the Nation-State: Culture and Conflict in Ireland, Israel and Palestine* (Cambridge: Cambridge University Press: 2004), p. 21.
16 *Ibid.*
17 *Ibid.*, p. 29; see also James Anderson and Liam O'Dowd, 'Imperialism and Nationalism: The Home Rule Struggle and Border Creation in Ireland, 1885–1925', *Partition and the Reconfiguration of the Irish Border* 26:8 (2007), pp. 934–50.
18 David McKittrick and David McVea, *Making Sense of the Troubles: A History of the Northern Ireland Conflict* (Chicago, IL: New Amsterdam Books, 2002), p. 5.
19 John Whyte, 'How much Discrimination was there Under the Unionist Regime, 1921–1968?', in Tom Gallagher and James O'Connell (eds), *Contemporary Irish Studies* (Manchester: Manchester University Press, 1983) is an unusually even-handed account which stresses unevenness and contingency in mechanisms of discrimination, but also insists on its actuality and power; for an engaging contemporary account of discrimination in this period by a nationalist-minded author see Ultach, *Orange Terror: The Partition of Ireland* (Dublin: The Capuchin Annual, 1943).
20 For an exhaustive account of the Special Powers Act as a discriminatory formation, see Laura K. Donohue, *Counter-Terrorist Law and Emergency Powers in the UK, 1922–2000* (Dublin: Irish Academic Press, 2001).
21 Thomas Hennessey, *Northern Ireland: The Origins of the Troubles* (London: Gill & Macmillan, 2005), p. 378.
22 On poverty and sectarianism in Belfast in the 1930s see Ronnie Munck and Bill Rolston, *Belfast in the Thirties: An Oral History* (Belfast: Blackstaff Press, 1987).
23 For an interesting analysis of housing policy in Belfast in this period see Ron Wiener, *The Rape and Plunder of the Shankill – Community Action: The Belfast Experience* (Belfast: Farset Co-operative Press, 1980).
24 Brian Dooley, *Black and Green: The Fight for Civil Rights in Northern Ireland and Black America* (London: Pluto Press, 1998).
25 Simon Prince, 'The Global Revolt of 1968 and Northern Ireland', *The Historical Journal* 49:3 (2006), p. 861; on the largely women-led housing activism of this early period see Tara Keenan-Thomson, 'From Co-op

to Co-opt: Gender and Class in the Early Civil Rights Movement', *The Sixties* 2:2 (2009), pp. 207–25.
26 McKittrick and McVea, *Making Sense*, p. 28.
27 Sam Wetherall, *Foundations: How the Built Environment Made Twentieth-Century Britain* (Princeton, NJ: Princeton University Press, 2020).
28 Marc Mulholland, *Northern Ireland at the Crossroads: Ulster Unionism in the O'Neill Years, 1960–9* (London: St Martin's Press, 2000); for an excellent analysis of the intersection between national and regional interests in O'Neill-ism see Martin Joseph McCleery, 'The Creation of the "New City" of Craigavon: A Case Study of Politics, Planning and Modernisation in Northern Ireland in the Early 1960s', *Irish Political Studies* 27:1 (2012), pp. 89–109; Gerry Downes (ed.), *Brits, Balconies and Bin-Lids: Residents Remember Life in Divis Flats* (Belfast: Divis Study Group, 1998); for a recent analysis of the memory of two of these modernist developments see Garikoitz Gómez Alfaro and Fearghus Roulston, 'Nostalgia for "HMP Divis" and "HMP Rossville": Memories of the Everyday in Northern Ireland's High-Rise Flats', *Journal of War & Culture Studies* 14:1 (2021), pp. 25–44.
29 Quoted in Mulholland, *Northern Ireland at the Crossroads*, p. 1.
30 For a classic analysis of the relationship between immigration, race and capital in post-war Britain see Ambalavaner Sivanandan, *Catching History on the Wing: Race, Culture and Globalisation* (London: Pluto Press, 2008), especially pp. 65–90.
31 On O'Neill-ism as a response to the Northern Ireland Labour Party see Mulholland, *Northern Ireland at the Crossroads*, especially chapter 2.
32 Brendan O'Leary, *A Treatise on Northern Ireland Volume 2: Control – The Second Protestant Ascendancy and the Irish State* (Oxford: Oxford University Press, 2019), p. 166.
33 Daniel Finn, *One Man's Terrorist: A Political History of the IRA* (London: Verso, 2019), p. 63; Mulholland, *Northern Ireland at the Crossroads*, p. 193.
34 McKittrick and McVea, *Making Sense*, p. 62.
35 Elliott, *Catholics of Ulster*, p. 422.
36 Orla T. Muldoon, 'Children of the Troubles: The Impact of Political Violence in Northern Ireland', *Journal of Social Issues* 60:3 (2004), p. 459.
37 Mark McGovern, *Counterinsurgency and Collusion in Northern Ireland* (London: Pluto Press, 2019).
38 Alan Ford, 'Living Together, Living Apart: Sectarianism in Early Modern Ireland', in Alan Ford and John McCafferty (eds), *The Origins of*

Sectarianism in Early Modern Ireland (Cambridge: Cambridge University Press, 2005), p. 12.
39 Desmond Bell, *Acts of Union: Youth Culture and Sectarianism in Northern Ireland* (London: Macmillan Education, 1990), p. 48.
40 Robbie McVeigh, 'The Undertheorisation of Sectarianism', *Canadian Journal of Irish Studies* 16:2 (1990), p. 121; see also Robbie McVeigh, *Sectarianism in Northern Ireland: Towards a Definition in Law* (Belfast: Equality Coalition, 2014).
41 David Cairns, 'The Object of Sectarianism: The Material Reality of Sectarianism in Ulster Loyalism', *Journal of the Royal Anthropological Institute* 6:3 (2000), pp. 437–52; see also John D. Brewer, and Gareth I. Higgins, 'Understanding Anti-Catholicism in Northern Ireland', *Sociology* 33:2 (1999), pp. 235–55, for an account of anti-Catholicism as a discursive formation. The phrase 'a lived experience defined by relationships of power' is recontextualised from Selina Todd, 'Class, Experience and Britain's Twentieth Century', *Social History* 39:4 (2014), p. 501.
42 Frank Burton, *The Politics of Legitimacy: Struggles in a Belfast Community* (London: Routledge & Kegan Paul, 1978), p. 37.
43 *Ibid.*, p. 49.
44 Claire Mitchell, *Religion, Identity and Politics in Northern Ireland: Boundaries of Belonging and Belief* (London: Routledge, 2017), p. 15.
45 A similar point about the mobilisation of sectarianism in a different context is made in the illuminating study of Fanar Haddad, *Understanding 'Sectarianism': Sunni–Shi'a Relations in the Modern Arab World* (Oxford: Oxford University Press, 2020).
46 On empire as part of popular culture and urban space in mid-Victorian Belfast, see Mark Doyle, 'The Sepoys of the Pound and Sandy Row: Empire and Identity in Mid-Victorian Belfast', *Journal of Urban History* 36:6 (2010), pp. 849–67.
47 Alan Parkinson, *Belfast's Unholy War: The Troubles of the 1920s* (Dublin: Four Courts Press, 2004); Niall Cunningham, '"The Doctrine of Vicarious Punishment": Space, Religion and the Belfast Troubles of 1920–22', *Journal of Historical Geography* 40:1 (2013), pp. 52–66.
48 Alvin Jackson, *Home Rule: An Irish History, 1800–2000* (Oxford: Oxford University Press, 2003), p. 248.
49 Jim McDermott, *Northern Divisions: The Old IRA and the Belfast Pogroms 1920–22* (Belfast: Beyond the Pale, 2001), p. 34.
50 Sean Farren, 'A Lost Opportunity: Education and Community in Northern Ireland 1947–1960', *History of Education* 21:1 (1992), pp. 71–82; Stephen Roulston and Ulf Hansson, 'Kicking the Can down the

Road? Educational Solutions to the Challenges of Divided Societies: A Northern Ireland Case Study', *Discourse: Studies in the Cultural Politics of Education* 42:2 (2021), pp. 170–83.
51 Northern Ireland Housing Executive, *More Than Bricks: 40 Years of the Housing Executive* (Belfast: Northern Ireland Housing Executive, 2011).
52 Finn, *One Man's Terrorist*.
53 Jonathan Bardon, *A History of Ulster* (Belfast: Blackstaff Press, 1992), chapter 15; Kathleen A. Cavanaugh, 'Interpretations of Political Violence in Ethnically Divided Societies', *Terrorism and Political Violence* 9:3 (1997), pp. 33–54.
54 For an ethnography of these kinds of practices (concentrating on contemporary Northern Ireland) see Heather Hamill, *The Hoods: Crime and Punishment in Belfast* (Oxford: Princeton University Press, 2011).
55 Laura McAtackney, 'Peace Maintenance and Political Messages: The Significance of Walls During and After the Northern Irish "Troubles"', *Journal of Social Archaeology* 11:1 (2011), pp. 77–98.
56 Tim Cunningham, 'Changing Direction: Defensive Planning in a Post-Conflict City', *City* 18:4–5 (2014), p. 459.
57 Mark Hackett, 'Driving the Social Divide: Planning in Belfast Reinforces the City's Segregation', *The Architectural Review* (2019), online at: www.architectural-review.com/essays/driving-the-social-divide-planning-in-belfast-reinforces-the-citys-segregation (accessed 18 April 2021).
58 Jon Coaffee, *Terrorism, Risk and the Global City: Towards Urban Resilience* (London: Routledge, 2006), p. 23.
59 *Ibid.*, p. 27.
60 Neil Jarman, 'Intersecting Belfast', in Barbara Bender (ed.), *Landscape: Politics and Perspectives* (Oxford: Berg, 1993), p. 115.
61 HC Deb 09, November 1978, Vol. 957, cols. 1161–62.
62 *Belfast Telegraph*, 25 January 1980, p. 4.
63 See the interview with Graeme Mullan in Chapter 6, for instance.
64 See John Bell, *For God, Ulster, or Ireland?: Religion, Identity and Security in Northern Ireland* (Belfast: Institute for Conflict Research, 2013), pp. 17–35, for a useful overview of the literature on religious identification in Northern Ireland.
65 Jonathan Bardon, *The Struggle for Shared Schools in Northern Ireland: The History of All Children Together* (Belfast: Ulster Historical Foundation, 2009). The Belfast punk band Ruefrex, known for their political sloganeering and especially for the 1985 single 'Wild Colonial Boy', a caustic attack on Irish-American support for republican violence, played a benefit gig for Lagan College in the mid-1980s as part of their wider attempt to address issues of sectarianism. Sean Campbell and Gerry

Smyth, 'From Shellshock Rock to Ceasefire Sounds: Popular Music', in Colin Coulter and Michael Murray (eds), *Northern Ireland After the Troubles: A Society in Transition* (Oxford: Oxford University Press, 2008), p. 243.
66 R. J. Cormack and R. D. Osborne, 'The Belfast Study: Into Work in Belfast', in R. J. Cormack (ed.), *Religion, Education and Employment* (Belfast: Appletree Press, 1983).
67 Bernadette Devlin, *The Price of My Soul* (London: Pan Books, 1969), p. 108.
68 Raymond Williams, *Marxism and Literature* (Oxford: Oxford University Press, 1977), p. 132. On generations and temporality see David Scott, 'The Temporality of Generations: Dialogue, Tradition, Criticism', *New Literary History* 45:2 (2014), pp. 157–81.
69 David Wilkinson, *Post-Punk, Politics and Pleasure in Britain* (Basingstoke: Palgrave Macmillan, 2016); Matt Worley, *No Future: Punk, Politics and British Youth Culture, 1976–84* (Cambridge: Cambridge University Press, 2017).
70 David Wilkinson, Matthew Worley and John Street, '"I Wanna See Some History": Recent Writing on British Punk', *Contemporary European History* 26:2 (2017), p. 410; see also John Street, Matthew Worley and David Wilkinson, '"Does It Threaten the Status Quo?" Elite Responses to British Punk, 1976–1978', *Popular Music* 37:2 (2018), pp. 271–89.
71 Worley, *No Future*, p. 254.
72 Popular Memory Group, 'Popular Memory: Theory, Politics, Method', in Robert Perks and Alistair Thomson (eds), *The Oral History Reader* (London: Routledge, 2003), p. 78.
73 Wilkinson, *Post-Punk*, p. 21.
74 Todd, 'Class, Experience and Britain's Twentieth Century', p. 508.

2

The Belfast punk scene in cultural memory

In Belfast's Cathedral Quarter, the site of extensive redevelopment over the last two decades and one of the emblematic locations of 'post-conflict', tourist-friendly Northern Ireland, there is a small blue plaque commemorating the city's punk scene, and specifically the celebrated impresario of that scene Terri Hooley. The plaque was unveiled near the end of 2012, as the finale of Belfast Music Week, following an early screening of the loosely fictionalised biopic of Hooley, *Good Vibrations*.[1] Speaking at the unveiling of the plaque, the then Lord Mayor Gavin Robinson said of Hooley:

> He is a remarkable man who came out of difficult times in Belfast. In the 1970s he set up a record shop in the city when many other people were going out of business: he provided an open and welcoming space when much of Belfast was closing down. He was a living example of how to survive beyond sectarianism and mistrust ... he discovered a new generation of bands in the town who were inspired by the ideals of punk rock.[2]

This is a striking peroration, not least in coming from an MP for the extremely socially conservative Democratic Unionist Party or DUP, notorious among other things for their intense opposition to same-sex marriage legislation and to the liberalisation of abortion laws in Northern Ireland.[3] His party's deserved reputation for antediluvian attitudes to gender and sexuality sit strangely with Robinson's apparent enthusiasm for the ideals of punk rock and for Hooley, who prior to his role in the punk scene had been a fixture in the hippy demi-monde of 1960s Belfast, and known as much for his diverse hedonistic enthusiasms as for his anti-establishment world view.

But we can see an important facet of the dominant popular memory narrative of punk in the North in Robinson's speech. For the mayor, punk is understood as a fundamentally entrepreneurial endeavour, in which Hooley's business acumen creates an 'open and welcoming' space within the 'difficult' landscape of 1970s Belfast, when much of the city was closing down and becoming non-commercially viable.

There are echoes here of former New York mayor Michael Bloomberg's 2008 speech at the Northern Ireland Investment Conference, in which, marking a decade since the Belfast/Good Friday Agreement, he said: 'The historic cultural barriers between the two communities are slowly coming down, and the sooner they do – and the sooner the physical barriers come down too – the sooner the floodgates of private investment will open.'[4] Tony Blair and Bill Clinton had already set the tone for this approach with their comments during the agreement negotiations ten years prior, and much of the discourse around peacebuilding in the North could be described as adhering to a model of what Mark Fisher would call capitalist realism.[5] Peace and a neoliberal construction of prosperity, as Aaron Kelly and others have shown, are fundamentally entangled in post-conflict Northern Ireland, particularly in terms of the production of space and the urban environment. The way in which the punk scene has been memorialised is part of this entanglement.[6]

This chapter will consider a number of cultural texts and events to make sense of the way in which the popular memory of punk has been mobilised in Northern Ireland since the 1980s, and of the way in which this memory is related to 'post-conflict' temporal politics. In a thoughtful review of the fortieth anniversary exhibition of the London punk scene in the austere setting of the British Library, arguably an equally uncomfortable pairing as that of the DUP and Terri Hooley, the historian Lucy Robinson says that thinking about the memorialisation of punk can teach us something through its evocation of 'an itchy sort of heritage'.[7] She adds: 'Of course the British Library exhibition was in the wrong place. That's what made it so punk rock. Punk was always in the wrong place.'[8] Arguing that punk's ambivalent relationship to commodification, capital and the past was present from its earliest iterations – that this ambivalence is part of what it is, not a contemporary graft onto it or a consequence of its incorporation into the nostalgia industry. Robinson proposes that we attend to the itchiness and the discomfort that punk heritage and commemoration can evoke, and to the meaningful contradictions these feelings might bring to light. As I explain in the concluding sections of this chapter, my particular interest here is in how my interviewees draw on popular memory narratives of the scene in describing punk's structure of feeling as they experienced it, and on how they narrate their own feelings about seeing their memories and their past experiences translated into this itchy sort of heritage.

Community history: *Shellshock Rock* and *It Makes You Want to Spit*

Determining a point at which a scene passes from the contemporary to the historical is tricky. In a sense, as Lucy Robinson's comments above suggest, music scenes are always historicising themselves. Richard Cabut and Andrew Gallix posit that at the very beginning punk was constantly in the process of forming, and while this is true, so is the inverse – something in the constant process of forming is also in the constant process of ending, and the kind of sharp, delineative periodisation that is characteristic of modern European historiography is also characteristic of how participants in music scenes rank, curate and order songs and bands.[9] For instance, the lead singer of Rudi, Brian Young, told me:

> Once 'God Save the Queen' came out sorta '77, people forget, the press, the Pistols were on that Bill Grundy show [...] the press hyped it up something rotten ... Punk had sort of ... once it got popular like that and it got popular very quick through late '76 right into '77 ... there were a lot of, it actually lost it, it became more of a – I mean it was still, don't get me wrong, it was still brilliant, it was still really exciting, it was still the really early days over here – but it sort of in a way, in England certainly, it had lost its innocence.[10]

In that sense, punk was already in the process of becoming historical, becoming an object of nostalgia, while it was still happening. Songs, in particular, are portals for this kind of nostalgic engagement with the recent past, and in that sense it is not fanciful to suggest that the first historians of punks were the punks themselves, collecting and playing records alone or in groups or in bars.[11] Zines, too, as Red Chidgey suggests in her analysis of feminist zine-writing, 'are primarily memory texts, documenting, interpreting, sharing and archiving the current cultural moment'.[12] For our purposes here, though, the first document that gives us access to a coherent sense of the nascent popular memory of punk's beginnings in Belfast is *Shellshock Rock*, the 1979 documentary by John T. Davis.[13]

What is instantly notable about the film, especially when compared to the later representations of the scene discussed below, is its refusal to establish an easy dichotomy between the punk scene and Northern Irish society. This refusal is evident in a vox pop section where middle-aged and elderly shoppers on Great Victoria Street are asked what they think about the punks. Rather than espousing the kind of moral panic or hostility inspired – among some journalists, at least – by the Sex Pistols' appearance on Bill Grundy in 1976, their reactions are alternately bemused, sanguine and supportive; one older man tells the interviewer that 'they're only young and enjoying themselves, sure it's all part of the life, part of the game … wish I was young myself I'd have been one!' The film's commitment to a non-dogmatic portrayal of punk (and of the North in general) is also apparent in the snippets of conversation with the young punks themselves. Stiff Little Fingers, unsurprisingly, offer up an alarmingly coherent political reading of the punk scene as a rejection of the sectarian politics of the state; some interviewees offer more diffuse expressions of anti-authoritarianism, one saying that punk in Northern Ireland is 'people saying honest things … we're just tired of the shit your ma and da tell you, it's a load of balls'. Others explicitly reject the political sloganeering of Stiff Little Fingers, with the lead singer of Protex telling the interviewer: 'We can't sing about Ulster, I'm fed up. We all live in it.'

The Troubles are only fitfully visible in *Shellshock Rock*, notably in an aerial shot of the Bogside in Derry taken from an army helicopter and in a few interstitial shots between the footage of bands and gigs. The director John T. Davis told me:

> I think everybody else who came over here to do that [film the punk scene] had put it back-to-back with Pigs and Saracens and patrols and bombs going off and whatever you have it. You know, which it was a pretty determined effort not to do that, it would have been easy to do that. To show that – but why would I want to do that – it's every bloody night on the TV and when you're making a little film like that you're not – it's kids, the music, that's going to inspire, and

what the music is saying. Maybe it's different for people who come here to do that because then they're – they see it all in a different way. But it was from the inside, *Shellshock* was done from the inside if you like. From within.[14]

John made two more films about the punk scene (*Protex Hurrah*, about the eponymous band playing in New York, and *Self-Conscious Over You*, about the Good Vibrations benefit gig in 1980) before moving on to an eclectic range of other topics.[15] Agnès Maillot argues that the form of these early punk documentaries mirrors the subject matter in its raw and scrappy approach; I would go further in arguing that the form Davis adopts across this set of films represents a deliberate refusal of simplistic or mono-directional narratives both about the punk scene and about Northern Ireland as such.[16]

Throughout the 1980s and 1990s ephemeral heritage activities continued to exist, sometimes in connection with the continued presence of the Warzone Collective as a space for gigs and community activities. Bands reformed and toured – Stiff Little Fingers, for instance, released *Tinderbox* in 1997, and The Undertones reformed in 1999 with Paul McLoone replacing former lead singer Feargal Sharkey. In 2003, Sean O'Neill and Guy Trelford published what was billed as the definitive guide to punk in Northern Ireland, *It Makes You Want to Spit: An Alternative Ulster, 1977–1982*. This marked the first real wave of commemoration of the punk scene in Northern Ireland, coming around five years after the Belfast/Good Friday Agreement and shortly after the second election to take place since the devolved assembly was established in 1998. Henry McDonald, writing for the *Observer*, said the launch of the book in the Empire pub and venue brought together:

> Some of the best people to emerge from this still divided society, people who broke the sectarian taboos, tore off the tribal placards placed on their heads since birth, the people that first showed that there was another life beyond the narrow confines of orange and green.[17]

This bitter-sweet celebratory tone is broadly representative of the book itself, although the polyphonic, zine-like form it takes makes space for a slightly more complex image of punk and of the society in which it existed. The introduction sets the scene in describing Belfast in 1977 as a 'ghost town', but one in which 'a fledgling teenage rebellion was being hatched'; one in which 'disenchanted youths from all across the city brought up on a diet of violence, bigotry and sectarianism, paramilitary and police oppression, bad housing and the highest unemployment in the UK, had had enough'.[18]

In this introductory section, the punk scene is placed squarely within a political context that is not purely reducible to sectarian animosity, but that incorproates economic and material concerns as well as the violence of the state. The remainder of the book comprises photographs, scanned gig flyers and posters, texts about specific Northern Irish punk bands and autobiographical or historical reflections by fanzine writers, gig-goers and other figures associated with the punk scene – John Peel, the DJ who first played 'Teenage Kicks' on the radio, wrote the afterword. It is arranged in alphabetical order, moving from one band, venue or topic to the next (so from the Androids to the Bankrobbers, for instance); this has the effect of eschewing a chronological narratavising of the scene in favour of nimble pogoing across spaces, moments and decades. It also avoids critical hierarchy-making – bands that achieved a degree of national or international celebrity are unfussily placed along counterparts who did not. A little like Davis' *Shellshock Rock*, the book's cacophony and jumble suggests a formal consonance with what is being represented; no single image or representation of the punk scene emerges from the overlaying of different voices and narratives. This is also clear in the different ways in which contributors conceptualise or politicise the scene. Guy Trelford's piece, for example, opens with an effective piece of montage situating punk in the context of the Troubles:

> Belfast 1970 – carnage and destruction – the Abercorn, McGurk's Bar, Bloody Friday, Shankill Butchers, soldiers on the streets, police with guns, tartan gangs, paramilitaries, segregation, martial law, curfews, no-go areas, rings of steel around the city centre, deserted streets after 6pm – Welcome To The City of the Dead![19]

This approach contrasts with that of another contributor, the punkishly pseudonymised Mr Puke, who emphasises the hedonistic and nihilistic abandon of punk, as well as its relationship to adolescent sexuality:

> I never played in a band, never set any trends in punk fashion, was never much use in a fight and never managed to pull many girls (even real punk girls didn't like the smell of vomit). In fact I just used to

get drunk, sniff solvents, get arrested and get beaten up. I realise I was a particularly sad and pathetic figure – but hey, at least I wasn't a poser![20]

The 'sad and pathetic figure', mainly concerned with avoiding the calumny of being branded a poser, is some distance away from the heroic cross-community *bricoleurs* described by Henry McDonald. Mr Puke's later descent into serious addiction or abjection – he says 'I was a chronic alcoholic and crazy guys were trying to catch me to blow my kneecaps away' – is a further allusion to darker elements within the lives of Belfast punks.[21]

Deborah Withers, in her compelling reading of the Women's Liberation Music Archive, describes it as creating 'a time travelling, affective historical encounter that can bring history alive in a continuous present where past, present and future interweave'.[22] This vivacity (and its attendant muddling of temporality) are part of the affective appeal of *It Makes You Want to Spit*. This is particularly apparent in the sections on Belfast's contemporaneous punk scene of the early 2000s. These pieces draw a clear line of connection between the punk scene of the 1970s and 1980s and punk's newer manifestations in the city, which despite their sonic and aesthetic divergences from the past are seen as products of a similar animus against the status quo.[23] It is also apparent in the individual narratives throughout the book, in which (like many of my interviewees) people describe the lasting impact of punk on their lives, even as their life courses splinter off in new directions. Mr Puke, notably, retains a complex attachment to his memories of the punk scene despite a 'genuine, honest-to-God Damascus road miracle conversion' which has led him to become 'a bishop and an International Evangelist in a Pentecostal Church'.[24]

In the specific context of Northern Ireland, *It Makes You Want to Spit* is also immediately relatable to Catherine Nash's essay on local history in the North. Nash notes that local or community history has been mobilised in the post-conflict North as a vehicle for peace-building initatives, but also that there is nothing inherently inclusive, agonistic or deconstructive about a focus on locality – 'these ideas can be used in attempts to undermine as well as to reinforce separatist and culturalist understandings of "community"'.[25] The most innovative attempts at local history (and those that succeed in transcending binary oppositions between Protestants and Catholics), she argues, have found 'ways of imagining a history that includes a shared history of conflict, shared histories of common experience, and distinctive experiences of those patterns of commonality and conflict for specific localities in Northern Ireland'.[26] *It Makes You Want to Spit* represents an exemplary attempt at generating this kind of pluralised or polyvocal local history, as does the archival and reissuing work continued by Sean O'Neill on the Spit Records website.[27]

Good Vibrations, punk and the Troubles

As the previous section suggests, then, a small but dedicated group of former punks have maintained a popular memory of the scene throughout the 1990s and 2000s and up until today. This memory is localised and mobile, articulated through different forms of heritage activity (websites, gigs, club nights), through records, YouTube clips and so on, and through the overlapping memories of participants. Of particular interest to the analysis here, however, is the increased public visibility that fell upon Northern Irish punk following the release of *Good Vibrations*, a biopic of Terri Hooley by Lisa Barros D'Sa and Glenn Leyburn, in 2012.[28] The film was popular and successful in both Northern Ireland and the rest of the United Kingdom, with the influential British critic Mark Kermode describing it as his 'favourite film of the year so far' in the *Guardian*.[29] Along with the other texts discussed below, it can be understood as forming something like a second wave of popular memory of punk in Northern Ireland. While this wave is not entirely distinct from what is described in the previous section (many of the participants in the development and maintenance of punk commemoration are part of both waves, for example) some subtle shifts in inflection and tone are visible.

I conducted my interviews for this book in 2015 and 2016, meaning that many of my participants had already seen *Good Vibrations*. It was often a topic of discussion. In this sense it occupies a similar centrality in this project to that of Peter Weir's 1981 film *Gallipoli* in Alistair Thomson's *Anzac Memories*, where Australian veterans of the First World War draw on the film to recount their memories of the conflict, or to *Dad's Army* in Penny Summerfield's oral histories of British home front workers during the Second World War.³⁰ But this is not to suggest that the film provided a script that my interviewees passively reproduced. Rather, it was variously a point of comparison against which their own experiences could be measured and described, a site of memory they could draw on to translate their memories into narratable or hearable stories, and an historical representation to be argued with, critiqued, amused by or enjoyed.³¹ This aspect of the film – my interviewees' different engagements with and responses to it in the context of their own memories – will be discussed in more detail in the analysis chapters to follow. For this chapter, what I want to highlight are the ways in which *Good Vibrations* (along with some other fictional and biographical texts dealing with Northern Irish punk) represent the punk scene, the conflict and Northern Irish society more widely.

The critic and theorist Richard Kirkland, writing specifically about post-conflict cinema in Northern Ireland, argues that it does not view the war only as a period of incomprehensible misery. Instead, it 'revisits that period through the techniques of narrative leaps, flashbacks and flashforwards in order to find there a concealed potentiality that will be seen to enable and justify the later peace process'.³² It is this dynamic that I want to draw out of a consideration of *Good Vibrations* and some other, auxiliary texts which also refer to the punk scene.

In *Good Vibrations*, the 'concealed potentiality' that Kirkland suggests post-conflict cinema is pursuing is connected to older periods in Belfast's history. The film focuses on the figure of Terri Hooley, who as noted above had been a feature of 1960s countercultural life in Belfast before opening a record shop in the 1970s that became a hub for the punk scene, and later recording several important albums by local bands. By placing Hooley at the centre of the narrative, the film draws a connecting thread between the political possibilities of pre-Troubles Belfast and the political possibilities represented by the punk scene; punk is a new manifestation of an old resistant tendency, with Terri, played charismatically by Richard Dormer, acting as both midwife to the new and bridge to the old. This thread is visible in an early scene where Terri meets his future wife, who has stepped into a pub to find him DJing a reggae set to a depressingly empty pub. They talk at the bar, where she makes gentle fun of his performance, describing him as someone who seems like they don't have many friends. 'Do you want to know the truth of it?', Terri says. 'I used to have lots of friends. Lots of anarchist friends, and Marxist friends, and socialist friends, and pacifist friends, and feminist friends, and friends who were fuck all.' When the Troubles started, he goes on, he suddenly found that he only had Protestant friends and Catholic friends – the hopeful multiplicity of the early 1960s, in the film's account, curdling into the zero-sum binaries of the 1970s.

In this context, Terri's decision to open a record shop appears to be a quixotic one, although (in an echo of Gavin Robinson's entrepreneurial reading of punk, mentioned above) he does establish a friendly relationship with a bank manager, who tells him he is the first person in years to request funding for a new business. Despite the bank manager's encouragement, the shop is shown to be struggling to attract custom in the context of the Troubles, which are presented via a montage of documentary and news footage featuring violence and exploding bombs. This nervous interlude is interrupted, though, when Terri is startled by a young man asking him if he stocks 'Orgasm Addict' by the Buzzcocks, to his obvious bemusement, and then demanding that he put up a poster for an upcoming gig, a prospect that leaves him similarly bemused. Nonetheless, he sticks up the poster, putting it on a pinboard to replace a yellowed flyer for a Rolling Stones gig at the Ulster Hall, in a further nod to the temporal connection being drawn between 1960s radicalism and the punk scene.

Terri attends the gig with Dave Hyndman, and is delighted to discover a community that appears to reject the Protestant–Catholic binary he deplored earlier in favour of an inchoate anti-authoritarian attitude that mirrors his own. This is reinforced when a brief row with a policeman is defused by Rudi starting to play 'Cops', and the audience breaking into a chant of 'SS RUC'. Terri is absorbed into the bouncing crowd, with a close-up on his face showing his excitement as the band move into 'Big Time', one of the best-loved songs of the punk era in Northern Ireland. At the end of the concert, a drunk but enthused Terri tells the sceptical band that he wants to help them put out a record.

Punk, as we see it presented here, is not so much about politics as it is about the rejection of politics, or at least of politics as it manifests itself in party-driven antagonism and demands, and of the seizure of power.³³ What Terri is impressed by is the young people's capacity for refusal. This is dramatised in several scenes throughout the film. A British soldier is baffled when the punks, their van having been stopped by the army on their way back from a gig outside of the city, reveal themselves to be both Protestant and Catholic; later, a sleazy English record executive is equally baffled by the lack of gritty, Troubles-driven realism in the music of The Undertones, telling Terri that if anything they sound like they're having too good of a time.³⁴ The image of the scene as inoculating young people from a commitment to the ethno-sectarian divide is further illuminated by mirroring the punks with two antagonistic loyalist skinheads, who seem to represent the malign effect of Northern Irish society on some young people; if the punks are magically immune to sectarianism, the skinheads are suffused with it. At the start of the film, Terri placates the local paramilitaries – both loyalist and republican – by offering them a selection of rare 1960s records. One of them warns him that it isn't them he has to worry about, but their younger counterparts, the ones 'coming up behind them' – they don't even remember a time before the conflict, he warns Terri, rendering them the implacable products of a decontextualised or depoliticised culture of violence.³⁵ This is emphasised when they beat Terri up and wreck his shop, telling him: 'You made such a big deal about not letting me in here. And look at it. It's fuck all. You're fuck all. You fucking lost.'

Particularly in this scene, the skinheads could be understood as embodying violence in Northern Ireland as such, the dark forces that Terri is attempting to keep at bay. But more narrowly, they evoke the anxious prophecies of early studies of childhood in Northern Ireland during the conflict, such as those of the American psychologist Rona Fields, who worried that exposure to violence and deprivation was creating a generation of traumatised and unstable young people.³⁶ In this sense they are the inverse of the punks, who absorb the same raw material as the skinheads but turn it to other ends – as Terri puts it in a speech on the stage of the Ulster Hall, in a final scene portraying the Punk and New Wave Festival of 1982, 'New York has the haircuts, London has the trousers, but Belfast has the reason'. Unlike the skinheads, passive receptacles of violence and irrationality, the punks are *bricoleurs* who 'disrupt and reorganise meaning', reworking the stuff of Northern Irish society through their anarchic aesthetic choices and their messy sociality.[37] This is a narrative that broadly coheres to the reading of punk offered by historian of Northern Irish music Martin McLoone, who portrays the scene as offering 'opposition ... to the status quo as well to those aggressive and violent opponents of the status quo who had reduced daily life to the abject'.[38]

To return to Richard Kirkland's argument, *Good Vibrations* fits into his category of post-conflict cinema that returns to the past in order to find the seeds of the political settlement among the debris and violence of the Troubles. It is notable that, beyond the 'SS RUC' chant and the very fact of their contiguity as Protestant and Catholics, the punks do not express any political position whatsoever – in this sense, they could be understood as ideal auguries for what Colin Coulter has denounced in post-Agreement Northern Ireland as 'a political culture that increasingly seems capable only of asking ordinary people to name the constitutional arrangement under which they would like to be unemployed'.[39] Their politics, that is, are reducible to those of good relations between polarised ethnic groups, with little possibility for thinking outside of or beyond this model.

At the same time, the film has elements of what Kirkland sees as a characteristic of a previous period of cinematic representations of Northern Ireland, in which the conflict was presented as 'an ineffable world of sadistic violence'.[40] The visions we are offered of the conflict against which punk takes place, and against which Hooley rails, are flat and vague, although no less affecting for that; an explosion on a city street, a brief and horrible glimpse of someone killed in a bombing, perhaps Bloody Friday, a shot of the wreckage following the Miami Showband massacre. There is little sense of stakes, or history, in what we are shown. Although this does not obviate the film's touching and powerful representation of punk as a form of resistant sociality, or its status as what Caroline Magennis astutely describes as 'one of the most notable expressions of Northern Irish joy on screen', it does make the question of what the punks are resisting and why somewhat difficult to answer.[41] This is an ambivalent inscrutability; it could be a precursor to the blank, bloodless politics of community relations, but it could also signify a kind of fugitivity or refusal, a rejection of the terms of Northern Irish society within which the political can be rendered visible.

The other post-2000s texts considered here are also attempts to make sense of the punk scene in the context of the Troubles. Terri Hooley's memoir, *Hooleygan: Music, Mayhem, Good Vibrations*, co-written with the journalist Richard Sullivan, focuses on punk's relationship to and rejection of tradition and moral conservatism in Northern Ireland during the conflict.[42] Published in 2010, the book is a kaleidoscopic juxtaposition of Hooley and Sullivan's text with photographs, drawings, pages of zines and so on, as well as brief interludes between chapters in which various luminaries –from Greg Cowan of The Outcasts, to Brian Young of Rudi, to the DJ and producer David Holmes – describe their encounters with Terri, giving the text a polyphonic, commemorative appeal comparable to *It Makes You Want to Spit* and disrupting a linear biographical narrative in favour of the synchronic, fragmentary effect of a collage or a zine.[43] The book begins with Terri's early childhood, noting the influence of his father's socialist politics and of his own youthful involvement with the Campaign for Nuclear Disarmament or CND; the latter campaign shaped his rejection of the parochialism of Northern Irish politics, where 'even in the late sixties it was becoming increasingly obvious that no matter what cause, project or principle you became involved in, it came with a sectarian tag'.[44]

This despairing portrayal of Northern Ireland during the war did not discourage Terri from setting up a record shop on Great Victoria Street, 'which, in the 1970s, was probably the most bombed piece of real estate in the world'.[45] Initially, this was as part of a cooperative endeavour including a health food shop called Sassafraz and a printing press run by Dave Hyndman, as is alluded to in *Good Vibrations*. Terri remembers the building from the sixties, 'when it was sandwiched between an antique shop with a big old cannon sitting outside on the pavement, and a shop which sold Lambeg drums'.[46] This is a nice bit of staging on Hooley's part, juxtaposing the radical possibilities of the cooperative with the attenuated militarism and Orangeism of the post-partition state. It sets the scene nicely for the emergence of punk, of which Terri says: 'I loved the energy and I loved the fact these kids didn't seem to give a shit about the cops and were prepared to take them on. Punk was anarchy, and I had been waiting for it all my life.'[47] The final clause there is temporally interesting, highlighting both the disruptive novelty of punk and Terri's status as the ideal facilitator for this exciting new scene. This is the focus of the remainder of the book, which largely hits the expected beats of a music memoir, describing encounters with bands and labels, notable gigs and interludes of drink, drugs and debauchery.

The specificities of life in Northern Ireland are only intermittently visible and often rendered with dry comedy. When Terri stays in Feargal Sharkey of The Undertones' childhood bedroom, for instance, he finds it bedecked with religious paraphernalia, allegedly including a 3D picture of the Last Supper. In the morning, he emerges from the room to tell the singer that he's proud of being a Protestant for the first time in his life. 'Feargal seemed taken aback and replied "What are you talking about Terri? I've never heard you talk like that." "Take a look around", I said, "How could you have a wank in a room like this?"'[48] This is a comic vignette, but as in the example above about the location of his first record shop, it is one that both sketches a picture of Northern Ireland (as mired in the pleasureless confines of religious dogmatism) and positions punk in relation to it (as a space where both the dogmatism and its attendant sectarian division can be made fun of and disrupted).

A similar tack is followed by the journalist Henry McDonald in his writing about the punk scene, which he took part in as a young man in Belfast. McDonald has expressed a nostalgic enthusiasm for the possibilities engendered by punk in columns for the *Observer* and in his 2004 memoir *Colours*.[49] In one article, McDonald reminisces about being stopped by the police:

> When an old cop started taking our names and addresses he looked flummoxed. There were punks from the Glencairn estate, Divis Flats, Ardoyne, the Lower Shankill and the Markets. It must have been the first time since 1969 that he had encountered a large group of youths from working-class republican and loyalist areas that were not trying to kill each other.[50]

Here we have, in utero – the article was published in 2002 – a variation on the scene in *Good Vibrations* where the army search a van stacked with bedgraggled punks from all over Belfast. As Martin McLoone says, 'McDonald's "old cop" may be a rhetorical flourish but it is significant'.[51] In the context of a post-conflict Northern Ireland where segregation of young Protestants and Catholics remained the norm in Belfast, he is evoking a world of non-sectarian sociality that is incomprehensible to the eyes of the state.

In his recent novel, *Two Souls*, McDonald takes a similar approach, although his representation of punk here is more phlegmatic and markedly less utopian.[52] This is partly manifested through the cross-cutting of punk with football fandom – the novel centres around the 1979 Irish Cup final between Portadown and Cliftonville, allowing McDonald to highlight sectarian animosity as expressed between the two groups of fans, in contrast to the relatively non-sectarian spaces of the punk scene. In a pub before the game kicks off, for instance, the narrator, Robbie Ruin, is surprised to recognise a fellow punk:

> We have spoken before in Terri Hooley's shop in Great Victoria Street while flicking through the boxes of singles and albums, searching for left-field bands such as Television, Magazine and Cabaret Voltaire. We didn't speak about Cliftonville, the Red Army and all the associated aggro of the season. Good Vibes wouldn't have been the place for such a discussion.[53]

The juxtaposition of the two subcultures is effective in generating a more nuanced vision of punk's role in people's lives; its capacity to challenge normative social relations in Northern Ireland is presented here as both geographically and temporally bounded, a dimension of the narrative that becomes especially clear through the narrator's increasing involvement in republican politics, activism and violence. McDonald also achieves this effect through the working-class, Catholic narrator's relationship with a middle-class Protestant woman, Sabine, whom he meets in the Pound bar. Their whirlwind romance is initially driven by a shared rejection of sectarian identifications that is reminscent of the teenagers in *Good Vibrations* – she explains to him: 'You are not of them the way I am not one of them, Mr Ruin. We are not like any of them. Our so-called sides. I could tell that about you almost right away.'[54] But a chance encounter with Sabine's family draws out some of the tensions that cannot be exorcised through this verbal disassociation from the 'sides' of the conflict, leading to a row in which Robbie says: 'Just tell them I am one of those unclean Fenians from the reservation down below. Tell them I'm one of the natives.'[55] As in the encounter with the fellow Cliftonville fan, it seems that McDonald's sense of the structure of feeling of the punk scene is of something that is fleeting and fragile, that can hold some of the contradictions and violences in Northern Irish society in abeyance but that ultimately cannot transcend them. This is emphasised by the deconstructed thriller plotline that comes to the fore in the second half of the book, which centres the complicating presence of the Troubles in the lives of the young people being depicted.

McDonald frames the punk scene with a wider lens than the other representations considered above; the election of Margaret Thatcher in 1979 is a topic of discussion among his protagonists, as are East and West Berlin and the ongoing Sino–Vietnamese War. The narrator's father is a communist who has broken with the mainstream republican movement as a consequence of his commitment to the workers' movement, and this generates another horizon for McDonald to set the punk scene against. In one scene this tension is explicitly staged, when the father argues with his son about the inadequacy of youth culture and politics, responding to Sabine's question about whether he's really a communist.

> Yes love, I certainly am. So is Marty here and some of the other comrades in the bar today. So was your boyfriend too, for a while, before he discovered all that posy anarchy, chaos and destruction malarkey. When he grows up he might become a good Marxist again. He could have a great future in the party.[56]

Here and throughout, McDonald is having some fun with the doctrinaire spiel of the 'old' left, although this is comingled with both fondness and admiration; similarly, his portrayal of the punk scene mixes an awareness of limits and internal tensions with an enthusiasm for the vitality and defiance of the young people involved.[57]

In general, though, this is a markedly less optimistic portrayal of punk than the others discussed so far – like *Good Vibrations*, it sees the present and the future in the past, but what it sees is no longer hopeful. The temporal jumps undertaken in the final sections of the novel make this clear, moving forward to 1994 and the ceasefire, which occurs alongside the death of the narrator's father. It is clear that he is still affected by the events of the book and of the conflict, and his complicity in them – 'I was heading to another trench – one I think I never left', the chapter ends.[58] The pessimism that is apparent here is to some extent a function of the (admittedly somewhat askew) thriller form that dominates the second half of the book, with the narrator becoming involved in republican paramilitary activity. As Laura Pelaschiar argues, 'the thriller, with its stereotyped generic mechanisms ("goodies" against "baddies") does not allow for any open interplay between characters and circumstances and leaves very little space for an articulated contextualisation of the Northern Irish reality'.[59] While there are no obvious goodies or baddies in McDonald's self-aware rendering of the genre, his approach has a similar effect in generating a despairing, bleak portrait of the North. In that sense, the novel is also notably a product of 2019, published in the middle of the three-year suspension of the executive at Stormont and fresh anxieties around Brexit and the border; the optimistic tenor of previous representations, including McDonald's own, have been replaced with something more anxious and uncertain.

Punk, heritage and space in Belfast

Uncertainity and ambivablence also characterise the remants of punk in the built environment of Belfast. Laura Oldfield Ford, in her elegiac zine collection *Savage Messiah*, summons up the ghosts of London's radical countercultures – punk, rave, squats, the free party scene – to occupy the seemingly blank spaces of the 'regenerated', neoliberal city. She evokes 'collective moments of euphoria, like Reclaim the Streets, parties taking over the Westway, blocking roads … [moments of] breaking out of this atomised despondency and actually achieving something really empowering', and situates them in the context of the 'sinister harmony' of the rebranded and sanitised London of the 2010s.[60] Aaron Kelly, writing in the wake of the Belfast/Good Friday Agreement, percieves a related atmosphere in the new urban landscape of Belfast, one that for him reflects the new economic and political dispensation of the North. 'This drawing and quartering of Belfast by urban planning, private enterprise and the state … hangs upon the occlusion rather than the inclusion of working-class experience and participation in civic and commercial life in Belfast', he adds.[61] This occlusion goes hand in hand with the mobilisation of culture as both an explanation of and a panacea for conflict – 'culture, in this guise, is employed to create a fantasy space in which we all share equally a regenerative diversity, which in fact masks specific social and economic disadvantage'.[62]

The heritage of punk functions ambivalently within this narrative. As the lionisation of Hooley and the installation of the plaque in the Cathedral Quarter suggest, it is one of the cultural wellsprings that can be drawn from in the ongoing attempts to rebrand the city as a tourist and investment-friendly space. As is often the case with top-down regeneration of cities, the Cathedral Quarter generates much of its cachet and its appeal from cannibalising the remnants of the past; in addition to being a central site for the punk scene, where several of the bars frequented by my interviewees were situated, this part of Belfast was a hub for the vestiges of bohemia that persisted in the city throughout the Troubles, facilitated by 'the decline of commercial premises, increase in vacant sites and availability of short-term leases and low-priced rent'.[63] Its image as the 'artistic' quarter has persisted even as rents have risen and private sector investment, intially driven by the Laganside Corporation, has increased.[64] At the beginning of 2020, Castlebrook Investments were granted outline planning approval for a proposed £500 million regeneration of the area, a plan which they are, ludicrously, calling 'Tribeca Belfast'.[65]

The cultural memory of punk, then, is one of the friendly ghosts that are conjured and diffused across this part of the city by developers and politicians keen to capitalise on its status as a cool or artistic location. This creates a strange spatial context for the memories expressed by my interviewees, who are describing the places of the punk scene to me at a moment where these spaces are both visible and invisible – so, for instance, there is a new Harp Bar in the Cathedral Quarter very close to the old site of the Harp Bar that hosted punk gigs, although the modern one is a psuedo-traditional pub of a style familiar to anyone who has visited Temple Bar in Dublin, drawing on the decontextualised signifiers of Irishness that Mark McGovern describes as 'anaesthetising the Irish social and cultural experience to a reified portrait'.[66] The original site of the Harp Bar is also expected to be turned into a boutique hotel.[67] Most of the shops and bars that my interviewees describe are now gone, with some exceptions – Lavery's, Queen's Student Union (although it now has a different name), the Ulster Hall – and while public spaces like the Cornmarket still exist, the context of the city around them is indelibly changed. In general it would appear that the little that remains of the punk scene in the built environment of the city has been enlisted into processes of top-down urban redevelopment and rebranding.

But there are some spatial remainders of punk that are, arguably, more difficult to assimilate into the arc of regeneration and prosperity followed by Castlebrook Investments and their ilk. In 2018, following a campaign by Dee Wilson and other former punks, a blue plaque was unveiled at the former site of the Trident bar in Bangor to commemorate what it describes as the birthplace of punk in Northern Ireland; unlike the plaque in the Cathedral Quarter, this was an unofficial act of commemoration, and is attributed to the 'Alternative Ulster Historical Society' in a reference to the famous Stiff Little Fingers song 'Alternative Ulster'.[68] The official Ulster Historical Circle had refused to countenance the idea of a plaque, arguing that it did not fit with their criteria 'because it was not for a specific individual or achievement'. Dee Wilson, contesting their claim, said: 'This plaque clearly celebrates a building (that is no longer standing) as well as an era. It's middle-class snobbery and elitism to ignore the contribution of punk here.'[69] It is interesting that the Ulster Historical Circle explicitly stated that the plural or non-individual aspect of the plaque is what renders it invalid – this chimes with the comments of some of my interviewees that *Good Vibrations*, because of its focus on Terri Hooley as a faciliatator of the scene, tended to occlude the collective agency of the young people who made the punk scene happen by themselves.[70] The Warzone Centre, a spin off of the Warzone Collective organised by Petesy Burns and friends, still exists near Great Victoria Street station, and although operating on an irregular basis remains the city's only autonomous social centre; the Just Books collective, initially founded by Dave and Marilyn Hyndman among others, still has a presence in the city via the Belfast Solidarity Centre.

And in 2004, following the death of the radio DJ John Peel, a piece of graffiti appeared on the Bridge End flyover in east Belfast bearing a snippet of lyrics – 'teenage dreams / so hard to beat' – from The Undertones' 'Teenage Kicks', famously Peel's favourite song. In 2013 it was removed by the Department of Social Development as part of a £300,000 improvement scheme for the area, but following an outcry from various cultural luminaries and many former punks,

a new version was designed and painted by young people from both the Short Strand and the lower Newtownards Road areas under the aegis of the East Belfast Partnership.[71] This back-and-forth seems like a microcosmic version of the ambivalent status of punk in the redeveloped city: on the one hand, it is part of the past that is defended by community groups seeking to defend against the erasure of the complexities of the past by a combination of private investment and the state-led quartering of Belfast indicted by Kelly and others; on the other, it is grist to the mill of that process, drawn on as a way of producing a usable narrative of the past that elides the continued legacies of the conflict and of social deprivation in the North.

Popular memory and oral history in Northern Ireland

How, then, do these interlinking narratives about the past relate to the conversations I had with my interviewees? This will be considered throughout the next four chapters with reference to specific interviews, but in this section I will offer a brief theoretical account of the relationship between the memory cultures described above and oral history.

As I explain at the start of the chapter, I am not suggesting that the existence of dominant narratives about the past means that we can see these narratives being reproduced wholesale in oral history narratives. But these narratives do, as the Popular Memory Group (PMG) suggest in their groundbreaking work on the relationship between past and present, provide the neccesary material, or the conditions of expression, for the construction of individual memories – 'memories of the past are, like all common-sense forms, strangely composite constructions, resembling a kind of geology, the selective sedimentation of past traces'.[72] In the context of the punk scene in Belfast, this composite is the meeting of various streams – the representations described in some detail above, but also a wider, transnational memory of punk as a global subculture, along with the popular memory of the Troubles in Northern Ireland, which is obviously in itself not a unified field.

What I am interested in is how my interviewees engage with this confluence of possible narratives when telling me stories and sharing memories about the punk scene, and when trying to express what (via Raymond Williams) I have described in Chapter 1 and elsewhere as the structure of feeling of this scene.[73] The PMG highlight how representations of the past provide a comprehensible language in which individual memories of the past can be expressed, and how the production of these narratives is enmeshed in questions of politics and power. In the context of my research, the punk scene offers a way to speak about memories of growing up in Northern Ireland during the Troubles, memories which (with some exceptions) are less visible than other aspects of the conflict; as Oonagh Murphy and Laura Aguiar argue in their analysis of the public sharing of Bronagh McAtasney's teenage diary from the 1980s, 'very little has been heard about the everyday lived experiences of those on the periphery of this conflict, particularly children and adolescents'.[74] The relative visibility of the punk scene in cultural memory means it is a space where various aspects of everyday life during the conflict can be addressed. Talking about being a punk and about what that entailed, as will be apparent in the interview chapters across the book, was also a way of discussing what it was like to grow up in the North, without always addressing those experiences directly; the familiar beat of stories about punk sometimes makes it possible for more dissonant elements of individual memories to be expressed, sometimes obliquely or at a slant angle. However, this can also be a process of delimiting or of constraint. Narratives that do not fit into the parameters of the memory cultures of the punk scene described above might be harder to express, or harder to understand on the part of the listener or interviewer. My analysis of the interviews in the following chapters will be attentive to these dynamics.

They are particularly relevant when thinking about the meaning interviewees assign to punk in relation to the composure of their own lives and subjectivites, to use Graham Dawson's important concept, in describing what it means to have been a punk in the context of Northern Ireland's unsettled present.[75] As Hilary Young has suggested in analysis of her oral history interviews with Glaswegian men on masculinity and fatherhood, composure does not entail the existence of a completely fixed or stable sense of self.[76] Interviewees are offering us brief and partial glimpses of a complex and shifting thing, as Lucy Newby has shown in her work on memories of childhood in Belfast.[77] What they offer is shaped both by existing narratives of the past and by intersubjective dynamics in the moment of the interview – the importance of this last factor is considered in more detail when it comes up in the interviews discussed in the following chapters.

Drawing on the work of critical oral historians such as Luisa Passerini and Alessandro Portelli, as well as Graham Dawson's work on temporality and memory in Northern Ireland, my analysis of the interviews in the following four chapters will seek to consider the presence and the function of representations of the past in the stories of my interviewees.[78] For my project, there are three key points to be taken from Portelli, Passerini and Dawson's approach. Firstly, when my interviewees describe the punk scene, they are reconstructing a narrative that draws on cultural memories and shared symbolic structures of expression, cultural memories that have different layers (public and private, for instance) and that are themselves contested rather than fixed. Secondly, the presence of this reservoir of cultural memories and discourses means that individual memories are never entirely individual; instead, they are social products, in which people make sense of their experiences through an engagement with these wider frames. Finally, it also means that my interviewees' memories are expressions of their understanding of and position in the present as well as the past.

Methodologically, these three points entail a particular kind of engagement with my interviewees' narratives. My approach is to listen to individual memories for their social echoes, and for their imbrication in and evocation of a particular structure of feeling; to pay attention to the form and style of the memories as well as to their content; and to frame and narrate the analysis in a form that makes the present-driven formulation of the accounts, and the intersubjective dimension of this formulation, apparent. In taking this approach, the analysis hopes to provide an insight into the politics of memory in contemporary Northern Ireland as well as into the structure of feeling of punk in the 1970s and 1980s.

Conclusion

From *Shellshock Rock* in 1979 through to *Good Vibrations* in 2012 and to the Alternative Ulster Historical Society's plaque outside the

Trident in Bangor in 2018, the punk scene in Northern Ireland has been the subject of representation, historicisation and commemoration. These processes intersect with a wider, transnational popular memory of punk as such. They also intersect, importantly, with memories of the conflict in Northern Ireland, memories which continue to be contested and unsettled.[79] This chapter has charted the development of the popular memory of punk through from its earliest moments up to the crystallisation or the coherence of this memory around projects such as *It Makes You Want to Spit* or *Good Vibrations*. Broadly speaking, post-conflict representations of the scene have viewed it as a non-sectarian or cross-sectarian youth culture, a view which was also expressed by my interviewees.

This representation has two effects, I would suggest. On the one hand, it can be used to reinforce a reading of the conflict in Northern Ireland as *primarily* the product of interpersonal sectarian animosity, a reading that occludes other structural factors in the conflict as well as the role of the British state as an actor in the conflict, as suggested in the previous chapter. On the other hand, it can make it harder to envisage or narrate different stories about the punk scene, whether those be ones that show the ways in which sectarianism continued to exist within it, or ones that shift the focus to other political possibilities or engagements within the scene (around gender, class or sexuality, for instance).

Good Vibrations is the text that pushes the primacy of sectarianism the harderst, although this does not mean it is unamenable to alternative readings such as that of Caroline Magennis. It contrasts with the more polyvocal approaches seen in *Shellshock Rock* and *It Makes You Want to Spit*, and the more pessimistic approach evident in Henry McDonald's recent novel *Two Souls*. The following four chapters will consider how a series of interviewees describe their memories of the scene, in conversation with some of the representations and popular memories analysed above.

Notes

1 Lisa Barros D'Sa and Glen Leyburn, *Good Vibrations* (London: Universal Pictures UK, 2012).

2 'Hooley All Smiles as Belfast City Council Honours "The Godfather of Punk"', *Belfast Daily*, 11 November 2012, online at: www.belfastdaily.co.uk/2012/11/09/belfast-city-council-honours-godfather-of-punk-terri-hooley/ (accessed 20 December 2021).
3 Jonathan Tonge and Jocelyn Evans, 'Northern Ireland: Double Triumph for the Democratic Unionist Party', *Parliamentary Affairs* 71:1 (2018), pp. 139–54; James W. McAuley and Jonathan Tonge, '"For God and for the Crown": Contemporary Political and Social Attitudes among Orange Order Members in Northern Ireland', *Political Psychology* 28:1 (2007), pp. 33–52.
4 'Take Down Peace Walls, NY Mayor', *BBC News*, 8 May 2008, online at: http://news.bbc.co.uk/1/hi/northern_ireland/7390938.stm (accessed 20 December 2021).
5 Mark Fisher, *Capitalist Realism: Is There No Alternative?* (London: Zero Books, 2009); for an application of this work to the Northern Irish context see George Legg, *Northern Ireland and the Politics of Boredom: Conflict, Capital and Culture* (Manchester: Manchester University Press, 2018).
6 Aaron Kelly, 'Geopolitical Eclipse', *Third Text* 19:5 (2005), pp. 545–53; Phil Ramsey, '"A Pleasingly Blank Canvas": Urban Regeneration in Northern Ireland and the Case of Titanic Quarter', *Space and Polity* 17:2 (2013), pp. 164–79; for a fascinating account of the attempts to utilise urban design as a peacebuilding tool in Belfast since the 1970s and a set of proposals for how this should be done in the future see Frank Gaffikin *et al.*, *Making Space for Each Other: Civic Place-Making in a Divided Society* (Belfast: Queen's University Belfast, 2016).
7 Lucy Robinson, 'Exhibition Review Punk's 40th Anniversary – An Itchy Sort of Heritage', *Twentieth Century British History* 39:2 (2017), p. 313.
8 *Ibid.*, p. 315.
9 Richard Cabut and Andrew Gallix (eds), *Punk is Dead: Modernity Killed Every Night* (London, Zero Books, 2017).
10 BY, 2016.
11 Raphael Samuel, *Theatres of Memory: Past and Present in Contemporary Culture* (London: Verso, 2012), is the classic text on non-professionalised historical practices. This will be discussed further in my analysis of Graeme Mullan's interview in Chapter 6.
12 Red Chidgey, 'Reassess Your Weapons: The Making of Feminist Memory in Young Women's Zines', *Women's History Review* 22:4 (2013), p. 669.
13 John T. Davis, *Shellshock Rock* (Hollywood Films, 1979).
14 Interview with John T. Davis, conducted by Fearghus Roulston, 2016.

15 Harvey O'Brien, 'Somewhere to Come Back to: The Filmic Journeys of John T. Davis', *Irish Studies Review* 9:2 (2001), pp. 167–77.
16 Agnès Maillot, 'Punk on Celluloid: John Davis' Shellshock Rock (1979)', *Historical Journal of Film, Radio and Television* 20:3 (2000), pp. 375–83.
17 Henry McDonald, 'Punk's Lost Vision', *Observer*, 9 November 2003, online at: www.theguardian.com/uk/2003/nov/09/northernireland (accessed 16 December 2021).
18 O'Neill and Trelford, *It Makes You Want to Spit*.
19 *Ibid.*, p. 46.
20 *Ibid.*, p. 120.
21 *Ibid*. On abjection in the Northern Irish punk scene see Timothy Heron, '"We're Only Monsters": Punk Bodies and the Grotesque in 1970s Northern Ireland', *Etudes irlandaises* 42:1 (2017), pp. 139–54.
22 Deborah Withers, 'Re-Enacting Process: Temporality, Historicity and the Women's Liberation Music Archive', International Journal of Heritage Studies 20:7–8 (2014), p. 699.
23 O'Neill and Trelford, *It Makes You Want to Spit*, p. 260.
24 *Ibid.* p. 120.
25 Catherine Nash, 'Local Histories in Northern Ireland', *History Workshop Journal* 60:1 (2005), p. 49.
26 *Ibid.*, p. 65.
27 www.spitrecords.co.uk (accessed 30 September 2020); for a theoretical account of the relationship between popular memory and reissued music see Andrew J. Bottomley, 'Play It Again: Rock Music Reissues and the Production of the Past for the Present', *Popular Music and Society* 39:2 (2016), pp. 151–74.
28 Barros D'Sa and Leyburn, *Good Vibrations*.
29 Mark Kermode, 'Mark Kermode's DVD Round-Up', 4 August 2013, online at: www.theguardian.com/film/2013/aug/04/good-vibrations-trance-blancanieves-dvd (accessed 17 August 2020).
30 Thomson, *Anzac Memories*; Summerfield, *Reconstructing Women's Wartime Lives*.
31 Lucy Newby, 'Troubled Generations? (De)Constructing Narratives of Youth Experience in the Northern Ireland Conflict', *Journal of War & Cultural Studies* 14:1 (2021), pp. 6–24.
32 Richard Kirkland, 'Visualising Peace: Northern Irish Post-Conflict Cinema and the Politics of Reconciliation', *Review of Irish Studies in Europe* 1:2 (2017), p. 19; on temporality and agency in post-conflict films see also Lucy Newby and Fearghus Roulston, 'Innocent Victims and Troubled Combatants: Representations of Childhood and Adolescence in Post-Conflict Northern Irish Cinema', in Ingrid E. Castro and Jessica Clark (eds), *Representing Agency in Popular Culture: Children and*

Youth on Page, Screen and In Between (London: Lexington Books, 2018), pp. 23–41.

33 The hard-to-define concept of 'politics', as used here, is understood as something like what Fred Moten and Stefano Harney describe as a 'correctional institution', or as that which is antagonistic to 'actually existing social life': Stefano Harney and Fred Moten, *The Undercommons: Fugitive Planning and Black Study* (Wivenhoe: Minor Compositions, 2013), p. 16.

34 The Undertones were staunch in their refusal to write about the political situation in Northern Ireland, as is ironically signified in their 1980 release 'More Songs About Chocolate and Girls'. This refusal was also a topic of discussion in contemporaneous interviews with the band – see for instance Harry Doherty, 'The Undertones: Putting on the Anti-Style', *Melody Maker*, 10 March 1979. It's worth noting that the later project of principal Undertones songwriter John O'Neill, That Petrol Emotion, took a much more explicitly political stance in their aesthetics and lyrics.

35 On the general tendency to view young people in this way in post-conflict representations of the Troubles, see again Newby and Roulston, 'Innocent Victims and Troubled Combatants'.

36 Rona Fields, *Northern Ireland: Society Under Siege* (London: Routledge, 1980); for an overview of this early literature in Northern Irish childhood studies see Ed Cairns, *Caught in the Crossfire: Children in the Northern Ireland Conflict* (Belfast: Appletree Press, 1987).

37 Dick Hebdige, *Subculture: The Meaning of Style* (London: Penguin, 1979), p. 106.

38 Martin McLoone, 'Punk Music in Northern Ireland: The Political Power of "What Might Have Been"', *Irish Studies Review* 12:1 (2004), p. 32.

39 Colin Coulter, 'Under Which Constitutional Arrangement Would You Still Prefer to Be Unemployed? Neoliberalism, the Peace Process, and the Politics of Class in Northern Ireland', *Studies in Conflict & Terrorism* 37:9 (2014), p. 774.

40 Kirkland, 'Visualising Peace', p. 16.

41 Caroline Magennis, '"Bubbles of joy": Moments of Pleasure in Recent Northern Irish Culture', *Etudes irlandaises*, 42:1 (2017), p. 165.

42 Richard Sullivan and Terri Hooley, *Hooleygan: Music, Mayhem, Good Vibrations* (Belfast: Blackstaff Press, 2010).

43 Annette Kuhn, 'Memory Texts and Memory Work: Performances of Memory in and with Visual Media', *Memory Studies* 3:4 (2010), pp. 298–313.

44 Hooley and Sullivan, *Hooleygan*, p. 40.

45 *Ibid.*, p. 52.

46 *Ibid.*, pp. 52–53.
47 *Ibid.*, p. 63.
48 *Ibid.*, p. 99.
49 Henry McDonald, *Colours: Ireland from Bombs to Boom* (Edinburgh: Mainstream Publishing, 2004).
50 Henry McDonald, 'Safety Pins Will be Worn', *Observer*, 2 June 2002, online at: www.theguardian.com/observer/comment/story/0,6903,726218,00.html (accessed 17 August 2020).
51 McLoone, 'Punk Music in Northern Ireland', p. 32.
52 Henry McDonald, *Two Souls* (Newbridge: Merrion Press, 2019).
53 *Ibid.*, p. 7.
54 *Ibid.*, p. 32.
55 *Ibid.*, p. 91.
56 *Ibid.*, p. 154.
57 For an account arguing that punk 'evidenced the turn away from prior forms of working-class organization toward other modalities of struggle' see Stuart Schrader, 'Rank-and-File Antiracism: Historicizing Punk and Rock Against Racism', *Radical History Review* 138 (2020), pp. 131–43.
58 *Ibid.*, p. 234.
59 Laura Pelaschiar, *Writing The North: The Contemporary Novel in Northern Ireland* (Trieste: Edizioni Parnaso, 1998).
60 Robert Barry, 'Zones of Sacrifice: Drifting Through London With Laura Oldfield Ford', *The Quietus*, 2017, online at: http://thequietus.com/articles/21820-laura-oldfield-ford-interview (accessed 17 August 2020); see also Laura Oldfield Ford, *Savage Messiah* (London: Verso Books, 2011).
61 Kelly, 'Geopolitical Eclipse', p. 547.
62 *Ibid.*, p. 548.
63 Carla McManus and Clare Carruthers, 'Cultural Quarters and Urban Regeneration – the Case of Cathedral Quarter Belfast', *International Journal of Cultural Policy* 20:1 (2014), pp. 78–98.
64 Many of the city's cultural organisations – the Black Box venue, the Belfast Exposed photography gallery and workshop space, the MAC theatre – are still based in this area.
65 Michael Kenwood, 'Council Wants 'Respect' Shown for Belfast's Writer's Square as Tribeca Development Begins', *Belfast Telegraph*, 3 February 2021, online at: www.belfasttelegraph.co.uk/news/northern-ireland/council-wants-respect-shown-for-belfasts-writers-square-as-tribeca-development-begins-40046204.html (accessed 17 December 2021); see also Stephen Baker, 'Tribeca Belfast and the On-Screen Regeneration of Northern Ireland', *International Journal of Media and Cultural Politics* 16:1 (2020), pp. 11–26.

66 Mark McGovern, '"The 'Craic' Market": Irish Theme Bars and the Commodification of Irishness in Contemporary Britain', *Irish Journal of Sociology* 11:2 (2002), p. 95. The Harp Bar has now shut down in the wake of the Covid-19 pandemic.

67 Ryan McAleer, 'Boutique Hotel Planned for Original Site of Belfast's Premier Punk Venue', *Belfast Telegraph*, 8 March 2019, online at: www.belfasttelegraph.co.uk/business/northern-ireland/boutique-hotel-planned-for-original-site-of-belfasts-premier-punk-venue-37890077.html (accessed 17 August 2020).

68 Ann-Marie Foster, 'Alternative Ulster: Marking Punk's Bangor Birthplace', *BBC News NI*, 10 September 2018, online at: www.bbc.co.uk/news/uk-northern-ireland-45317415 (accessed 17 August 2020).

69 Henry McDonald, 'Four Decades On, "It's Time to Honour" the Punk Dreamers of an Alternative Ulster', *Observer*, 18 February 2017, online at: www.theguardian.com/uk-news/2017/feb/18/alternative-ulster-punk-dreamers-trident-bar-bangor-stiff-little-fingers (accessed 17 August 2020).

70 See Chapter 4 for an extended discussion of this point in relation to my interview with Petesy Burns.

71 Helen Jones, 'Teenage Kicks Mural Reinstated in Belfast After Outcry', *BBC News NI*, 16 March 2015, online at: www.bbc.co.uk/news/uk-northern-ireland-31909136 (accessed 17 August 2020).

72 Popular Memory Group, 'Popular Memory', p. 78; see also Lynn Abrams, *Oral History Theory* (London: Routledge, 2010).

73 Raymond Williams, *The Long Revolution* (London: Pelican, 1965), p. 64; a later formulation comes in Williams, *Marxism and Literature*, pp. 128–36.

74 Oonagh Murphy and Laura Aguiar, 'When a 1981 Diary Meets Twitter: Reclaiming a Teenage Girl's Ordinary Experience of the Northern Irish Troubles', *British Journal for Military History* 5:1 (2019), p. 55. An exception to this absence in the academic literature is Bill Rolston, *Children of the Revolution: The Lives of Sons and Daughters of Activists in Northern Ireland* (Derry: Guildhall Press, 2011).

75 Dawson, *Soldier Heroes*; see also Michael Roper, 'Re-Remembering the Soldier Hero: The Psychic and Social Construction of Memory in Personal Narratives of the Great War', *History Workshop Journal* 50:1 (2000), pp. 181–204.

76 Hilary Young, 'Hard Man, New Man: Re/Composing Masculinities in Glasgow, c.1950–2000', *Oral History* 35:1 (2007), pp. 71–81.

77 Lucy Newby, 'Troubled Generations? An Oral History of Youth Experience of the Conflict in Belfast, 1969–1998' (unpublished PhD thesis, University of Brighton).

78 Luisa Passerini, *Fascism in Popular Memory: The Cultural Experience of the Turin Working Class*, trans. Robert Lumley and Jude Bloomfield (Cambridge: Cambridge University Press, 2010 [1984]); Alessandro Portelli, *The Battle of Valle Guilia: Oral History and the Art of Dialogue* (Madison, WI: University of Wisconsin Press, 1997).

79 Graham Dawson, *Making Peace with the Past?: Memory, Trauma and the Irish Troubles* (Manchester: Manchester University Press, 2007); Bill Rolston, 'Ambushed by Memory: Post-Conflict Popular Memorialisation in Northern Ireland', *International Journal of Transitional Justice* 14:2 (2020), pp. 320–39.

3

Epiphany, transgression and movement

My interview with Alison Farrell, in a busy cafe close to Belfast City Hall, began with a disavowal. She told me that when a friend had sent her my call for participants, she had been unsure if she qualified. Expanding on this doubt, she said:

> Well we weren't like punks, like, shaved heads and Mohicans as such, we were punks to what was a kind of … we're from Dungannon [laughter] and punk wasn't big in Dungannon, it wasn't big at all, so there were a crowd of us that sort of hit that age at that time, and we all went into that together I suppose, so I sort of, he'd [her friend] seen the advert and said you should contact this, OK, and I said what about yourself, and he said no because he can't remember any of it! [laughter].[1]

Alison's doubt is a helpful starting point for three reasons. Firstly, it is a reminder of the loudness of a certain hegemonic memory of punk, a memory encompassing 'shaved heads and Mohicans', the Sex Pistols, spitting, safety-pins and so on.[2] Alison's own memory differs from the dominant one because of her age – she became interested in punk in 1980, well after the period from 1976 to 1978 generally taken as the high watermark of British punk – and because she was in Northern Ireland rather than London, the epicentre and transmitter of those hegemonic images.[3] After becoming popular slightly later in Northern Ireland than in the rest of the United Kingdom, the punk scene enjoyed a late flowering that would last up until the mid-1980s, incorporating some stylistic and musical variations. One effect of this slightly delayed engagement with punk was that the boundary drawn between punk and post-punk in Britain was blurrier in the North.[4] The central English band in Alison's account are Echo & the Bunnymen, Liverpudlians who are very much part of the post-punk scene Mark Fisher describes as marking a break from 'lumpen punk R'n'R', but most of the Northern Irish bands she mentions maintained a sound and an aesthetic indebted to The Clash and other exemplars of 'first wave' punk.[5] This is a reminder of the need to maintain an awareness of geographical and temporal differentiations across the punk scene, but also a reminder of the transnational dynamics of the cultural memories analysed in the previous chapter.

Secondly, Alison's emphasis on living in Dungannon foreshadows the importance of the specificities of rural or semi-rural life, and of the movement between town and city, to her narrative. Dungannon is a mid-sized town in County Tyrone, about forty miles away from Belfast, and about ten miles away from the border between the north and south of Ireland. The nearby village of Caledon staged a seminal moment in the civil rights movement when young Nationalist MP Austin Currie squatted a house there in 1967, to draw attention to discriminatory housing practices intended to maintain electoral dominance for Unionist politicians.[6] Dungannon was also the intended destination of the first major civil rights march in Northern Ireland, which left from Coalisland in County Tyrone and walked to the town some weeks after Currie's protest. This march presaged future patterns of violence after it was confronted and attacked on the outskirts of Dungannon by Ian Paisley's Ulster Protestant Volunteers, who also attacked later marches, most famously at Burntollet in 1968.[7] As the Troubles developed, Dungannon formed a notorious 'murder triangle', along with Armagh and Portadown, becoming a base of operations for loyalist and republican paramilitaries and for state forces.[8] It is often associated with the Glenanne Gang, a loose organisation composed of loyalist paramilitaries and state security forces and a byword for collusion between these groupings during the Troubles.[9] Alison's narrative is only occasionally explicit about the tapestry of violent incidents that occurred in or around Dungannon in this period, or about the deeper history of discrimination and structural sectarianism that animated the protests of 1967 and 1968, but they exist as a frame throughout as well as a spectral presence informing the structure of feeling she describes.

The third bit of the quote to draw out here is Alison's comment that although punk wasn't big in Dungannon, 'there were a crowd of us that sort of hit that age at that time, and we all went into that together'.[10] The sense of collective and generational sociality hinted at here is an important part of how Alison composes her narrative and describes the structure of feeling of the punk scene, through reference to a group and a collectivity; the epiphanic moment she refers to is not individual but plural, and the structure of feeling is collectively felt. This is emphasised by the story of her friend convincing her to take part in the project, as someone who can remember what happened, but who is remembering not just for herself but on behalf of others.

The punk scene and epiphany

After our initial discussion of how she found out about the project, Alison explained that she had become interested in the punk scene after her and some friends auditioned for a school play in lower-sixth (so when she was sixteen or seventeen). The play represented a rare opportunity for the students in her all-girl, de facto Protestant school to mix with the students of the all-boys school nearby. 'So we auditioned for the school play and through that we met ... boys! And it just all sort of coincided that the boys that we met were all into, they had a garage band and that sort of thing, so we sort of fell into, obviously we were all into the music scene by that point', she explained.[11]

> Um, and that's how it's all sort of, how we got into that. And again it also was one of the few things in Dungannon that crossed other divides. So not only did we meet boys for the first time but we also found that we met people from other schools, which definitely didn't happen at the time in Dungannon. And it was quite hard to find somewhere that we could meet. So there was a cafe that was not even in a neutral place but a very neutral cafe so we all used to meet there, and then sort of any of the bands, you know, there was a couple of the bands formed around town and it didn't matter where they played everybody went to see them so we crossed religious divides, all sorts of divides. It was quite exciting.[12]

This is an epiphanic story about transgression – about crossing, as Alison says, 'all sorts of divides'. The oral historian Lynn Abrams describes the epiphanic as a narrative strategy mobilised by a narrator 'attempting to align past and present selves, to make a smooth or coherent story from a disjointed or incoherent life'.[13] In this aligning or smoothing movement between past and present it is a technique of composure, in the double sense given to this term in the work of Graham Dawson, Alistair Thomson and Penny Summerfield as relating both to the composition of a self and the composition of a narrative.[14] Specifically, the epiphanic mode is a way of incorporating a break or a change in the narrated self into the interview – a way of explaining and making sense of how and why you have changed over the course of time. Abrams says it allows us to identify 'moments of acute self-recognition which occur both in the narrator's life experience (as a significant event remembered, recounted and used to explain something) and in the moment of the oral history interview, expressed not just in the words said but in the ways in which those words are expressed'.[15]

In Alison's narrative above, the school play and the friendships that come out of that, and the engagement with the punk scene these friendships lead to, generate an exciting moment of self-recognition where she begins to question the structuring of her social world. For Abrams's interviewees, a group of British women who grew up in the years following the Second World War drawing on competing discourses of liberation and respectability to construct their identities, the epiphanic moments in the interview 'enabled them to make a bridge in their own minds between two selves ... enabled women to *show* how they made the transition to a modern female selfhood that they now inhabit'.[16] One interviewee, for instance, remembered quitting her steady teaching job and moving to work at an international school in Spain; another wearing red stockings to church as a teenager despite the opprobrium of her mother.

Similarly, Alison positions her past self as one that existed within competing discourses and institutions (segregated schooling; religion and sectarian identity; popular culture and punk), and that negotiated a path through them to narrate her present, composed self – 'it didn't matter where they played everybody went to see them so we crossed religious divides, all sorts of divides. It was quite exciting.'[17] I am particularly interested here in the temporality of epiphany, its capacity to shuttle a story between the past and the present, and in its capacity for expressing collective affects or structures of feeling. In the context of my interviews, epiphany is less like a discrete moment, a hinge, and more like an electric charge distributed across the whole discussion, but felt and expressed with more intensity at certain critical times, and at moments where the past-in-the-present dimension of what is being told becomes especially important.

This movement between past and present was apparent near the end of the interview, for instance, when Alison returned to the way in which punk allowed her to experience space differently in Dungannon. She said:

> Suddenly you had this new thing where you were neither Roman Catholic or Protestant you were this individual that listened to punk music and that suddenly became your label, you were the girl that was seen up town wearing her pyjamas – cool – that was better than being said that I was the girl that was up town that was a Protestant, in my view. And that's what I did. And I'm proud of it![18]

Here we see a very explicit connection between the three moments of self-recognition in the narrative – the pre-punk Alison, who was implicitly conscious of herself as a Protestant and as someone interpellated as a Protestant; the punk Alison, who can reject this identification via the transgressive movement of being 'seen up town wearing her pyjamas', in a telling muddling of the public and the private or domestic; and the Alison who is telling the story and who is both marked by her past actions and affected by them – proud in the final story, and excited in the previous one. The shift is premised on the possibility punk offered to transgress the boundaries of identity – 'suddenly you had this new thing where you were neither Roman Catholic or Protestant' – and to challenge the process of telling that positioned the young Alison as belonging to one part of the community. As Abrams explains, the epiphanic moment is related to both the past and the present, or the moment of telling. Alison's vivid recollection of this sudden shift in possibilities upholds this interpretation. The long, excited sentence in which she explains how punk allowed her to resist interpellation as a Protestant was followed by two shorter, summative statements – 'that's what I did. And I'm proud of it!' – stamping the narrative with the imprimatur of composure.

Crossing boundaries – transgression – is central to the epiphanic power of punk in Alison's narrative.[19] Transgression is a fleeting, unstable kind of movement, difficult to pin down; but what it does reveal is the felt, tangible existence of symbolic and material boundaries and orders. In Alison's stories about Dungannon, two connected symbolic orders are apparent – sectarianism and respectability.

Transgression, sectarianism and respectability in Dungannon

These connected structures of sectarianism and respectability were immediately apparent in Alison's initial description of the nascent punk scene in Dungannon. In the narrative quoted in full at the top of the previous section, she said: 'And again it also was one of the few things in Dungannon that crossed other divides. So not only did we meet boys for the first time but we also found that we met people from other schools, which definitely didn't happen at the time in Dungannon.'[20] As the account of segregation in the first chapter suggested, meeting people from 'other schools' is a circumlocutory description of meeting people from the other religious community – or Catholics in Alison's case. Bearing that in mind, this narrative does several things. It claims that both Catholics and Protestants participated in the punk scene; it suggests that the punk scene allowed boys and girls to meet in relatively unconstrained circumstances; and by describing the exceptional – things that 'definitely didn't happen at that time in Dungannon' – it describes a norm – segregation, the institutionalised maintenance of segregation through the education system, single-sex schooling and spatial division. And it is also an account that is attentive to both the limits of spatial segregation and the limits of transgression, in that the place Alison describes as their usual meeting place is a precarious island within a sectarian geography, 'a cafe that was not even in a neutral place but a very neutral cafe'.

In his work on collusion and the 1994 Loughinisland murders, Mark McGovern makes the important point that nearly all of the existing work on sectarianism in Northern Ireland has focused on the two largest cities in the North: Belfast and Derry. It is necessary, he claims, to widen the scope of this research to consider the nature of division in rural areas. These divisions, which are not simply a product of the conflict but in many cases precede it, are 'deeply rooted in a history of colonial conquest, appropriation and settlement, [and] have always been just as stark and real in many rural areas of the North, if often less visible to those unfamiliar with the signs, signals and local social knowledge of the sectarian *habitus*.²¹ It is important that (while, as I will suggest below, Alison's narrative moves between Belfast and Dungannon and cannot be easily split across the two spaces) the epiphinal transgression generated by her engagement with punk is both initially and primarily apparent in rural or semi-rural spaces, where she appears to feel the weight of both the sectarian telling process and of a network of familial relationships more heavily than she did in the city.

Both sectarianism and respectability, in Alison's account, are maintained through everyday practices of surveillance and control. Allen Feldman's work on the surveillance of difference in Northern Ireland as a 'scopic penetration that contaminates private lives and spaces' goes some way to describing what she is talking about.²² But Feldman concentrates on Belfast, and in particular on interface areas in the centre of the city like the Short Strand, where sectarian telling processes were accompanied and abetted by spectacular and non-spectacular forms of violence. Alison's lower-key focus on quotidian boundaries is attentive to sectarian division, but also allows her to make visible other manifestations of power and boundary-setting in Northern Ireland, partly in terms of gender and sexuality. This was initially apparent in a conversation we had about clothes and fashion, and in her enthusiastic description of the do-it-yourself (DIY) culture of modifying clothes to make them punkier. As nearly all of my interviewees attested to, DIY fashion practices were particularly important in Northern Ireland given the relative difficulty in buying readymade punk clothes without going across the water to London or other regional British cites. Alison said:

> We would've had evenings in where we just sat and fixed clothes. We got a doctor's coat, one of my friends was doing medical science and we got a doctor's coat and tie-dyed it bright fluorescent pink and sewed a feather boa on to it ... you could not be seen dead ... with purple pixie boots, what was I trying to ... and a miniskirt somewhere in the middle of it, but you know, I thought, I'm cool tonight. So, uh, you were getting jam-jams [pyjamas] and ripping them up²³

The freewheeling, associative way Alison spoke about this process of DIY tailoring is suggestive, reflecting both the bricolage form of the process itself and the epiphinal excitement of dressing up as transgressive performance; her bashful, ironic interjections ('what was I trying to ... you know, I thought, I'm cool tonight') indicate the difficulty and the pleasure of describing this excitement after the fact, in the present. Importantly, this is again a communal process, collectively undertaken with friends in the evenings in before a night out or a gig. Another of my interviewees, John Callaghan from west Belfast, evocatively described the first wave of Belfast punks as 'works of art'.[24]

> And I kind of got caught up in that for a bit of crack so the next week in school again shopping, my best mate C who was a fellow punk at the time, we're going to have to get into this, so what do we do, what do punks wear, went through the newspapers and everything. So we came up with the sliced T-shirt, this lovely white t-shirt, Adidas t-shirt, and I just sliced here and pinned it together, scribbled the names of a few of the bands on it. This is brilliant, this is mean! No hair gel or anything at the time, no way of spiking the hair up, you'd try and get it wet, so someone suggested using your father's Brylcreem. Which didn't quite work but we tried it anyway, just messed the hair as much as possible.[25]

John also remembered his efforts to find chains to attach to his school trousers, in a complicated process which echoes with Alison's torn up pyjamas in its repurposing of domestic items: 'I got a chain, a chain that came off the plug for the bath. You take the plug off, pulled the chain down the side of the trousers – that looks great, what about the other side. The only thing I could come up with was my mum's necklace, 18-carat gold.'[26] As in Alison's account, John gave a vivid and affective sense of the excitement of the DIY process as entailing some movement between public and private, with the chain from his bath becoming a vehicle for the performance of a transgressive identity.

Discussing these early engagements with punk and with punk clothing, I asked Alison if she felt that being a girl in the scene had any bearing on her experiences. She dismissed this question initially: 'It wasn't, being a girl wasn't really, I mean when we went to gigs I had to haul stuff out the same as the guys. Being short probably was a bigger problem than being a girl!'[27] But a moment later, she reformulated this response in a way that seemed to speak to both the cultural memory of the punk scene in Northern Ireland and to the inelegant or imprecise framing of my initial question. She said:

Epiphany, transgression and movement

'The music sort of crossed so many barriers and we were all finding out, we were all 17 or 18, we were all finding out an awful lot, you were forming your own views about what it was like to be in Northern Ireland at the time.'[28]

> The big thing that was happening around you is that there were shootings, you know, Dungannon was fairly badly hit. I mean all towns were, but that would've been a big thing, you know, so you're trying to get your head around what side's right and what side is wrong, and for somebody like Stiff Little Fingers to come on and sing 'Barbed Wire Love' made you stop and think, there's an alternative – 'Alternative Ulster', you know – that sort of, that was the big big thing, more so than gender issues, but gender issues also came into that because you had like the Au Pairs and The Slits, Patti Smith, women were finding a place – Toyah was there, OK, she wasn't punk really but she was as punk as I was – you were finding there were females coming out who weren't like Bucks Fizz females, you could wear black leather and not be ... you know, you could be wearing black leather because you wanted to, you could wear ripped trousers, you could wear pyjamas, basically you could wear anything. Like I wore a tutu to a disco made out of a poncho.[29]

There is a gendered dimension to the composure of this narrative. I initially read it as expressive of a silence – as the hegemonic cultural memory of punk-as-non-sectarian, or punk-as-response-to-the-Troubles, making other stories about the scene harder to talk about or to mould into a shareable narrative shape.[30] But on rereading the transcript I think instead that Alison is making a point here about intersectionality, or about the interconnectedness of the structures of sectarianism and respectability that her narrative is describing, in a way that pushes against the edges of this cultural memory and that gently redirects the movement of my initial question about gender.[31] The structures and the transgressions overlap and to try to isolate one of them is to fail to grasp the complexity of what is being expressed. This overlapping is apparent in the form of her response, which begins by stressing the violent context I outlined at the start of the chapter – 'Dungannon was fairly badly hit. I mean all towns were, but that would've been a big thing' – before segueing into the question of being a woman in the punk scene –'that sort of, that was the big big thing, more so than gender issues, but gender issues also came into that'. Alison remembers the punk scene as allowing her to transgress the boundaries of sectarianism and the boundaries of respectable gender performance, both by wearing outrageous or unusual clothing, and by repudiating the claim that clothes were a means of attracting male attention: 'you could wear black leather and not be ... you know, you could be wearing black leather because you wanted to', she said. The Au Pairs, The Slits and Patti Smith provide models for this kind of transgression; Bucks Fizz, the colourful and clean-cut 1981 Eurovision winners, are a countermodel. In their winning Eurovision performance, the two male singers of Bucks Fizz tore off the floaty skirts the two women singers were wearing, revealing miniskirts underneath – they are a telling evocation in this context, evoking both the ambient misogyny of 1980s Britain and the sense of difference Alison wanted to express through her DIY clothing.[32] In a context where 'the position of Northern Irish women has ... been profoundly affected by ... (para)militarism; the ideological dominance of constitutional debates; and the limited impact of feminist politics within the province', Alison's double transgression takes on a particular weight.[33]

The complex dynamics of transgression also featured in Alison's account of travelling from Dungannon to Belfast as a teenager to see Echo & the Bunnymen, who are the central band in her account much as The Stranglers are in Graeme's and Crass are in Petesy's. She said:

> Yeah, most people you knew, there would've been a whole crowd from Dungannon that would've gone down that you'd have known. There was the ones that were like, really punky – we had a couple that got on to the local news for being, you know, they would carry a kettle like a handbag and had their hair all done, you know, we weren't quite that extreme, we were all Bunnymen freaks so we were different, we didn't fit into Dungannon but I don't think we were that outrageous. But I do know that two of my relatives would've walked across the street and pretended they didn't know me, so maybe we were more outrageous than what we thought, I don't know.
>
> F: So did it feel different, Belfast from Dungannon, in terms of...
>
> A: You were more accepted down in Belfast, it was a lot cooler down in Belfast. You could sort of get away with wearing what you wanted in Belfast.[34]

The kind of look performed by Alison here is not one that fits with the hegemonic memory of punk (as entailing a very specific image and style) and so can only be expressed with a pre-emptive disclaimer; but this disclaimer is immediately undercut by the positioning of the look into a particular time and place, that of Dungannon in 1981, which is implicitly cast as somewhere that rigorously maintained the bounds of decorum through the boundaries of respectability – even if the 'really punky' crowd took this transgression further than Alison and her friends. The story of someone using a kettle as a handbag, which suggests a muddling of domestic and public similar to Alison's story about wearing her pyjamas in town, seems to carry a particularly potent symbolic freight in the popular memory of punk in Belfast – the outré accessory was mentioned in the *Belfast Telegraph* as part of the outfit of someone caught up in the Battle of Bedford Street after The Clash's cancelled gig in 1977.[35]

The conversation here also captures a subterranean moment of intersubjectivity, in which, as someone who is also from a small Northern Irish town, I share with Alison the recognition of just how minor a deviation from the norms of acceptability needs to be to make an unfavourable impression in small Northern Irish towns. This implicit description of the mechanisms of respectability-maintenance in Dungannon is made explicit when Alison, having suggested that her and her friends were not particularly outrageous compared to the newspaper-baiting antics of some of their peers, remembers that 'two of my relatives would've walked across the street and pretended they didn't know me'. Particularly in the context of a small town like Dungannon, the family is a critical site for the production and reproduction of discourses of respectability; as Alison says, things felt slightly different in Belfast.

Alison associated the city with a relative cosmopolitanism and indifference, constructing it as a place where it was easier to perform your gender differently and not to adhere to the Catholic–Protestant bifurcation that was formative of her early life in Dungannon.[36] If Alison's teenage engagement with punk is the hinge from which her narrative opens, going to university and renting a flat in south Belfast creates the possibility of mobilising her newly minted punk identity in different ways.

From the country to the city – anecdote and movement

Alison was a punk in Dungannon before she was a punk in Belfast. Or perhaps more precisely, she was a punk in Dungannon at the same time as being a punk in Belfast, given the relative ease with which she was able to travel between the two locations – for instance, by staying in her older boyfriend's flat in the city after going to gigs there. These plural and recursive trajectories are an important corrective to the simplistic rendering (visible in the title of this book, and elsewhere) of the 'Belfast punk scene' – the material infrastructure of punk in Belfast may have made it an especially important site for the performance of punk identities, but those doing the performing often came from other parts of Northern Ireland and returned to their towns and villages after gigs or Saturday afternoons hanging out in Good Vibrations or the Cornmarket. This is evident in Alison's movement between Dungannon and Belfast. It is also apparent in a story John Callaghan told me about meeting punks from around the North, a surprising and enjoyable experience for someone who grew up in west Belfast.

> A couple of times I remember around town just seeing three or four strangers – what are you doing here lads, where are youse from – Ballycastle, where's that – just you had something in common, they had the same thing, the same sense of being on the outside, you just hit it off straight away. It was easy, it was so easy to make friends in those days. And the whole thing in the middle of a bloody civil war! Went to school every morning – do anything at the weekend? – just arsing about town, who were you with, a couple of punks from Lisburn – you know, Prods – and nobody ever said anything, so much bitterness and sectarianism but you never got a bite. You know I just threw it out there, just to see! Never got a bite at all – people expected that you would be behaving like that as punks, you know.[37]

As well as emphasising the point that punks came from across Northern Ireland to be part of the 'Belfast' punk scene, John's narrative is a compelling account of the structure of feeling of the scene as formed by a shared sense of 'being on the outside'. He remembers that 'it was so easy to make friends in those days', in a touching formulation that evokes the collective sociality of the scene and the possibilities allowed for by this collective sociality. Finally, the slightly bathetic deflation at the end of the narrative suggests something that will also be relevant to Alison's account. On the one hand, you have the 'bloody civil war' and on the other hand, John's desire to shock his schoolmates by describing his day out with some 'Prods' from Lisburn is thwarted – 'Never got a bite at all – people expected that you would be behaving like that as punks, you know.' This is an important reminder that a simplistic rendering of the relationship between punks and their society is impossible – the formula of punk as non-sectarian and Northern Irish people in general as sectarian does not hold together. But the main point I want to draw out from his story is that punk offered both the young people he met from Ballycastle and Lisburn, and him and his friends from a majority-Catholic enclave of west Belfast, a different sense of geography, of the possibility for movement, a possibility that 'is both meaningful and laden with power'.[38]

Mobility and movement were also central to Alison's account, particularly in her memories of living in Belfast as a student. As she explained, she felt more comfortable marking herself out as different in Belfast, both in terms of sectarian identity and in terms of her general aesthetic or look. This is clear in the quote above where she suggests that 'you were more accepted down in Belfast, it was a lot cooler down in Belfast. You could sort of get away with wearing what you wanted in Belfast'.[39]

This was a slightly startling narrative for me, given the conditions of segregation and violence I described in the first chapter, and a salutary reminder not to reify those conditions and bear in mind their uneven distribution across the city and across the people of the city. I was also surprised when she dismissed my suggestion that passing through the checkpoints set up around the city centre would have been a frightening or discomfiting experience. 'That was never, you know, I lived on the Lisburn Road. I left Dungannon in '82 and came down to Belfast. And lived up the Lisburn Road and there was never issues as long as you were civil and polite I always thought', she said.[40] This is to some extent a marker of her position as a Protestant university student. Her experiences, as she recognises at points in the narrative, are those of someone who lived in the relatively safe and relatively middle-class south Belfast area around the Lisburn Road, which was a popular residential area for students at the nearby Queen's University and remains something of an aberration in the overall geography of the city because of its transient student population and mixture of Protestant and Catholic residents. It is also a reminder that the social world of 1970s and 1980s Northern Ireland is not reducible to the Troubles and to the structures that made the Troubles possible.

But in spite of this evocation of Belfast as a safe place as long as you kept your head down and adhered to some norms of polite behaviour (even while challenging or transgressing others), Alison's memories of movement across and outside of Northern Ireland suggest a more anxious and equivocal sense of the relationship between power, space and violence. This anxiety was apparent in three stories she told me, which both develop the epiphanic weight Alison gave to her encounter with the punk scene, and trouble its too-neat distinction between one self and another, by suggesting both the limits to transgression as a spatial practice and the limits to punkness as a non-sectarian identity.

These stories are anecdotes, in Daniel James's sense – that is, they 'represent the relationship of the individual to dominant social models and attitudes. They express in a synthesised form, on a local scale, the transgression or acceptance of hegemonic values.'[41] If the epiphanic mode is used by interviewees to describe how their sense of self has changed over time in relation to their social and cultural worlds, the anecdote shifts the focus to dramatise the moments where the narrator encounters particular aspects of these worlds. There are many different types of anecdote, and they do not all do the same thing. As Lionel Gossman puts it in his entertaining genealogy of the anecdotal form in historical writing, they 'may reduce complex situations to simple, sharply defined dramatic structures, but they may also, if more rarely, prise closed dramatic structures open by perforating them with holes of novelistic contingency'.[42] But along with the epiphanic mode already discussed they are important mechanisms for conveying a relationship between self and society. In my interviews they are usually used to express a feeling of dissonance or contention with one of the structures of Northern Irish society described in Chapter 1, although this dissonance is sometimes felt as a pleasure rather than a discomfort.

In terms of Alison's interview, I will consider three anecdotes in sequence. The first involves a trip to Blacklion, a small border town; the second an encounter with some policemen on the motorway out of Belfast; the third, a hitchhiked journey to London to see Echo & the Bunnymen.

A cottage in Blacklion

The first anecdote describes Alison and her friends spending a weekend in Blacklion, a border village on the southern side of the line separating County Cavan, in the Republic of Ireland, from County Fermanagh, in Northern Ireland.

Alison said:

> So, we all spent a weekend in this house, it was a pump with running water and we had a couple of radios – so we were going to listen to the radio – and candles. And that was it. And yet if you look at it now you've got Blacklion on the border there [indicates on the table] and we were staying somewhere about there, so you crossed the border about twenty times[43]

The actual border being transgressed here is suggestive of a particular politics of place, one that combines a performative awareness of the artificiality of the split between the north and the south of Ireland with an equally performative bravado. This is maintained throughout the story, which continued with Alison and her friends being stopped on the way back from the pub by an army patrol.

> It was sort of like, have you got any proof of identification ... my handbag was like from one end of the street to another ... 'No, we haven't' ... and then go through what's your name again, where are you from, and nobody knew we were there anyway so it was hilarious. But they let us go, we weren't arrested.[44]

The border location is important here for the double-edged inflection of the narrative. On the one hand – in terms of showing the narrator's relationship to established values – Alison's story of her and her friends drunkenly criss-crossing the border line renders the existence of the line absurd, in an approach that is a staple of stories about border life and (for instance) the minor acts of smuggling many people living between the two states undertook after partition.[45] But on the other hand, the presence of an army patrol and the account of their bemused encounter with a group of out-of-place punks gestures towards the darker edge of the narrative and of the militarisation of the borderlands, as a site where everyday life 'was shaped by the heavy military presence and the high level of paramilitary violence' that existed in this area throughout the 1970s and 1980s.[46]

How does this narrative function to 'represent the relationship of the individual to dominant social models and attitudes?'[47] On one level, it suggests that punk as a licence for mobility had definite limits – 'I couldn't find ID because I was completely out of my tree, we looked all punky and they weren't used to sort of punky type people there'[48] – and loses its effect in Blacklion, reiterating the idea that behaviours and movements were more heavily policed in rural parts of Ireland, at least in Alison's account. In terms of composure, it turns what might have been a frightening memory into a broadly comic story, taking what could be a bald statement of the geography of fear and constraint that operated in the border region of Northern Ireland in the 1970s and 1980s, and brightening its darker edges with a picaresque account of youthful transgression. Alison and her friends were not arrested, but in raising that as a foreclosed possibility at the end of the account her story transmits a transitory sense of the pervasive anxiety of everyday life and everyday movement during the Troubles.

Driving to Portrush

This entangling of anxiety and humour was also present in Alison's account of being stopped by the police when driving to Portrush from Belfast. Portrush is a seaside resort town in County Antrim, closer to Derry than it is to Belfast. An encounter with the police would have been frightening under any circumstances – Alison noted in passing that she was far more frightened of the police than of the army, although unfortunately we did not discuss why that would be the case.[49] In this instance, the situation was freighted with additional anxiety because they had some freshly picked mushrooms of indeterminate status in the back of the car, although Alison was at pains to stress to me that they turned out to not, in fact, be hallucinogenic.

> The police put their head in you know, where are you going, where are you from, all that, so my friend P, so she said [her full name], Dungannon, address, and asked me, Alison Farrell, Dungannon, gave my address, put your head in to the back and B said that his name was … used to play for Liverpool … really famous … Kenny Dalglish! We sat in the front sort of going why the fuck did he just do this. So

they asked C his name and he said Jean-Jacques Burnel ... what the fuck are these two at, because the last thing we wanted was to be taken out of the car, we just wanted to get on our way and make some mushroom soup.[50]

After the boys wind the police up some more – 'So, "where are you from Mr Dalglish?", and he said "Oh I'm from Anfield Road, Liverpool" ... and the more that this went on the more they did the whole winding up thing' – they're allowed to go on their way. Alison neatly deflates the remembered excitement and alarm she displayed in recounting this story by summarising the situation as having been a 'close shave'.[51] As in the Blacklion anecdote, there is a potent sense here of fear or danger, potentially disruptive or discomposing feelings, being contained in the broadly comic form of the story; she is dramatizing or performing her sense of the police as a malign and frightening force – 'we were stopped by the police – that was worse, you hated being stopped by the police' – without allowing this to capsize the narrative entirely.[52]

In terms of mobility both stories describe Alison and her friends on the move – to rural Blacklion, on the motorway to Portrush – and in describing that trajectory show the rules and practices of surveillance that mark out its accepted boundaries. 'While the bounded territories of planners impose structure and order on the world, the ability to move through, within, and between these spaces constitutes a kind of almost-free will', suggests the geographer and poet Tim Cresswell.[53] That final clause is important – the moving figures in Alison's stories are only almost-free, pushing against the bounds of accepted mobility in Northern Ireland in the early 1980s while still constrained by them.

Hitchhiking to London

A final story about hitchhiking from Belfast to London (via ferry) offers another illustration of punk's status in Alison's narrative as a metaphorical passport offering licence for new kinds of mobility. 'We got over ... we hitched down to the ferry in Larne and then we hitched from Stranraer the whole way down to see the Bunnymen gig', she said.[54] They then waited outside the BBC studios to meet the DJ John Peel, whose evening show on Radio 1 was a fixture of and important tastemaker in the punk and post-punk scenes. Hitchhiking is a form of transgressive mobility *par excellence*, one that conjures up a particular cultural imaginary that (as in the stories above) involves both anxiety and freedom. This was not really drawn out in the story, though, which was a short one and mainly concentrates on the excitement of meeting Peel.

She said:

> I can remember the night he played Billy Bragg and you sat up and went [sits bolt upright, wide-eyed, parodically rhapsodic] what was that, you know! It was such an influential part of your night because there wasn't social media or stuff, you listened to John Peel to know what was going on [...] And it was sort of ... you knew that you weren't just this little isolated dot in Belfast anymore, John Peel knows who I am! Not.[55]

The mobility attested to here is slightly different than that of the previous two stories in that it is more poetic or metaphorical than material or spatial. Existing as part of a transnational imagined community of punks and post-punks – a feeling that is heightened by having actually met John Peel when visiting London – allows Alison to exist in a structure of feeling that extends outside of Northern Ireland, one that means she isn't just 'this little isolated dot in Belfast'. This is mobility as the possibility of joining yourself up with other parts of the world – London, Manchester, New York – and of feeling that possibility as freeing, even while remaining bounded by the material and social constraints of life in Belfast in 1982. It is also an account that is reminiscent of the way in which Petesy and Damien, in the following chapter, connect Belfast to cultural and political currents coming from other parts of the world.

Punk as structure of feeling in Alison's narrative

Alison's account offers an initial evocation of the structure of feeling of the Belfast punk scene. Her account is equivocal and ambivalent, describing the pleasures of transgression and mobility, but also an awareness of violence and of boundaries that cut across these pleasures. This anxious, knotted sense of imaginative freedom and material constraint is a central component of what it felt like for her to be a punk in Belfast and Dungannon in the early 1980s.

In the closing moments of the interview, Alison considered the persistence of this structure of feeling, particularly in the context of contemporary Northern Ireland. Reflecting initially on her parents' response to the punk scene, she said:

> Our parents were very good ... tolerant, yes ... and again had a lot to cope with very quickly. Now I'm a parent, and looking back they had to cope with a boyfriend, they had to cope with a change in clothes, a change in attitude, this crazy thing about writing quotes all over the bedroom, um, you know, having been sort of going to an all-girls school and being quite conservative I suppose and suddenly going into wearing these outrageous clothes, having blue hair at times, they coped with it, and they coped quite well. My mum was never keen on me staying in Belfast but I think that was more to do with boyfriends than security. I think so. [Laughter] And I know certainly if my daughters did a quarter of the things I know I did, we would not be...[56]

This is a temporally complicated narrative, where Alison sees her parents' tolerant response to her adolescent transgressions through the lens of her relationship with her own children. As in the stories discussed above, her dissection of parental relationships links the imposed structures of respectability with the way in which violence and the threat of violence shaped everyday life in Northern Ireland – 'My mum was never keen on me staying in Belfast but I think that was more to do with boyfriends than security. I think so.'[57]

Alison expanded on this temporal complexity in the final exchanges of the interview, when we discussed the Terri Hooley biopic *Good Vibrations*.[58] In many of my interviews, as the following chapters will discuss and as was suggested in Chapter 2, the film functioned as an exemplary site of memory. Interviewees responded to it in complex ways, often combining a thrill of recognition with a less easily expressed feeling of uneasiness, a sense that the narrative of the film tended towards an elision of the messiness of their own stories. John Callaghan, for instance, said: 'I found it really emotional to be honest. Just right at the end they showed pictures. I knew a couple of people in it, not great friends but just part of the big fraternity, a couple of them are dead, you know what I mean, Jesus Christ was that really 30-odd years ago.'[59]

In Alison's case the film functioned as a way to discuss the past with one of her two daughters. She said:

> But watching the film [...] [one of my daughters] watched it and found it hilarious and she wanted to talk about the Miami Showband [massacre], and explaining to her ... she's interested enough in history to know that it was wrong and you know, "Can you remember that mummy?", and there are several instances that I remember that made me sit in my bedroom and cry my heart out, you know, you could not come through the Troubles and not cry, you know, you just, you could not be human. And there are still incidences that haunt me for want of a better word, I suppose music sort of helped, you know, forget about it. So we talked about the Miami Showband and I said you've got to understand [...] you know, Dungannon was so different and Northern Ireland was so different and this brought us all together. It brought us to a safe place, now she would be quite you know, quite a few of her friends, I think young people have this weird thing about sexuality anyway, I think you have to sort of ... this fluidity about sexuality ... but her friends tend to be fluid more one way than the other. But I don't know, they just don't seem to have this thing about saying if they're heterosexual or homosexual, they're just sort of fluid about it all the time, which I think is cool, but I sort of say ... your friends, you know, everybody accepts that now ... growing up you were Roman Catholic or you were Protestant, that was it, it didn't matter, that was it bottom line.[60]

This is a dense story, bringing together the various narrative strands that have been unspooled throughout Alison's interview. It suggests, firstly, the capacity of *Good Vibrations* to act as a prompt for the transmission of intergenerational memory, bridging the years between mother and daughter by making Northern Ireland's history tangible, if not quite comprehensible. Watching the film together creates a space for memory work and for discussion of the past; it makes it easier to find a frequency for transmitting memories across generational lines.[61]

As she explains, Alison and her daughter talked about the Miami Showband massacre after watching the film.[62] This is the name given to the killing of Fran O'Toole, Tony Geraghty and Brian McCoy, three members of the popular Miami Showband, a touring group who had various number one records on the Irish singles charts, in a 1975 attack in which two of their bandmates – Des McAlea and Stephen Travers – were injured but survived. The band were stopped at a checkpoint near Newry on their way home from a gig in Banbridge by a fake army patrol made up of members of the loyalist Ulster Volunteer Force (UVF). The UVF members attempted to place a time bomb on the back of the band's bus; when the bomb exploded prematurely they opened fire on the members of the band. While the circumstances surrounding the event remain unclear, a 2011 report by the Historical Enquiries Team suggested that it had been planned with the collusion of the RUC.[63] Stephen Travers, one of the survivors, has claimed that the attack was planned and carried out by the Glenanne Gang, a coalition of loyalist paramilitaries that have become a 'byword for collusion' between state and non-state forces, especially in the mid-Ulster area where Alison grew up.[64] This highly complicated event, now a focal point for contentious post-conflict memory politics and particularly for the amnesiac desires of the British state, is a powerful evocation in this context; it seems to stand for the difficulty of translating the difference of the past into the present for her daughter, as well as for the difficulty of making sense of the violence of the conflict more generally.

This flash of discomposure is heightened through Alison's admission that 'there are several instances that I remember that made me sit in my bedroom and cry my heart out, you know, you could not come through the Troubles and not cry, you know, you just, you could not be human'. There are two limits made tangible by her statement here: the limits of the punk scene's amelioration of the difficulty of everyday life in Northern Ireland, of bringing Alison and her friends to a 'safe space', and the limits of the epiphanic narrative mode, as Alison accedes to the unsettling presence of memories that do not fit within this way of talking about the past. Music, she suggests, allowed her to forget about the material conditions of existence in 1970s and 1980s Northern Ireland, but remembered violence exists at the margins of the story and of punk's structure of feeling.

Finally, there is an apparent digression at the end of the narrative as Alison describes changing attitudes to sexuality among young people in Northern Ireland, before making an apparently oblique comparison to her own childhood: 'growing up you were Roman Catholic or you were Protestant, that was it, it didn't matter, that was it bottom line'. In the moment of the interview I found myself somewhat blindsided by this change of tack, and did not quite grasp Alison's meaning. On reflection, this seems like a meaningful anacoluthon, a 'breakdown of grammar or syntax that is often mistakenly treated as though its manifestation reveals nothing about language'.[65] Alison is making a connection here between her daughters' friends' desire not to be placed into a binary category of sexuality (straight/gay) and her own desire not to be read as a Protestant, or as 'not-a-Catholic'. This also serves to draw together the different boundaries she sees herself as transgressing as a young woman – those of sectarianism but also those of respectability. Earlier in the interview, she had described going to the Orpheus, a bar frequented by punks but also a venue for Belfast's small gay scene. Alison said:

> And again, it wasn't even to do with …. Two of my friends were gay at the time, well, they still are, but it was sort of again just, crossing all boundaries. Like the smell of poppers as you walked in would have absolutely blown your head off, it was disgusting, um, yeah, so, it was sort of like…[66]

Here, and in the conversation with her daughter remembered above, we get a powerful sense of the complexity of punk as structure of feeling and its relationship to Northern Ireland then and now.

Conclusion

This chapter has analysed interviews with Alison Farrell and John Callaghan to consider epiphanic memories of the punk scene in Northern Ireland. For Alison, this epiphany relates to how being a punk changed her relationship to sectarianised (and gendered) space in Dungannon and Belfast. In her narrative, developing a punk identity within these spaces entailed a newfound capacity for transgression. This capacity does not erase the architecture of surveillance and control she describes, or the 'sediment of history' that makes sectarianism manifest in everyday life, but it does allow her to negotiate the boundaries in a new and exciting way.[67] The following chapter will suggest a different, though similarly spatialised, sense of punk as a structure of feeling, expressed in interviews with Petesy Burns and Damien McCorry.

Notes

1. Interview with Alison Farrell, conducted by Fearghus Roulston, 2015.
2. Robinson, 'Punk's 40th Anniversary'; this is also a useful text for thinking about how this friction can be productive rather than simply prescriptive.
3. The tension between punk as myth and punk as lived experience is comparable to the tension between personal memories of the 'swinging sixties' and the potent cultural memory of this period in Britain analysed here: Helena Mills, 'Using the Personal to Critique the Popular: Women's Memories of 1960s Youth', *Contemporary British History* 30:4 (2016), pp. 463–83.
4. Mark Fisher, *Ghosts of My Life: Writings on Depression, Hauntology and Lost Futures* (London: Zero Books, 2014); Wilkinson, *Post-Punk*.
5. Fisher, *Ghosts of My Life*, p. 109.
6. See Keenan-Thomson, 'From Co-op to Co-opt', both for an account of Currie's action and an account of how discriminatory housing practices in Dungannon were challenged by a group of working-class, female activists in the 1960s, who called themselves the Homeless Citizens League. Keenan-Thomson argues that this activism was eventually co-opted by the middle-class and male-dominated Campaign for Social Justice, a co-option that culminated in Currie's attention-grabbing action.
7. Richard Bourke, *Peace in Ireland: The War of Ideas* (London: Pimlico, 2012), p. 63.
8. Anne Cadwallader, *Lethal Allies: British Collusion in Ireland* (Cork: Mercier Press, 2013).
9. Mark McGovern, *Counterinsurgency*, p. 28.
10. AF, 2015.
11. *Ibid.*; see Chapter 1 for an account of the segregated education system in Northern Ireland.
12. *Ibid.*
13. Lynn Abrams, 'Liberating the Female Self: Epiphanies, Conflict and Coherence in the Life Stories of Post-War British Women', *Social History* 39:1 (2014), p. 21.
14. Dawson, *Soldier Heroes*; Thomson, *Anzac Memories*; Summerfield, *Reconstructing Women's Wartime Lives*.
15. Abrams, 'Liberating the Female Self'.
16. *Ibid.*, p. 35.

17 AF, 2015.
18 *Ibid.*
19 For a general account of transgression see Tim Cresswell, *In Place/Out of Place: Geography, Ideology and Transgression* (Minnesota: University of Minnesota Press, 1996); for a specific account of transgressiveness as a quality or a potentiality attributed to young people in Northern Ireland see Newby, 'Troubled Generations? (De)Constructing Narratives'.
20 AF, 2015.
21 Mark McGovern, '"See No Evil": Collusion in Northern Ireland', *Race & Class* 58:3 (2017), p. 55; for more work on rural sectarianism see Anna Bryson, '"Whatever You Say, Say Nothing": Researching Memory and Identity in Mid-Ulster, 1945–1969', *Oral History* 35:2 (2007), pp. 45–56; Brendan Murtagh, *Community and Conflict in Rural Ulster* (Coleraine: University of Ulster, 1999); Kelleher, *Troubles in Ballybogoin*.
22 Allen Feldman, 'Violence and Vision: The Prosthetics and Aesthetics of Terror', *Public Culture* 10:1 (1997), p. 27.
23 AF, 2015.
24 Interview with John Callaghan, conducted by Fearghus Roulston, 2016.
25 *Ibid.*; I have abbreviated the name of John's friend here.
26 *Ibid.*
27 AF, 2015.
28 *Ibid.*
29 *Ibid.*
30 Penny Summerfield, 'Culture and Composure: Creating Narratives of the Gendered Self in Oral History Interviews', *Cultural and Social History* 1:1 (2004), pp. 65–93.
31 Kimberlé Crenshaw, 'Mapping the Margins: Intersectionality, Identity Politics, and Violence against Women of Color', *Stanford Law Review* 43:6 (1991), pp. 1241–99.
32 Julia Downes, 'The Expansion of Punk Rock: Riot Grrrl Challenges to Gender Power Relations in British Indie Music Subcultures', *Women's Studies* 41:2 (2012), pp. 204–37.
33 Karyn Stapleton and John Wilson, 'Conflicting Categories? Women, Conflict and Identity in Northern Ireland', *Ethnic and Racial Studies* 37:11 (2014), p. 2073.
34 AF, 2015.
35 Ian Cobain, *Anatomy of a Killing: Life and Death on a Divided Island* (London: Granta, 2020), p. 58.
36 Fran Tonkiss, 'The Ethics of Indifference: Community and Solitude in the City', *International Journal of Cultural Studies* 6:3 (2003), pp. 297–311.
37 JC, 2016.

38 Tim Cresswell, *On the Move: Mobility in the Modern Western World* (London: Routledge, 2006), p. 10.
39 AF, 2015.
40 *Ibid.*
41 Daniel James, *Doña María's Story: Life History, Memory and Political Identity* (Durham, NC: Duke University Press, 2001), p. 178.
42 Lionel Grossman, 'Anecdote And History', *History and Theory* 42:2 (2003), p. 145.
43 AF, 2015.
44 *Ibid.*
45 Peter Leary, *Unapproved Routes: Histories of the Irish Border, 1922–1972* (Oxford: Oxford University Press, 2016), especially chapter 3.
46 Catherine Nash and Bryonie Reid, 'Border Crossings: New Approaches to the Irish Border', *Irish Studies Review* 18:3 (2010), p. 276.
47 James, *Doña María's Story*, p. 172.
48 AF, 2015.
49 For an extensive sociological account of state and non-state harassment of young people in the North, mostly focusing on the late 1980s and early 1990s, see Robbie McVeigh, *It's Part of Life Here: The Security Forces and Harassment in Northern Ireland* (Belfast: Committee on the Administration of Justice, 1994).
50 AF, 2015. I have abbreviated the names of Alison's friends in this account. Kenny Dalglish was a celebrated centre-forward who played football for Liverpool and Scotland; Jean-Jacques Burnel is a member of The Stranglers; Anfield is the home stadium of Liverpool FC.
51 *Ibid.*
52 *Ibid.*
53 Cresswell, *On the Move*, p. 213.
54 AF, 2015.
55 *Ibid.*
56 *Ibid.*
57 *Ibid.*
58 Barros D'Sa and Leyburn, *Good Vibrations*.
59 JC, 2016.
60 AF, 2015.
61 Kuhn, 'Memory Texts', p. 304; see also Annette Kuhn, *Family Secrets: Acts of Memory and Imagination* (London: Verso, 2002).
62 Stephen Travers and Neil Fetherstonhaugh, *The Miami Showband Massacre: A Survivor's Search for the Truth* (London: Hodder Headline, 2007).
63 Anon., 'Miami Showband Massacre: Report Points to RUC Collusion, Families Say', *Belfast Telegraph*, 15 December 2011, online at:

www.belfasttelegraph.co.uk/news/northern-ireland/miami-showband-massacre-report-points-to-ruc-collusion-families-say-28692254.html (accessed 18 March 2021).
64 McGovern, 'See No Evil', p. 51.
65 Jan Mieszkowski, 'Who's Afraid of Anacoluthon?', *MLN* 124:3 (2009), p. 648.
66 AF, 2015.
67 Burton, *The Politics of Legitimacy*, p. 49.

4

Making affective and political spaces

Both of the interviews discussed in this chapter, with Petesy Burns and Damien McCorry, took place several months apart in the Linen Hall Library in central Belfast. I had chosen the library as a pragmatic alternative to the small cafe a few yards away on the corner opposite City Hall, where most of my previous interviews had been conducted. The initial reason for the change was simply that the library cafe was quieter, with no music playing and only a genteel clattering of cups and plates to be heard when listening back to the recording. On reflection, though, it felt like an apposite choice of location. The Linen Hall Library is an important national institution. Former librarian and founding member of the United Irishmen, Thomas Russell, was arrested in the building in 1796 and later executed.[1] It holds a remarkable selection of documents, pamphlets and ephemeral material about the Troubles – the Northern Ireland Political Collection. The library feels historic, in Lauren Berlant's sense, affectively and materially; the steps from the street are worn and scuffed by generations of feet. Talking about punk with Petesy and Damien in the refined, Victorian-ish cafe of the Linen Hall Library felt generative, jarring, upsetting. It created a situation, 'a state of things in which something that will perhaps matter is unfolding amidst the usual activity of life'.[2]

Berlant's poetic sense of what it might mean to feel historical, to pause and to think differently in the unfolding activities of life, is a useful starting point for the interviews I consider in this chapter, and the attempts to make or remake space that both interviews describe. Petesy and Damien remembered the structure of feeling of punk as an intervention in the classed, sectarianised geography of Belfast. Like Alison in the previous chapter, both interviewees here evoke spaces and boundaries in their recollections of the punk scene and of the Troubles, but their focus is less on transgression and more on the discovery of what could be made in the gaps that were afforded them.

The arc of their interviews is in part a consequence of how they participated in the scene – they were both in successful bands that played across and outside of the city, and Petesy in particular remains a well-known figure in the remnants of the scene and on the live circuit, most recently touring in a reformed version of The Outcasts. It is also related to their explicitly political conceptualisation and narrativisation of the scene. Both see punk as allowing them to express a critique of the Northern Irish state that is not reducible to the nationalist or republican ideologies that dominated the areas in which they grew up. This political mode takes different tacks in both cases. Petesy's affiliation with an anarchist milieu, his local organising, and the influence of anarcho-punk bands like Crass and Poison Girls inflects his understanding of punk and politics. Damien instead draws on the leftist politics of The Clash and Rock Against Racism to make sense of his own experiences in west Belfast and to develop his own reading of the conflict in the North.

Growing up in Belfast

At the start of the interview Damien described growing up in the majority-Catholic community of Andersonstown, in west Belfast, an area that was heavily affected by the Troubles.

> Interesting, really, I suppose um the period you're interested in is my teen years. It was funny because it was just what you knew, you don't know any different, you're a kid, you don't know that everybody's life is not the same as yours. You go to school, you go out and play with your mates, you see the army, there's riots, there's, you know, trouble – you try and stay out of trouble like any kid – and all that is going on around you so it was kind of very interesting times. And that was our norm, we didn't know any different, so you just adapt very well being a kid to that.[3]

At the end of the interview he returned to the way in which his engagement in punk stretched the relatively constrained horizons described above.

Making affective and political spaces 93

You know it enabled me as a person to step outside my small horizons and boundaries and it enabled me to ... obviously, you get confidence through playing in bands, being on stage and that, and to express yourself, artistically, 'cos we wrote our own songs and all of that, it was very good, very good.[4]

For Petesy, from the majority-Catholic New Lodge area of north Belfast, his initial encounter with the Harp Bar had a similar resonance to Damien's experience of joining a band.

> P: The Harp was great, it was good for me because it was like – from where I lived it was about 15 minutes' walk. Sorta down into the city centre on the north side, Hill Street, which is the Cathedral Quarter now. You know, I mean, on first sight it looked like a lot of other bars around – I mean where I grew up all the bars had grills around them, sorta you know security measures.
>
> F: The only, I've seen the Sunflower has kept theirs up, so I've seen it there.
>
> P: Yeah, all the bars used to be like that. And you had buzzers on the doors and stuff like that for getting in like. So, it looked like any other bar except the place, the whole area round it was completely rundown and derelict, that part of town was completely dead. But once you get in it was just, wow, you know, wall-to-wall punks, and not only punks, there were people who went there who weren't punks, but it was just like you know – it felt like quite a homely and safe environment. And people you would never have dreamed of meeting in your life, from different parts of town and different classes and religions. So, it was really interesting in that respect having grown up in this single identity area all of my life, all of a sudden to be just in a place where you knew, you just knew people from all over the town and it didn't really seem to matter.[5]

This is a thick description in which the material markers of the conflict and Belfast's securitised architecture (grills, buzzers, security doors) and the material conditions of deprivation on Hill Street are deliberately contrasted with the inside of the bar and its 'wall-to-wall punks'. The contrast is heightened by the arresting description of the Harp Bar as 'quite a homely and safe environment'; in offering up an unexpected, jarring image that sidesteps the classic macho imaginary of punk as aggressive or confrontational to instead emphasise dynamics of care or safety, Petesy gives a vivid sense of the unhomeliness and unsafe environment prevailing elsewhere in the city. The Harp, he says, was somewhere you met 'people you would never have dreamed of meeting in your life'; somewhere 'where you knew, you just knew people from all over the town and it didn't really seem to matter'. The final clause proposes an understanding of the spatial politics of the Belfast punk scene as not being predicated on ignoring difference – which in Petesy's account is not a neat Catholic–Protestant bifurcation but also complicated by the vector of class – but as instead entailing certain ways of navigating and exploring difference.[6]

Petesy's tone was animated throughout this story, and his expressive language was paired with an expressive demeanour and a fixing gaze; as in Alison's narrative about taking part in the school play and meeting both boys and punks for the first time, this seems like an epiphanic moment, conveying within the moment of the interview the passage from one possible self to another. The temporal complexity that is implicit in epiphany as a narrative mode is made explicit here, partly via my interjection about the grill outside of the Sunflower pub – 'all the bars used to be like that', Petesy said, gesturing both to the way in which the built environment of the city has changed since the 1970s and to the muddling of past and present his narrative composure entails.[7] As in Alison's account, the epiphanic encounter with the punk scene that he describes here is not discrete, or contained within this one moment of the interview. For instance, Petesy returned to the idea of punk as a turning point near the end of our discussion, again explicitly relating it to his childhood and adolescence in the New Lodge.

> It [being involved in the punk scene] took me out of a lifestyle that I would have, for not knowing any better, that I would have just followed and done what everyone around me was doing. And followed that track. That everyone was following you know. It sorta took me away from that and showed me other possibilities.[8]

Both the interviews discussed in this chapter are expressions of the affective relationship between place, politics and self, and of the efforts to change this relationship that punk entailed for the interviewees. In these opening extracts, Damien describes the 'norms' of growing up in Andersonstown – rioting, state violence, the presence of the army; Petesy describes the securitised bars around where he grew up and the (metaphorical) openness of the Harp in contrast to that. I will draw these strands out of each interview in turn, beginning with Petesy's, then conclude by returning to their common points.

The Anarchy Centre and Stalag 17

Petesy's first intimations of the punk scene were imaginative rather than musical, gleaned through the news that the Sex Pistols' 'God Save the Queen' (at number two in the charts in 1977) would not be broadcast on the radio because of its shocking content. 'It sort of had that effect on a lot of people, you know, if it was banned ... what better publicity could you get you know. And then I sort of sook that out and just really loved the whole spirit of the whole thing and wanted to know more and more about it.'[9] He reflected on the spatial constraints of the period in describing how that initial period of discovery happened.

> Yeah at that time again sort of life was very self-contained and you didn't really go out of that area too much. And there was a record shop near to Carlyle Circus – about five minutes from where I lived – I was skint then anyhow, so I just went in by chance and there it was – the single, 'God Save the Queen', you know. Yeah, so, and that was it. And then from there I think just the more you got involved and the more bands you went to see – uch there was a lot of record shops in the town centre so the likes of Caroline Music and then [I] eventually discovered Good Vibrations and places like that, there was quite a few independent record shops in the mid to late '70s in Belfast you know so there was never really an issue getting anything. You know but it was just, as you say, there was no internet – you had to physically go through the record collection.[10]

The self-contained, insular world that Petesy remembers here opens up into the enlarging possibilities of the punk scene. Eventually, these possibilities lead to him forming a band, initially with limited success.

> Like mates jumping up on the stage in between bands or something in the Harp and doing a cover of one of your favourite bands or something – chaos – but it was just a gradual process of you know, and then you know there was a couple of friends who had a band and their bass player left and they said do you want to join sort of

thing, so that was, it was just the start of that process, being involved in a different level.[11]

Finding places to gig and to rehearse was difficult, however. The Harp Bar closed in 1981 or 1982 – subjected to a short-lived Western-themed makeover, 'wagon wheels and nooses and things like that … quite embarrassing'.[12] The Pound, near Oxford Street, would occasionally put on punk gigs, but inconsistently, and without the sense of community that infused the Harp – Petesy described its ownership as distant from and somewhat puzzled by the various punk bands and fans who occasionally arrived for events there.

> Nah nah, definitely separate, so there wasn't a lot of opportunities – we would've had a few places, maybe the Manhattan, which is down near Victoria Street, just a regular venue. But sort of very early '80s, very little happening, so you found yourself playing wherever people could organise gigs. So they'd be all over the place, out of town, up the west, wherever, playing in youth clubs, whatever opportunity you could get to play. The Anarchy Centre was a great place [but] it was short-lived.[13]

The Anarchy Centre – or the A Centre – was only open for about six months in 1981 and 1982, but marks an intersection between the punk scene as a youth culture and the older, more politicised, but often more middle-class anarchist culture that coalesced around the Just Books collective and the university.[14] Petesy describes this intersection while reiterating its ephemeral nature, but it is apparent that the anarchist emphasis on DIY culture and mutual aid had a lasting effect on his sense of community and his personal politics and attitudes.

> Punks would always go on about anarchy and stuff like that … in a sort of incoherent and nihilistic way – but here were a bunch of theoretical anarchists who were sort of putting their money where their mouth was and actually it was – but having said that it was really very short-lived.[15]

Despite this (and despite the tension Petesy describes between the idealistic anarchists' desire to politicise the punks and the punks' continued commitment to hedonism, and particularly to sniffing glue), the nascent social centre takes on a central role in his narrative

Making affective and political spaces 97

as he describes his own conversion to a more politically active understanding of the punk scene and of his band's role within that scene. The epiphanic moment here occurs when the venue temporarily reopened in 1982, for gigs from two British anarcho-punk groups, Crass and Poison Girls.

> F: Did you see the Crass gigs and the Poison Girls gigs?
>
> P: Yeah we played with both of them, my band Stalag 17 played with the Poison Girls and played with Crass. And actually I was pretty much – at that point I was still firmly entrenched in the sorta, not what I would call the fashion end of punk but the apolitical, the hedonistic sorta chaos type thing, and that was the first time … and I would have always dismissed Crass … [long pause … F: Hectoring or preachy?] … Not even that, just the way, just took the line from the media, basically saying they were middle-class hippies. And just took that line without really having met them or thought about it, and then when they came I met them and saw how engaged they were just with people, outside of being on the stage, sitting about, not being stars, just being really interesting and interested, you know. And then seeing the band and the spectacle of it – because they had all their films and banners and them themselves, just completely engaging, it was just like a completely different kind of experience and you sorta thought, that's what punk's about.
>
> F: [You thought] there's something there?
>
> P: And it really grabbed you you know. And that really was a turning point for me personally.[16]

This is one of the moments in the interview where the epiphanic charge of punk was especially strongly present, in spite of the intersubjective fumble at the start where I clumsily filled a pause by imposing my own slightly jaundiced view of Crass onto the discussion. As in Petesy's description of the Harp Bar that opens the chapter, the felt experience of space is crucial here; he describes the way in which the band occupy everyday space in a particular way: 'Sitting about, not being stars, just being really interesting and interested.' They engage in a low-key, quotidian spatial performance –'being really interesting and interested' – which is fundamentally different from, for example, The Clash's much-maligned publicity shots from their first visit to Belfast, posing beside peace lines and army installations. George McKay argues that 'what was different about Crass was that here was a post-punk band whose sole reason for existence was that they were going to change the world'.[17] While sloganeering, banners and agitprop were part of this revolutionary ambition, it was also predicated on an anarchist micropolitics of space, disposition and affect, where how you engaged with your audience, how you behaved off stage and how you interacted with people on a day-to-day level were the necessary starting point for activism, organising and cultural production.[18] This means that, as McKay and Petesy both argue, Crass' aesthetic and politics were founded on a productive tension between their deliberately understated presence off stage and their highly choreographed and confrontational stage shows – 'the spectacle of it ... all their films and banners'. Petesy's story concludes with a highly physical sense of both of the ways in which Crass inhabited space – 'it really grabbed you ... that really was a turning point for me personally'.

Sara Ahmed asks: 'How do emotions work to secure collectives through the way in which they read the bodies of others? How do emotions work to align some subjects with some others and against other others?'[19] Her argument is that emotions and feelings –shame, pain, love, fear – are sticky in two senses; that is, they adhere to the body of the person who experiences them, but they also move between bodies and across groups like burrs, sticking to others through contact. 'The impressions we have of others, and the impressions left by others are shaped by histories that stick, at the same time as they generate the surfaces and boundaries that allow bodies to appear in the present', Ahmed concludes.[20] In Petesy's account of meeting Crass, he is arrested by their desire to occupy space in a particular way, creating what is for him a history that sticks. The epiphanic role that encountering anarcho-punk (rather than just punk as such) plays in his narrative was reinforced by his account of seeing another band from that small scene, Conflict.

> And they played in a wee small bar, Conflict were [stretches out in the chair to indicate the size of the members of the band] I mean, tall, and big spiky hair, it was just ... and Colin the singer was just so angry, you know. And it was such a spectacle to see the power of that anger. Of that sort of, someone who was really fucked off with the way things were and was going to do something about it. Stuff like that.[21]

Again, the emphasis here is on how they occupy space, emphasised by Petesy's spatial performance in the moment of the interview, stretching out in his chair; there is a nice sense of the ineffability of the structure of feeling he is evoking here, the difficulty of putting words on it, both in his recourse to embodying it and in the ellipsis afterwards – 'it was just …' As with Crass, performance and staging is also important – 'it was such a spectacle to see the power of that anger'. These two epiphanic encounters are consolidated in Petesy's narrative by his touring with Stalag 17 and his involvement in the Warzone Collective.

> Yeah the A Centre opened in '81 and Crass played in '82, that's right. So um they really sowed the seeds for what we all did later. After Crass and the politicisation thing, Stalag 17 went from being like a party band or just another punk band to having a bit more of a political or an anarchist slant. Even though I might not have quite understood it at the time [laughter] I still wanted to identify with that idea of doing things for yourself and all. And through that we met other people like the other band about locally that would have professed anarchism at that time was Toxic Waste, so they would've been based in Newtownards so they started to come into town and we would've shared gigs. And basically through that, through that came the catalyst, for what became the Warzone Collective. Now this was '83, '84. And again we were just starting to get our act together in terms of pooling resources and organising gigs. Sorta trying to educate people about what was going on in the world. And at that stage also the Just Books – there was a cafe in Just Books and the ones who had been running it gave it up. So we took it on.[22]

The Warzone Collective and Giro's

The model for the collective and the various offshoots that emerged from it came partly from conversations with the anarcho-punk bands that Petesy brought to Belfast – 'Dirt, Conflict, Subhumans'. It also came partly from a three-week European tour Stalag 17 and their similarly motivated friends Toxic Waste, from Newtownards, undertook in the early 1980s.

> Squats and social centres, and it was just … actually that was the basis for Giro's, for the Warzone Centre. Ourselves and Toxic Waste

had been away and we came back and we were talking about that model and going like, that's fantastic, it's fantastic, and it's within the realms of possibility. So yeah the, that's what I loved about, there was no rockstar attitudes, people came and just came for what they got basically.[23]

Inspired by the network of autonomous and anarchist social centres they encountered in mainland Europe, and increasingly unsatisfied with the vagaries of trying to work with commercial promoters and bar owners in Belfast, the group started to think about setting up a more permanent space for the Warzone Collective to work in.

And that was the whole thing and we were going everything we do here and everything we create – and we weren't really interested in making money ourselves – but everything we do it goes to someone else. And that fair enough where the bands are concerned, they deserve the money, blah blah blah. But we're giving this money to all these bars all the time, what the hell like, what about just having our own bloody place like. So that was from about '83 or '84, that idea of let's just try and do this.[24]

With help from a Rathcoole charity and the Unemployed Centre near Donegal Place, Petesy and other members of the Warzone Collective expanded their cafe into a fully fledged social centre and gig venue called Giro's (after the popular name for unemployment benefit). Petesy said:

This is '86, so I was 24. We'd nothing but time on our hands. So we went in and just completely refurbished this place, got the ground floor ready and turned it into a practice room. And within a few months we had like two practice slots a day, four at weekends or six at weekends something like that, they were booked out solid within a couple of months with just bands generally coming to the place. And then the cafe opened, we had a screen-printing workshop and stuff like that. And that happened within, we were in it about a year, less than a year before the cafe opened, and the cafe then was it. As soon as the cafe opened the place was established. People were coming – and not just punks – people were just coming to see what was going on.[25]

The pride and enthusiasm that tangibly permeated this account in the moment of the interview suggested the importance of Giro's to Petesy's narrative composure and to his sense of self. It is also suggestive of the structure of feeling he is evoking, one in which a group of people with 'nothing but time on our hands' were able to make a profound intervention in the spatial politics of Belfast, one which was of interest not only to punks but also to other people in the city wanting 'to see what was going on'.

His account here works to link punk in Belfast to a wider, transnational community of activism, politics and music, both in terms of the links with Crass and other British-based anarcho-punk bands already discussed, and in terms of the links with the European social centre scene. The 'prefigurative building of alternative institutions built on principles of shared ownership and democratic control ... co-ops, left trades councils, women's and community centres, independent printing presses, radical bookshops' was crucial to what David Wilkinson calls the 'libertarian left' strand of the 1980s punk or post-punk scene, and this is one of the contexts in which Petesy's narrative can be framed.[26] It is also part of the wider history of shifts in the economics and politics of space in Britain, and particularly the 1980s emphasis on privatisation and commercial regeneration as alternatives to costly state intervention or building programmes.[27]

Thatcherism and neoliberalism played out differently in Northern Ireland than in Britain because of the region's history of independent administration, the level of autonomy granted to successive secretaries of state and the backdrop of violence against which policy was conducted.[28] Public sector spending, for instance, remained relatively high in the North, as did public sector employment.[29] However, attempts to commercially regenerate Belfast are comparable to those seen in England. These policies (Enterprise Zones, the Laganside Development Order) are predicated on a logic of economic rationality based on a trickle-down model that assumes that private sector success will invigorate the whole city; as Frank Gaffikin and Mike Morrissey suggest in their analysis of Thatcherite policies in Northern Ireland, 'the process ... also involved considerable social costs, including community dislocation and effective disenfranchisement'.[30] In this sense, the Warzone Collective was not just an intervention in sectarian geography but in a city centre that was shaped by commercial and ideological imperatives as well as segregation and securitisation. In the context of the ongoing neoliberalisation of space in contemporary Belfast, Petesy's memory of making and maintaining Giro's held a particular valence and power, as memories of a time when this kind of spatial intervention seemed possible.

'But at the end of the day we were spending our time just doing nothing hanging about the town centre and there was a dire need, there was a dire need', Petesy concluded.[31] As the interview came towards an end we discussed the afterlife of the Warzone Collective, which maintains a limited presence in the city, although exclusively as an occasional venue for punk and metal music rather than as a social centre, cafe or rehearsal space. Petesy explained:

> There's a place now which is Warzone in name but it's not really ... it's not really like what we did. The place in Donegal Place lasted for five years and then we moved up to Donegal Lane, far bigger premises, and it lasted for twelve years. So seventeen in total. '86 it opened and 2003 it closed. There was a very temporary premises down on Linen Hall Street there [...] Ours was more like, our idea was to have a social centre, a place where you could utilise the building rather than just it being closed all week and having gigs at the weekend. Which is basically what it is, it's a venue now like. And a venue was only part of what we wanted to do, we never had a venue for years, we had the cafe and the practice room [...] It was the daily thing, it was the ... but then having said that we were all on the dole then and even towards the end of the Giro's that I was involved with it was becoming really difficult for people to volunteer, to find the time to volunteer, because they were just being pressured into schemes and into you know, so I mean, it may not be sustainable to have the model we had.[32]

The impossibility of maintaining the Warzone Collective under contemporary economic conditions – especially the more stringent restrictions on employment benefit that put claimants under pressure to show that they are applying for jobs –means that the possibilities for what the space can be are newly delimited. There is a sense in which the language of neoliberalism leaks into Petesy's account as well here, colouring the language he uses to describe the end of the centre – 'it may not be sustainable to have the model we had'. 'It really is, definitely, you know, and people – we just had very unique circumstances and grew up in a different culture', Petesy added.[33]

What is notable here is not simply the evocation of the culture of 1970s and 1980s Belfast as a different culture and a different time – this is a narrative trope commonly deployed in temporalising narratives of Northern Ireland's recent history – but as a different culture that connotes a positive rather than negative set of connotations.[34] If there is a kind of nostalgia at work here it is a critical nostalgia, 'a manifestation of utopian longing politically necessary in an era where substantive political change seems more or less impossible'.[35] This sense of possibility was reiterated at the close of the interview, where Petesy describes how he thinks being a part of the punk scene affected his life.

After a moment of hesitation at the scale of the question – at the difficulty of assessing the impact a moment or a series of moments can have on something as mobile and hard to pin down as a life – Petesy confidently said that punk had changed his life, acknowledged this to be a cliché, but avowed it anyway. It introduced him to positions and experiences he would never have encountered otherwise, he added, citing the gay-friendly nature of the scene as unusual for Belfast at that time.

> Totally, totally [unusual], as was meeting a Protestant, as was you know lots of things, cultural things, meeting people who had snooty accents from the Malone Road or wherever, but you never, you know, maybe in school, but in your daily life people who you were engaged with involved with people went on to get married across the divide and things like that so cliché though it is it was a total life-changing experience. Yeah, and still, I would carry those principles, try and carry your life in that way. Getting that sort of grounded ... and such an insight into so many different minds, there's a lot of sloganeering in punk about changing things, when you get to the likes of Crass and bands like that who just went into it you were reading them and you didn't understand half of it but it was really great, it was like an education, you were going this is taking that idea of sloganeering and going well actually look at the foundation of this.[36]

This relates to the statement quoted earlier where Petesy uses a spatial metaphor to describe how punk changed his sense of mobility and possibility. Punk, he says, 'took me out of a lifestyle that I would have, for not knowing any better, that I would have just followed and done what everyone around me was doing. And followed that track. That everyone was following you know. It sorta took me away from that and showed me other possibilities.'[37] Both descriptions offer an understanding of punk's structure of feeling as enduring, as having a continued resonance in how Petesy lives and thinks – how he carries his life, in his evocative phrase. This sense of the continued resonance of the scene was also a feature of my interview with Damien McCorry.

Bands, possibilities and limits

Damien's interview began with a reflection on the area where he grew up.

> West Belfast, place called Stewartsdown Park, it's in Andersonstown. So that's where we, I was brought up. Mum and Dad still live there to this very day and, ah, quite a few of the family still live around there, you know. I would go up and see them a couple of times a week and the street hasn't changed, the people haven't changed, you know, but that's the way it goes.[38]

He continued his description with the account quoted at the start of this chapter – 'You go to school, you go out and play with your mates, you see the army, there's riots, there's, you know, trouble' – and the suggestion that adaptation to this disruption was the norm for young people in west Belfast.[39] For Damien, this adaptation was aided by an interest in music, which quickly became an interest in both the politics and the culture of the punk scene.

> I think it's just it's a culture thing, it's what was happening musically at the time that was a good, it was all part of the youth culture at the time. I was very much interested in the whole political side of it. Which was, ok, you know there was the anarchist side of it but it was more Rock against Racism [RAR], Campaign for Nuclear Disarmament [CND], it was part of a youth movement, as much as just about the music and the bands [...] But we were very much, there was a movement there which felt you could change things, this idea that you didn't have to be signed by EMI, that you could do things yourself.[40]

In another echo of Petesy's account, Damien's interest in RAR and the CND renders Belfast cosmopolitan, not an atavistic remainder of internecine religious conflict but a site marked by the transnational eddies and currents of the 1970s and 1980s. Additionally, both campaigns (each of which contained much internal diversity and dissent) were spaces for the articulation of a critique of state power and state violence that was not reducible to the politics of Irish nationalism or republicanism.[41] This double sense (of punk as a welcome distraction from local and Troubles politics, but also as a way to make new sense of local and Troubles politics) was important throughout Damien's interview. His first band started to organise their own gigs around the city in the late 1970s, after a successful first gig at the Cosmos youth club in Andersonstown. This leads to encounters with difference that reorient the childhood perspective expressed at the beginning of the interview, and again returns to his sense of the global in the local.

> It was great, because one of the really interesting things about it was that certainly everybody in my band – I only can tell my experiences – I wouldn't have met a Protestant person [strong emphasis on the last word here] *ever*. Right? Didn't happen, there were none near me, didn't go to my school – we were in our ghetto, you know. And you knew what they were and they were supposed to be the enemy and that but you know whatever, you never met a real one. Until I started playing in the bands, and you came into the centre of Belfast, and I was meeting guys from the Newtownards Road, meeting guys from other parts of Belfast. Who you know, different tradition, et cetera, and then you realise these guys are just thinking, they're young people thinking the same as I do, they may be from a different faith or whatever. And how could we support things like Rock against Racism if you're holding kind of, you know, if you're having sectarian thoughts. You can't say well racism's wrong but sectarianism's ok, you can't do that. So it was really refreshing. And I know a lot of the other guys felt the same because the centre of Belfast and the places we played *were* non-sectarian. They were the only places ... I mean I couldn't have walked into a bar on the Sandy Row or on the Zetland Road, I'd have been in trouble. And equally, someone from there couldn't have gone into a bar in my place or they'd have been in trouble. But in the punk scene none of that featured at all. It was great, really refreshing. But the thing was that we couldn't really bring bands from other places into our area, you know, so when we were having gigs in that area it was bands that were kind of...[42]

This is a nuanced account that is suggestive of the politically transformative possibilities of making new spaces in the city, of the affective, refreshing nature of these possibilities in contrast to the stifling environment of sectarianism and violence Damien is evoking, but also of the material limits that this emergent structure of feeling invariably encountered in Belfast in the late 1970s. The punk scene's capacity to reinvent places is both temporary and contingent, and not a capacity that can be made manifest across the city as a whole – Damien's affiliation with the punk scene does not make him either safe or comfortable on Sandy Row or the Zetland Road. He adds that 'we couldn't really bring bands from other places into our area', trailing off rather than describing the 'bands that were kind of…', or the bands who were willing and able to play in the majority-nationalist community of Andersonstown and similar Catholic enclaves in west or north Belfast –presumably, bands from or associated with Catholic or nationalist communities.

The unspoken final clause here is partly just a typical apothegmatic strategy of polite Northern Irish conversation. But it also suggests, I think, the difficulty of incorporating this structural problematic into the overall narrative of the interview, a narrative that broadly cleaves with the collective memory among Northern Irish punks of the scene as non-sectarian in a way that transcended these kinds of structural divisions. Luisa Passerini says: 'Oral sources refuse to answer certain kinds of questions; seemingly loquacious, they finally prove to be reticent or enigmatic, and like the sphinx they force us to reformulate problems and challenge our current habits of thought.'[43] Damien's moment of reticence here spoke vividly and clarifyingly of how punk's possibilities were limited by the structural sectarianism and segregation of Belfast and of Northern Irish society. A further reflection on the spatial constraints involved in living in west Belfast followed. Damien describes the ring of steel, being searched coming in and out of the city, and the difficulty of transporting amps and guitars from home to gigs when public transport tended to stop running quite early.

> Well there was black taxis, there was – you know the black taxis ran later – although to be honest if you were walking late at night through town and up to the black taxi rank, I think it used to be on Castle Street, with a guitar and an amplifier – you'd better have about five or six friends with you. 'Cos otherwise [laughing] you weren't going to get as far as the taxi, certainly not with your guitar![44]

As with some of my other interviews, including Alison's – Hector Heathwood's interview, discussed in the following chapter, is another example – violence and the fear of violence are evoked here as a sort of environmental factor in the everyday life of teenagers and young people in Belfast.[45]

Damien's relative success in bands did not make an enormous impression on his parents, he explained, echoing the sense given at the beginning of his interview of the domestic sphere as relatively fixed in comparison to the multifaceted, shifting public sphere.

> My dad was happy that I was playing music, he liked music even if it wasn't to his ... I don't think to be honest they really appreciated the half of what was going on. I mean they were very busy, I come from a family of six children. So really when I wasn't around you were off the radar and that was fine.[46]

This benign parental indifference, however, was unsettled by an incident in his late teens.

> But I remember one night, oh man, I was thinking I was maybe 17, I definitely wasn't 18 I was still at school, we'd played in Belfast and I think it was up in Ardoyne, the Shamrock Bar. And one of the guys lived across the street from me. And we were all meant to get a lift home but this girl was like, girl, I mean, to me she was a woman, she was 21 or 22, took a shine to me and took me back to her apartment on Cliftonville Road. And I was happily spending the night there thinking this is great, living the dream, rock and roll blah blah blah, and what had happened was when my mate got home and mum knew I was out, wouldn't settle until you got home. Then she realised the big guy across the road was home so she says to my dad, where is he, so he had to go and get him up, who then took my dad and showed him where I'd gone, so I'm thinking I'm like real punk and living the dream and all this with this woman, but my dad starts battering on the door – about half two in the morning – to take me home. I was like [performs a sort of all-over, full-body adolescent cringe; laughter] he was gonna kill me, my mum was like where were you at this time of night, and to be fair that was a really tough time in Belfast. Late '70s, people were getting lifted off the streets and taken away and they were found up the Hightown Road or whatever. So I mean I get it but when you're 17 or 18 and you're getting [with] a girl you don't ... think about it, not at all, and we'd been drinking and playing and just whatever. And as I say this was pre-mobiles so you couldn't call or text or phone, he wasn't a happy bunny.[47]

This is an anecdote in Daniel James's sense. That is, it is a 'morality tale with both a social and an individual register ... about proper and improper behaviour, responsible and irresponsible actions, about the way the world is and the way it ought to be'.[48] An archetypal adolescent narrative of casual sex, performed in the conventional register of slightly bashful masculinity from the perspective of an older and wiser man, is interrupted by the memory of violence and fear. 'Late '70s, people were getting lifted off the streets and taken away and they were found up the Hightown Road or whatever', he says. The performance of 'thinking I'm like real punk and living the dream' is interrupted by a firm reminder of the performance's staging, and of the real threat of abduction.

It seems that the Hightown Road (which passes through the north of the city towards the back of Cave Hill) is being used here as an off-hand example of an isolated part of town. It is worth noting, though, that the Hightown Road is where the bodies of Paddy Wilson and Irene Andrews were found after they were murdered by the Ulster Defence Association (UDA) in 1973. John White, the commander of the UDA front organisation the Ulster Freedom Fighters, was convicted of the murders in 1978, around the time that this story is taking place in Damien's narrative.[49] This is suggestive both of the way in which cultural memories of the Troubles informs the way in which my interviewees remember the period, and of the way in which remembered fear marks the text of the interviews indelibly if sometimes near-imperceptibly. Peter Shirlow, describing Belfast after the peace process, argues that 'the narratives and reality of constantly protecting place and religious segregation are still interlinked devices in the whole enactment of discord and conflict' – Damien's evocation of moments of violence that seep into their narratives from other parts of the past highlight the way in which these narratives permeate the stories told about Northern Ireland's recent history.[50]

The almost-conventionality of the story (teenage hijinks; stretching the bounds of responsibility; parental strife; reflection on the parental relationship from the position of full adulthood) is troubled by the recognition that the late 1970s was 'a really tough time in Belfast'. As in some of the other interviews discussed later on, then, the potential violence of particular spaces is present in the interstices of the narrative, but not fully incorporated into it.

Directly after this story, still reflecting on how his parents felt about his involvement in the punk scene, Damien mooted that they did at least appreciate that it took up his time and prevented him from becoming involved in sectarian or violent elements of youth culture in west Belfast, or from joining the paramilitaries.

> It gives you an outlet and also it kept me out of trouble from any other paramilitary activity or anything like that, so whereas quite a number of my peers would've got involved in that kind of stuff – as happened to teenagers in west Belfast. But all the guys that played with me in bands they never had any because [F: All your free time, I suppose] well, we weren't hanging around the street corners to be preyed on by these people.[51]

The choice of words here – 'preyed on' – is suggestive, and reflects the dual spatial vulnerability that Damien's description of his adolescence evokes. On the one hand, the possibility of becoming a victim of sectarian or state violence, as in the first story; on the other, the possibility of responding to this threat by joining a paramilitary group like the Provisional IRA.

A final sense of the interaction between punk as a spatial practice and the forces of sectarianism and class that structured space in Belfast comes in Damien's story about his first job, in the laboratories at the Royal Victoria Hospital.

> The first day I started the guy, they put me into this lab with a guy who was a horrible person and he said to me here, take your earrings out. I said no, he said I'm telling you to take these earrings out, I said I was interviewed with these earrings in got the job with the earrings in and nobody mentioned it, I said girls are in here wearing earrings – so if they take theirs out, 'cos we need to for health and safety reasons [F, redundantly: Hygiene!] I've no problem, and he hated me forever after that.[52]

As in the account of how some bands could not play in west Belfast, we get an idea here of how punkness as a signifier of difference functioned differently depending on place and position.

DIY cultures and structures of feeling

Like Petesy, Damien's account of punk in Belfast is explicitly related to a broader, transnational structure of feeling. It is similarly related the idea of punk as having a DIY or do-it-yourself ethos, and although it is narrativised in a different way here, there seems to be a similar sense of the scene as a response to a feeling of being ignored or mistreated by social systems and structures.

> You know it enabled me as a person to step outside my small horizons and boundaries and it enabled me to … obviously you get confidence through playing in bands, being on stage and that, and to express yourself, artistically, cos we wrote our own songs and all of that, it was very good, very good. And that can-do mentality. I mean most of the guys that I know from way back then would be you know a lot of them went on. I mean I started a business a lot of my friends started businesses.[53]

The entrepreneurial verve expressed here takes a different form from the anarchist-minded ethos expressed in Petesy's interview, but the desires are roughly coterminous – to generate spaces and institutions that circumvent Belfast's existing spaces and institutions. This desire plays a role in composing the narrative and the subject both Petesy and Damien are presenting within the interview.

> And I'm not saying, that might have happened anyway, but it was this culture of we don't need you to give me a job, I can stand on my own two feet. I don't need you to give me a record contract, we can make our own music, do our own thing. And I think that's definitely been a thread through my life you know.[54]

This avowal of punkness as a 'thread' that has continued to unravel through the life course is a common theme in nearly all of my interviews.[55] Damien concluded our discussion by returning to the link between politics and place in the Belfast punk scene.

> And I think it, some of the ideas from punk were still very valid. The anti-nuclear thing, the anti-racism thing. I mean we were at a Rock against Racism gig in Divis flats, very near Divis flats, there was a big church hall there [F: I think I've seen a picture] yeah and that was amazing, St Comgall's Hall I think it was, and we did Rock for Cambodia, we did somewhere near there as well which was sponsored by Blue Peter, something like Blue Peter was involved in that, we did a Rock for Cambodia thing. That was quite novel you know and there were a couple of music festivals in west Belfast we played at there was a band called The Lids were really really good back in the day[56]

This account, again, links politics in Belfast to broader political currents – but it also stresses the importance of the local, the embodied and the specific. It is reminiscent of Eamonn McCann's proud assertion, when reflecting on Northern Ireland's sometimes-elided position in the global '68 protests, that 'we were part of that', internationally; it insists on seeing the problems facing nationalist communities in Belfast as part of a constellation of social and political issues without attempting to elide their complexity or specificity.[57] This was drawn out further in our final exchange, in which Damien set up a dichotomy between certain punk bands that he felt were more interested in the scene as a set of empty signifiers than as a set of political and spatial practices.

> I don't want to name names about some of the bands but some of the bigger bands that were getting a good bit of public recognition – some of them were from good schools and very well, you know, parents were very well sorted, from an upper-middle-class background shall we say. And I'm not saying what they were doing was invalid or being critical of what they did at all, but it wasn't quite, it didn't have the realism of we are actually from the streets of west Belfast, where it is really bad. And you've never experienced that because you go to Campbell College and your parents take you for two weeks to Spain every summer.[58]

There is an important corrective within Damien's critical narrative, both to totalising narratives of the punk scene in Belfast and to totalising narratives of punk in general as a form of working-class resistance. This was developed in his concluding comments, in which he returned to the way in which being in the punk scene had informed his political position and attitudes both then and now.

> I think we started to view some of the conflicts in a different way because we were probably very left-leaning then we looked at the situation and we didn't see it as a Catholic versus Protestant we kind of looked at it and thought you know the people on the Shankill Road who have no jobs, the guys above them the politicians and the leaders and all them, they're telling them that they've no jobs cos the Catholics have taken their jobs. Go over the Falls Road you're being told the Catholics have no jobs cos the Protestants, and we thought we saw it as maybe more of a class struggle, that that was what was wrong, and that punk maybe could – and it maybe changed but we certainly were anti-establishment we were certainly anti-government

but you know not much changed of that. I remember going to Ballynahinch, Enoch Powell with his famous Rivers of Blood speech, we were there protesting. We all went there and protested. And I'm sure it was Ballynahinch we went to we went protesting back then. So that was all part of what we did, certainly for me and my band that was integral to what we did.[59]

As Damien suggests, Powell is mostly remembered for a racist speech he made in April 1968 as a member of the Conservative Party's shadow cabinet, expressing fear and alarm about immigration into England.[60] However, in his later career he was also the Ulster Unionist MP for South Down, between 1974 and 1987. Damien appears to elide protests made against Powell at some point during his sojourn in Northern Ireland with the speech itself, which was made in Birmingham, but the nature of the action being described is unclear. Again, however, it is clear that Damien's memories of the punk scene connect it to a larger world of international political activism.

Conclusion

Petesy and Damien, like Alison, describe epiphanic encounters with the punk scene; like Alison, they stress the collective, affective and spatialised dimensions of this scene as a structure of feeling. The explicitly or capital-P political aspect of their memories may, in part, be the product of their specific position within the segregated and sectarianised geography of Belfast in the 1970s – certainly, both of them draw on slightly different parts of the cultural memory of punk to formulate a critique of the British state, but also of parts of the republican movement in their neighbourhoods growing up. They emphasise the hopeful feeling of possibility generated by trying to change the city, along with the frustration and fear generated by the difficulty of exercising this possibility. This feeling is visible in Petesy's desire for a venue that was not implicated in either capitalist or sectarian logics, but also the affective resonance he attributes to the Crass gig at the Anarchy Centre; and in Damien's evocation of urban political protest, but also of the excitement and novelty of meeting people from Protestant backgrounds: 'Who you know, different tradition, et cetera, and then you realise these guys are just thinking, they're young people thinking the same as I do, they may be from a different faith or whatever.'[61]

The following chapter will analyse two interviews (with Hector Heathwood and Claire Shannon) to consider how punk is remembered as challenging hegemonic discourses on gender and sexuality in Northern Ireland.

Notes

1. The United Irishmen, founded in 1791, were a revolutionary society aiming for the emancipation of Ireland and its independence from England. Their attempt at a military uprising, in 1798, was not successful. On Russell himself, see James Quinn, *A Life of Thomas Russell, 1767–1803: A Soul on Fire* (Dublin: Irish Academic Press, 2001).
2. Lauren Berlant, 'Thinking about Feeling Historical', *Emotion, Space and Society* 1:1 (2008), p. 5.
3. Interview with Damien McCorry, conducted by Fearghus Roulston, 2016.
4. *Ibid.*
5. Interview with Petesy Burns, conducted by Fearghus Roulston, 2016.
6. *Ibid.*
7. Tim Edensor, 'Mundane Hauntings: Commuting through the Phantasmagoric Working-Class Spaces of Manchester, England', *Cultural Geographies* 15:3 (2008), pp. 313–33.
8. PB, 2016.
9. *Ibid.*
10. *Ibid.*
11. *Ibid.*
12. *Ibid.*
13. *Ibid.*
14. Dave Hyndman, *The A Centre or The Lost Tribe of Long Lane* (Belfast: Northern Visions TV, 1981).
15. *Ibid.*
16. PB, 2016.
17. George McKay, *Senseless Acts of Beauty: Cultures of Resistance Since the Sixties* (London: Verso, 1996), p. 76.
18. Nick Montgomery and carla bergman, *Joyful Militancy: Building Thriving Resistance in Toxic Times* (Stirling: AK Press, 2017).
19. Sara Ahmed, 'Collective Feelings: Or, the Impressions Left by Others', *Theory, Culture & Society* 21:2 (2004), p. 25.
20. *Ibid.*, p. 39.
21. PB, 2016.
22. *Ibid.*
23. *Ibid.*

24 *Ibid.*
25 *Ibid.*
26 Wilkinson, *Post-Punk*, pp. 37–77; Simon Reynolds, *Rip it Up and Start Again: Post-Punk 1978–1984* (London: Faber & Faber, 2005).
27 Wetherall, *Foundations*, 2020, especially chapters 5 and 6.
28 Frank Gaffikin and Michael Morrissey, *Northern Ireland: The Thatcher Years* (London: Zed Books, 1990); see also Jennifer Curtis, '"Profoundly Ungrateful": The Paradoxes of Thatcherism in Northern Ireland', *PoLAR: Political and Legal Anthropology Review* 33:2 (2010), pp. 201–24.
29 Curtis, 'The Paradoxes of Thatcherism', p. 204.
30 Gaffikin and Morrissey, *Northern Ireland*, p. 125.
31 PB, 2016.
32 PB, 2016.
33 *Ibid.*, p. 10.
34 Graham Dawson, 'Memory, 'Post-Conflict' Temporalities and the Afterlife of Emotion in Conflict Transformation After the Irish Troubles', in Marguérite Corporaal, Christopher Cusack and Ruud van den Beuken (eds), *Irish Studies and the Dynamics of Memory: Transitions and Transformations* (Oxford: Peter Lang, 2017), pp. 257–97.
35 Andrew Burke, 'Music, Memory and Modern Life: Saint Etienne's London', *Screen* 51:2 (2010), p. 105; see also Svetlana Boym, *Common Places: Mythologies of Everyday Life in Russia* (Cambridge, MA: Harvard University Press, 1994), especially pp. 283–91, and Agata Pyzik, *Poor But Sexy: Culture Clashes in Europe, East and West* (London: Zero Books, 2014).
36 PB, 2016.
37 *Ibid.*
38 DM, 2016.
39 *Ibid.*
40 *Ibid.*
41 On the CND, see Christopher R. Hill, 'Nations of Peace: Nuclear Disarmament and the Making of National Identity in Scotland and Wales', *Twentieth Century British History* 27:1 (2016), pp. 26–50, and Christoph Laucht and Martin Johnes, 'Resist and Survive: Welsh Protests and the British Nuclear State in the 1980s', *Contemporary British History* 33:2 (2019), pp. 226–45; on RAR see Schrader, 'Rank-and-File Antiracism'.
42 DM, 2016.
43 Passerini, *Fascism in Popular Memory*, p. 91; see also Sean Field, *Oral History, Community and Displacement: Imagining Memories in Post-Apartheid South Africa* (London: Palgrave Macmillan, 2012), p. 127, for a thoughtful reflection on this dynamic.

44 DM, 2016; during the conflict, black taxis were used as an unofficial substitute for buses, especially for residents living in parts of the city where the transport network was often disrupted by violence. See Wendy Ann Wiedenhoft Murphy, 'Touring the Troubles in West Belfast: Building Peace or Reproducing Conflict?', *Peace & Change* 35:4 (2010), pp. 537–60.
45 Interview with Hector Heathwood, conducted by Fearghus Roulston, 2016.
46 DM, 2016.
47 *Ibid.*
48 James, *Doña María's Story*, p. 172.
49 Brian Rowan, 'Loyalist White a Police Informer: Special Branch Recruited Killer', *Belfast Telegraph*, 21 February 2006, online at: www.belfasttelegraph.co.uk/incoming/loyalist-white-a-police-informer-28108844.html (accessed 14 August 2018).
50 Peter Shirlow, 'Ethno-Sectarianism and the Reproduction of Fear in Belfast', *Capital & Class* 27:2 (2003), p. 93.
51 DM, 2016.
52 *Ibid.*
53 *Ibid.*
54 *Ibid.*
55 See, for instance, John Callaghan on watching *Good Vibrations* for the first time: 'Looking around and you see all these middle-aged men, dragging their partners … coming out, every single one of us misty-eyed, lump in the throat … I found it really emotional to be honest. Just right at the end they showed pictures. I knew a couple of people in it, not great friends but just part of the big fraternity, a couple of them are dead, you know what I mean, Jesus Christ was that really 30-odd years ago.' Interview with John Callaghan, conducted by Fearghus Roulston, 2016.
56 DM, 2016.
57 Eamonn McCann, quoted in Prince, 'Global Revolt of 1968'.
58 DM, 2016.
59 *Ibid.*
60 Shirin Hirsch, *In the Shadow of Enoch Powell: Race, Locality and Resistance* (Manchester: Manchester University Press, 2018); on Powell's later career in Ireland see Paul Corthorn, 'Enoch Powell, Ulster Unionism, and the British Nation', *Journal of British Studies* 51:4 (2012), pp. 967–97.
61 DM, 2016.

5

Gender, respectability and emigration

I interviewed Hector Heathwood in the near-empty smoking area of an upmarket bar in Dublin, just off the River Liffey, although it was early afternoon and we both stuck to coffee. A trace of this setting's weirdness has leaked onto the tape in the thumping dance music that can be heard over both of our voices. Hector, a freelance photographer who has been living in the Irish capital for some years after a stint in Edinburgh, was smartly dressed in a dark suit and winklepickers, evidence of an interest in clothes and fashion that he had also cultivated as a young punk; he described going over to London in this period to look (unsuccessfully) for Malcolm McLaren and Vivienne Westwood's infamous punk boutique SEX, and while there also 'looking to get one of those wee Jam suits, you know, three buttons, an Italian cut'.[1]

Born in east Belfast, he got involved in the punk scene in 1976 or 1977, initially introduced to the music of some English bands by a schoolmate before deciding to look for what passed for the local scene, inspired by his lack of enthusiasm for pre-punk popular culture:

> Cos you know like with Bowie dying recently and all this going on about it, but Bowie was one of the things that kept us all going during the '70s, cos him and Lou Reed that was it for originality. It was desperately bad in the early part of the '70s. All I remember is drizzle, drizzle and fucking Bob Dylan, possibly Yes, all those big super bands were out. Godawful, you know.[2]

Hector described the early days of the punk scene in Belfast bathetically and funnily, comparing it to the opening scenes of the 1986 Sid Vicious biopic *Sid and Nancy* in which a gaggle of punks wander, lost, around London, looking for like-minded people – 'where everybody's running around looking for this great punk scene that there's supposed to be, and that's what it was like you know, sorta going down town on Saturday going where the fuck is this, you know'.[3]

The first intimations of a fledgling local scene appeared, in his account, at the Trident bar in Bangor, which he described as a soul club that would occasionally play a solitary punk record near the end of the night, invariably 'White Riot' by The Clash. 'Wherever you were, the Trident was long and thin, so wherever you were when you heard the police sirens [at the start of the song] you made for the dancefloor, running over tables.'[4]

Bangor is a seaside town about 15 miles away from the city by car, and Hector also described the difficulties of travelling to and from the Trident in the context of the Troubles. He said:

> You had to get in the minibus but it was funny cos the whole of Bangor was like a warzone, and when you got into Mr Addison's Taxis it was like a truce. So all the spideys, as it was the name, and all the punks would be like [noise indicating convivial and drunken sentiments being shared] dancing to 'Rivers of Babylon', Boney M., but I remember like, I remember coming up there one night and there was a rain of bottles coming down on us, I'm thinking fuck, but when we looked over they were coming from the top of the local police station [laughter] so who do you fucking call [laughter]? Another night I was away down the street but there was a punk getting set upon by a couple of guys, you know, so we were all haring up the street, but by the time we got there a cop dog patrol had turned up. The guys, the spideys ran off, and then the cops set the fuckin' dog on the punk that was lying on the ground bleeding, you know.[5]

These two anecdotes, coming near the start of our interview, nicely sketch out the relationship between punk and Northern Irish society that Hector wanted to convey. Being a punk, he suggested, meant existing outside of the sectarian architecture of the conflict (epitomised here both by the 'spideys', Northern Irish slang for working-class adolescents constructed as 'rough' or 'unrespectable', and by the police); it also meant dealing with the ambient hostility that this outsiderness provoked and made possible. Hector performs the delineation between punk and its parent society especially vividly here, with both stories turning on the unexpected behaviour of the Royal Ulster Constabulary – the punchline of 'so who do you fucking call?', in the first anecdote, offers a nice encapsulation of the thesis that to be a punk was to be a pariah, as does the inverted expectations and alarming escalation of violence described in the second story. I am using the word punchline deliberately here. The wry, laconic tone he adopted to talk about what sounded to me like two quite fraught situations was characteristic of how Hector spoke throughout the interview, relating his memories with an air of mild amusement that suggested a desire to communicate both the saturated violence of the past (so commonplace as to be funny rather than upsetting) and the relative lack of impact it had on Hector himself (since in joking about it, he implicitly rejects moralising or trauma-focused readings of the effect of those early encounters with conflict). Following Lucy Newby, it seems like there is a rejection of dominant narratives of the conflict in the humorous tone of these stories, or at the very least a consciousness of their uncomfortably delimiting effects on subjective accounts of the past.[6] Anna Sheftel, in her work on dark humour in Bosnia-Herzegovina, suggests that 'humour is a way of remembering and representing [the violent] past in a subversive manner; it offers an alternative mnemonic paradigm that resists the ethnically divisive historical narratives that plague the region'.[7]

But these are dark jokes with a sharp edge, especially the second one; humour is often one of the ways in which aspects of the violent past can be made visible in oral history narratives without upending the emotional landscape of the interview.[8] Throughout our conversation, Hector returned to the question of violence repeatedly, and particularly to the question of quotidian violence as being part of life in Belfast in the 1970s and 1980s. The memory of these everyday patterns of violence created a space for exploring a second preoccupation of the interview, which was an engagement with dominant codes of respectable or acceptable masculine behaviour. Hector's interview offered an eloquent engagement with these codes and his position within them. As the narrative above suggests, there was an ambivalence to how he talked about and around them; on the one hand he described how punk allowed him to transgress or critique them, and on the other hand much of the bravado and the humour in his stories continued to draw on a particular masculine persona, one that treats the potentially disruptive or dangerous aspects of life in Belfast during the Troubles with phlegmatic unruffledness.⁹

I read Hector's interview in this chapter, alongside another interview with Claire Shannon, to consider punk's structure of feeling in relation to hegemonic constructions of gender, sexuality and respectability in Northern Ireland. Alison Farrell's interview, in Chapter 3, covered some similar ground in thinking about punk as a means of transgressing the boundaries of respectability she encountered in Belfast and Dungannon – the focus here will be less on transgression and more on the specificities of the boundaries themselves. A further distinction between Alison's narrative and these ones is that both of the latter interviewees have since migrated from Northern Ireland; the possible relevance of this trajectory to the way they remember punk and the North will be considered in the conclusion.

'Fuck, it was weird, but it was good fun'

The two stories Hector told about Bangor at the start of the interview also had an intersubjective dimension, again related to humour; under certain circumstances, joking about the conflict with another Northern Irish person can be a (risky) strategy for establishing a rapport, but it can also be a means of establishing a moment of cross-generational conversation or interaction. In describing his own experiences of Belfast, Hector seemed to be assessing my awareness of the conflict, checking how shocked or alarmed I would be by his blasé recounting of violent situations. I said that it seemed like there was little hope of help from the police in light of what he had said, and he responded:

> It was unbelievable. You know it was a pretty violent time anyway obviously, but [if you] marked yourself out as different you were fucked, you know. When the Harp started the IRA actually had a death threat out on punks and you were sort of sitting with them going you going to shoot me today, I might, you know. Fuck it was weird, but good fun.¹⁰

The sense of punkness as entailing difference from the fragmented society of Northern Ireland is again apparent here, with the IRA rather than the police serving as the referent to that fragmentation; also apparent is the continued nonchalance with which Hector evokes the threat of violence, particularly given that from 1977 or so onwards he was involved in an unofficial organising committee at the Harp along with his ex-wife, with Terri Hooley and some others, booking bands, promoting gigs and so on. Turning the Harp into a hub for the punk scene, he suggested, was an alternative to going to local discos and 'getting the shit kicked out of us, you know, this was great to have a place to go'.[11] It was also mixed in terms of Protestants and Catholics – 'it was pretty much like a refuge, it wasn't like dealing with cross-community animosity sorta like, you know it would've been my first real contact with a lot of Catholic people. In east Belfast there aren't any and it was great you know, we all got along fine in that respect', Hector explained.[12] But these unusual proximities did not exist outside of the city's pre-existing social networks – 'I'm from east Belfast, so an awful lot of the punks [from that part of the city] wouldn't go to the Harp [on the edges of what was considered a Catholic area] because they thought they would get fuckin' shot or whatever', he said.[13] Similarly, while the bar may have been a refuge from the specific kinds of cross-community animosity that characterised other social spaces in the city, it was not a refuge from violence as such, with Hector describing 'a few major fights' and an incident with a gun as specific moments when the uneasy peace of the Harp was broken.[14] He situated punk squarely within the structures and atmospheres of the city, rather than somehow outside or above them.

Two tensions, then, characterised Hector's initial account of the punk scene. The first is between his adherence to the conventional punk-as-refuge narrative, reminiscent of many of the cultural texts discussed in Chapter 2, and his unusual willingness to portray the more difficult and fractious aspects of the scene; the second is between his description of the atmospheric violence of the city in the 1970s, and his desire to avoid collapsing the complexities of this description into a trauma narrative, or a narrative in which he is a bystander rather than a participant in the thick atmosphere he is evoking. 'Sorry, this all sounds massively violent – it kinda was but it was like really exciting and you got a thrill out of it you know', he said, in a reflexive moment in which he recognised that his experiences and emotions might be challenging to translate to me as a listener in the 'post-conflict' present, and in the context of the cultural memory of the punk scene.[15]

> F: It really sounds like there was nowhere to turn, you're getting aggro from all sides.
>
> It just got to the stage, I'm sure a lot of punks did, it got to the stage where if somebody called you something on the street you just went for them cos half the time they would back off – oh he was pissing around, leave it – and then it was grand, but all of that, if you were gonna get a kicking you were gonna get a kicking anyway you might as well get the first smack in. What can I tell you, [jovially] what doesn't kill you makes you stronger. Yeah, yeah but I mean The Clash gigs, I always liken The Clash gigs to a bit like, have you ever been in, like a riot. [F, sounding slightly embarrassed: No, not really] Well I was in a fair few east Belfast riots at the time they were using baton rounds but The Clash gigs were a bit like a riot set to music. Kinda all this aggression, kinda going forward, not anything in particular, but in the end you come out like fucking Buddha cos you have no aggression left, you're just like [makes a cartoonishly ecstatic noise and face]. I remember being, after riots when I was younger, like you know everybody would be sitting there smoking how'd you go and all that, you know, it was real relaxed.
>
> F: Like a release of tension?
>
> H: Yeah, yeah, cos there was fuck all else to do, I mean round my way there was like one youth club which closed all summer – rioting season – and that was it, you were out on the streets, what else are you going to fucking do you know.[16]

Hector here is to some extent presenting his engagement in the punk scene as a continuation of his childhood in east Belfast, which he said entailed taking part in the so-called 'recreational rioting' that media representations and popular culture such as Yann Demange's Troubles thriller *'71* present as a central part of working-class youth culture in the city.[17] In linking his childhood encounters with street violence to the violence he encountered (and took part in) through the punk scene, Hector rebuts the cultural memory visible in *Good Vibrations*, where punk is clearly figured as an alternative to violence rather than another site for its expression; but he is also engaging in a performance of hegemonic masculinity in which an acceptance of violence is part of growing up. Specifically, he seems to be drawing on the image of the 'hardman', a figure identified by Allen Feldman as one of the poles of hegemonic masculinity in Belfast.[18] His tone remained laconic, operating very clearly within the frame of the street-fighting hardman, even if the violence he's describing doesn't have the same symbolic function – the hardman in Feldman and Sean O'Connell's readings of this archetype in the cultural memory of post-industrial Belfast was engaged in the maintenance of the sectarian boundaries between and within working-class communities, whereas as a punk, Hector suggested he was exposed to violence for moving across or not being contained within those boundaries.[19] The masculinised composure of this narrative was emphasised through the intergenerational moment where he described The Clash gigs as 'riots set to music', asking me if I've ever been in a riot; in establishing my generational (and spatial) naiveté or innocence, as someone from rural Northern Ireland who was born in the late 1980s, Hector is able to take on the role of the discerning practitioner of masculine violence, both in terms of the difference between punk gigs and riots, and the similarity in the (essentially) post-coital relaxation induced by both experiences.

But this relatively coherent performance of masculinity – one which adheres to what Fidelma Ashe calls the militarised masculinity of Troubles-era Northern Ireland, even as it partially steps outside of it in its rejection of the sectarian division these masculinities helped to reinforce – was not maintained throughout the interview. Slippages and shifts in tone suggested the consequences of the affective atmosphere Hector is describing, an atmosphere in which any explicit performance of difference exposed you to the possibility of violence. This violence is importantly spatial or territorial. The following reflection came at the end of an account of the difficulties of traversing the centre of Belfast, moving from the Harp Bar in what is now the Cathedral Quarter towards the Cornmarket in the middle of the city.

> H: But for that, coming from the Harp to that turnstile you had to go through Cornmarket, where there was a couple of the biggest spiderman discos on earth, so you had to sort of run the gauntlet before you got to the gates; sometimes you were just fighting your way through Cornmarket, others you just sort of slithered through

the shadows and got away with it. But that sort of stuff was constant, you were just, people having a go at you constantly.

F: It sounds exhausting.

H: It was, I do remember a guy breaking down one night just with the strain of it. Stress of it, he was a big guy you know, and he was just sort of sitting there crying just because he was stressed and strained, he was alright after that but you know that constant battering really knuckle down probably doing speed as well like you know [laughter] which doesn't help with your emotional state. Yeah.[20]

Hector's jocular tone changed slightly here, with this conversation coming a little bit later into the interview. He instead offered an admission, or half-admission, of the psychic strain that adopting the hardman persona described in the previous quote entailed. This is apparent in his choice of words, describing the experience of traversing the violent city as 'running the gauntlet' or 'slithering through the shadows', rather than through the active or pre-emptory violent role he described in the previous quote – 'if you were gonna get a kicking you were gonna get a kicking anyway you might as well get the first smack in'. It is also apparent in the different narrative structure he uses, where the violence of the city is understood as something atmospheric and enveloping – 'that sort of stuff was constant, you were just, people having a go at you constantly' – rather than through the tension-and-release model of the riots he talked about earlier.

Finally, he gives a displaced description of what existing in this environment could do to your emotional or psychological state – Hector remembers 'a guy breaking down one night just with the strain of it [...] he was alright after that but you know that constant battering really knuckle down probably doing speed as well like you know'.[21] The disintegrating syntax is notable in the final sentence, and expressive of the memory of violence as pervasive and unsettling – this seems to be a site where Hector is expressing a slight critique of the edicts of hardman hypermasculinity, or of the strain that embodying these edicts entailed in the context of the conflict in Northern Ireland. There is also perhaps a flash of discomposure here, as the jovial attitude he previously expressed towards conflict – 'what doesn't kill you makes you stronger' – comes into tension with a different understanding of the effects of violence; arguably this discomposed moment is partially resolved with the light-hearted reference to taking speed which caps the anecdote, indicating that a partial renunciation of masculine self-control was permissible on the grounds of temporary, substance-based derangement.

Sexuality, gender, respectability

In the moments of the interview where he discussed fighting and aggression, Hector was negotiating with the hypermasculine image of the hardman and the atmosphere that surrounded and fostered this image. This ambivalent movement between adopting the appropriate masculine persona and rejecting it was also characteristic of how he talked about sex and sexuality in the context of the punk scene. Here is an exchange which followed his mentioning the fact that underground gay bars in Belfast such as the Chariot Rooms were also welcoming to people dressed like punks, unlike many of the other bars in the centre of the city.[22]

> F: It's interesting that intersection between the gay scene, such as it was, and the...
>
> H: Well there were a good few gays within the punk scene as well. Cos again most people were accepted it was a place where they could come...
>
> F: Quite unusual in Northern Ireland in the 1970s.
>
> H: It was yeah because it was still illegal. Actually, as an aside, but when I was still married in '80 or '81 or something they made it legal and I came home and the auld boy next door to me who was a staunch Paisleyite type of a character [F: Save Ulster from Sodomy eh] and he was gomping up and down in his driveway you know really angry and I says 'Robert, you know what's wrong?' and he goes 'Ah, they made homosexuality legal today' and I goes 'They didn't make it compulsory Robert' [laughter]. It was just such a fucking reaction, you're not doing it, it doesn't concern you, what's your fucking problem.[23]

Hector is emphasising here the capacity of the punk scene to incorporate and welcome difference, whether sexual, religious or whatever, and contrasting this to the hostility of Northern Irish society more widely to difference. The anecdote about his Paisleyite neighbour then provides a funny illustration of the difference between the punk scene's ethics of indifference and wider society's curtain-twitching attempts to maintain the bounds of heteronormative respectability. It is a joke in the sense that Luisa Passerini understands jokes in her work on the memory of fascism in Turin – for her, laughter and comic stories about Mussolini among the workers she interviews represent 'pragmatic acceptance of daily compromise with the regime as well as rebellion at the symbolic level'.[24] Hector has remembered the date correctly here – in 1981, the Northern Irish gay rights activist (and later Unionist politician) Jeff Dudgeon brought a case to the European Court of Human Rights, which found that the law in Northern Ireland criminalising all male homosexual acts between consenting adults was a violation of the European Convention on Human Rights.[25] Hector's evocation of Ian Paisley, the evangelical Presbyterian minister and leader of the Democratic Unionist Party or DUP, known for his hysterical, millenarian oratory and virulent anti-Catholicism, is also apposite.[26] As my interjection suggests, the DUP had launched a 'Save Ulster from Sodomy' campaign in the mid-1970s as a reaction to the emergence of Cara-Friend, a charity supporting LGBTQ people in the North, and to the Northern Ireland Gay Rights Association or NIGRA.[27] Sean Brady says of this evangelical project: 'It was a concerted and persistent campaign, which advertised itself in the newspapers, and demonstrations and pamphleteering on street corners: it promoted itself as a religious crusade, and lasted for many years, though the height of its activity and prominence was between the mid-1970s and 1982.'[28]

In the context of the conversation we had been having about the relationship between punks and the circumscribed and beleaguered but nonetheless present gay social scene in 1970s Belfast, Hector's joke both established the hegemonic moral order of the North – one in which staunch Paisleyites 'gomp around' in an impotent rage about other people's sexuality – and dramatises or performs his rejection of that attitude towards sexual difference. In general, Hector's interview was marked by a sense of sexual freedom or licence that struck me initially as indebted to a 1960s-inflected, hippyish liberalism as much as to the cultural mores of the punk scene. He evoked a landscape of casual sex and romantic entanglements with a frankness that in a Northern Irish context registered as slightly startling, suggesting for instance that when teenage punks ran across the Trident in Bangor to enjoy the one punk song in the night, 'most people were up in the toilet fuckin' shagging, you know'.[29]

This element of his narrative seems to have a similar ambivalence to the element on violence and fighting already discussed. Hector's performance of sexual dissidence via his engagement in the punk scene allowed him to critique the atmosphere of repression generated by putative moral arbiters such as Ian Paisley. This dissidence, or transgression, is not inherently radical, or inherently deconstructive of fairly standard, rigid gender roles. There are traces of machismo here as there are in the accounts of fighting and violence discussed above, but also traces of a desire to find different kinds of relationships in the context of 1970s Northern Irish society; for instance, when talking about the period immediately after his period of intense involvement in punk, Hector touchingly described living with his first wife in Orangefield:

> She was still punk-looking you know, I had the blue hair and stuff, so we were still living our punk life and looking at things and communicating properly between two human beings and all that jazz so the ethos had stayed with us even though the thing [the punk scene] had long gone.[30]

In the context of a setting where, as Eamonn McCann suggested, 'if there's one thing Catholic and Protestant reactionaries in the North can unite on, it's that young people mustn't be allowed to enjoy sex', Hector's account is striking for the accent it places on pleasure and possibility.[31] David Wilkinson, in a thoughtful account of the relationship between politics, sex and transgression in punk, warns against a dehistoricised account of the complicated sexual politics of the scene, in that (for instance) the supposed transgressions of Vivienne Westwood and Malcolm McLaren often functioned 'squarely within the terms of the conservative orthodoxies they provoked'.[32] Despite this, 'transformative sexual liberation' was a current of punk, with Wilkinson citing Pete Shelley of the Buzzcocks' 'strong residual connection with the methods, preoccupations and institutions' of gay activism as one example of this.[33] Hector's

Gender, respectability and emigration 127

narrative speaks to this history, but also to the history of sexual politics in Northern Ireland, where 'a highly regulated sexual landscape characterised by limited sexual rights' was hegemonic throughout (and after) the Troubles.[34]

Post-industrial possibilities and labour

Hector's sense of punk as offering a wider range of possibilities was also related in his narrative to questions of work, labour and life course. As with the image of the hypermasculine hardman, the image of the industrial worker was central to the cultural imaginary of east Belfast in the period when Hector was growing up.[35] Reflecting on the way in which punk had enlarged his sense of the potential world, he said: 'But you know people were like, sorta performance art was creeping in [pauses], paintings and stuff, fanzines. So there was a lotta sorta possibilities were springing to mind where there had been effectively zero, like. You worked at the shipyard or Shorts.'[36] The shipyard, in the context of the working-class Belfast Protestant world Hector grew up in, teems with connotations – of masculine skill and bravery, of a capacity for wit and for debauchery, and of a half-imagined past when Northern Ireland was an economic powerhouse and a cornerstone in the edifice of the British imperium.[37] While Harland & Wolff was in the doldrums by the period Hector is talking about, the residue of the industrial past retained (and retains) a powerful weight in deindustrialised Belfast, especially in terms of the production of masculinities, as in similar contexts such as former mining towns in Wales or former mill towns in the north of England.[38] This weight is felt both proudly and oppressively in Hector's narrative. He talked fondly, for instance, of a photography exhibition he had organised in the mid-1980s with images of retired shipyard workers, who he had photographed when visiting their houses in his day job as a TV repairman. But his juxtaposition of the possibilities of the punk scene – performance art, paintings, writing – and the constraints of a life tethered to 'the shipyard or Shorts' comes through powerfully here, with the emphatic 'zero' at the end of the sentence signalling the potential foreclosure of possibility, followed by the clipped naming of the two industrial sites emphasising the heft of this residual imaginary.

We returned to the question of work and life course near the end of the interview, when I asked Hector to summarise the effects of punk on him as a person.

> H: I think it was that you sorta challenged accepted views, you know what I mean. Like you know a lot of stuff you were brought up you went to school you were taught do this this this and this then retire and fuck off, nobody cares, but you were suddenly able to challenge that you know – what do I want to do? You know, [inaudible], and I think like today that's pretty, that's quite normal, but then it was a pretty big thing you know, I mean like, I had people my age going … you know like kids today flying away to fucking Sri Lanka for this you know, fucking bastards, but that's what we wanted, you know like mad, I'm mad happy that happens for people now, I wish it had happened in my day but I'm not going to begrudge anybody else getting it, I wanted it you know.[39]

Firstly, this is a good summary of punk's relationship to the atmosphere of respectability and conformity Hector evoked throughout his interview – 'you were brought up you went to school you were taught do this this this and this then retire and fuck off, nobody cares', as he says, in a pithy and caustic summary of the masculine ideal of the responsible breadwinner. Punk allowed him to challenge this linear model of progression and life course (and this oppressive model of ideal masculine behaviour) and try to figure out his own desires and ambitions beyond the path he was expected to follow. Again, given the particular valence that industrial labour has in the popular memory of working-class, Protestant Belfast, Hector's dismissive description of the conventional school-work-retirement trajectory is conspicuous. This was heightened by the shift into a different temporal mode in the second section of the quote, where he moved rapidly between his youth and adolescence and the lives of 'kids today flying away to fucking Sri Lanka for this you know, fucking bastards'. There is a touching sense here both of the way in which Hector sees the punk scene as expanding his sense of possibilities and his sense of self, and of the material limits to what this could do – 'I wish it had happened in my day but I'm not going to begrudge anybody else getting it, I wanted it you know', he concluded.

Claire Shannon, punk and politics

A further interview with Claire Shannon offered related insights into the atmosphere of respectability in 1970s and 1980s Northern Ireland, its relationship to constructions of gender, and how the punk scene existed as a structure of feeling within this atmosphere. Claire is a bit younger than Hector, and thus was involved in a slightly later wave of punk in Belfast – that of the late 1970s and early 1980s. This partially explains the differences of emphasis in their accounts, and particularly the differences in the spaces and venues that they describe. Another major divergence between Hector's interview and Claire's is that Hector presented himself as a product of working-class east Belfast culture in a relatively uncomplicated way (although we did not in fact talk very much about his childhood prior to taking part in the punk scene); Claire, on the other hand, presented herself more as a 'born outsider' to the social world of Northern Ireland, partly through her early experiences of life and partly through her gender. Her experience of constructions of gender in the North is filtered through her experiences as a woman, and the subordinate position afforded to women in those structures.[40] However, what her account shares with Hector is a critical view of the moral universe of the North, and of the way in which mechanisms of respectability and conformity are mobilised to construct and maintain this universe.

Claire was born in Rathcoole, Newtownabbey, but moved to Belfast as a child and grew up there, mostly in the south of the city. Her parents had been communists in the 1950s and in the initial period of the Troubles were sympathetic to the republican cause, although as the conflict deepened they recanted on this affiliation, gravitating instead towards Belfast's small humanist movement. These family allegiances and a childhood spent with 'Catholic kids from the Ormeau Road and Protestant kids from the Cregagh and Woodstock Road' meant that Claire felt herself to be outside of the sectarian structures of the Northern Irish state long before her engagement with the punk scene.[41] However, this sense of distance or separation was experienced painfully at times, notably through her experiences of school. Despite her parents' humanism, she attended Carolan, all-girls grammar school, which she described as 'very, very religious, mostly Baptist'. 'It was a nightmare for me', she added.[42] Struck by this formulation and by the discrepancy between her parents' lack of religious adherence and the ethos of the school, I asked why she had been sent there, and she explained that her parents' options were limited.

> C: A lot of my friends ... a lot of my friends, people I'm in touch with who were in the punk crowd at the time nearly all sent their kids to integrated schools. So you thought it was odd for me to go to a Baptist ... I don't think my parents knew it was as religious as it was ... but what the other factor was it was one of the nearest grammar schools. My younger sister was very into punk as well – you might have seen from these photographs – she hated Carolan, it was a very restrictive sort of place. I think I said, there's a photograph of her the day she got expelled [laughter] she dyed her hair pink and went into school and was expelled.[43]

Claire was a thoughtful and reflective interviewee, and the ellipses here and throughout the transcript indicate the winding patterns of her speech as she carefully considers both the multiple directions in which her own memories move, and the best way in which to express this multiplicity in the context of the interview. Here, she initially does something temporally similar to the moment near the end of Hector's interview where he juxtaposes his options in the 1970s with the geographically widened options of many young people today, 'flying away to fucking Sri Lanka for this you know, fucking bastards'.[44] Similarly, Claire notes that many former punks have chosen to send their children to 'integrated' schools – that is, schools for both Protestant and Catholic pupils – but that this was not an option for her parents. Lagan College, the first integrated school in Northern Ireland, opened in 1981, although it did not receive any government funding or a permanent location until the mid-1980s.[45] She also manages to both sidestep my implicit question of why school was a 'nightmare' and answer it through the figure of her sister, a recurring presence throughout the interview as someone who was seemingly more ensconced in the punk scene than Claire herself.

On her own relationship with school, she said, somewhat elliptically: 'Became very unhappy and I dropped out in lower sixth. And just, well, it wasn't popular at home so that's when I moved into a flat to have more freedom and that's when I got more involved in hanging out in Lavery's and going to clubs and [inaudible] and stuff.'[46] This was the beginning of a year or so in which she immersed herself in the Belfast punk scene, as well as in left politics, eventually doing her A levels in the business college before leaving the North for England and university.

Throughout the interview, Claire expressed a nuanced sense of the punk scene as disruptive of the socially conservative world epitomised for her by the evangelical dictates of Carolan school, but as also a site for the reproduction of other norms and mechanisms of control. Her sense of the disruptive potentialities of the scene was especially clear in an account of going to Jules, a bring-your-own-booze underground nightclub in the centre of the city. As was often the case when specific places were mentioned in the interviews, we engaged in some cartographic back-and-forth around where exactly the club was in Belfast.

> Yeah, yeah, you know I can see in my mind where it is, North Street, sort of North Street running down ... there was a little bit ... you've got Smithfield over here and there used to be, for a few years there was a big cafe there on that sort of junction, but it's closed down now. Sorta where North Street came up towards High Street and Royal Avenue there, it was on a corner. And it was a whole carry-on getting ... you know everybody loved it.[47]

The final clause here about the 'carry-on' or rigmarole of getting into the club as adding to the excitement of going there points nicely to the multiple function of moments like these in oral history narratives. They are pragmatic, like the call-and-response conversations you have when giving directions; but they also have an intersubjective aspect in that they perform the connection between the interviewer and interviewee, in this case showing that both Claire and I remember the layout of central Belfast – although the nods, grimaces and noises of affirmation I was making throughout this process do not register in the transcript. Finally, they are also a technique of narrative or of storytelling that help to generate the epiphanic charge carried by her description of the nightclub – Claire's enunciation of place names and streets here is a way for her to share the excitement and pleasure she felt at finding this hidden, secret space, and the way in which – as she says – the 'whole carry-on' of finding and getting into it complemented this mood.

F: It sounds quite exciting.

C: It was ... I remember the first night I went there. Was a ... I was you had to get up a lot of stairs so I got to the sort of top landing just before you went into the club and there was a little serving hatch or something and this guy just sorta crawled out of it in front of me, he was very gay, and he had a ribcage on ... and I think that was quite normal for the first time I went there, I was 17, and I was shocked, but like pleasantly, I just thought this is mad, it's fantastic, you know, so I think it was my favourite venue but as I say it was a bit of a carry-on getting into it. You'd get queues ... there was a massive big staircase and you had to say you were a member of a club or something and you'd go up to the doorman and sign something to get in. And then when you got into the actual club bit it was a couple of rooms, couple of rooms to sit in, and a sort of dance floor bit, and then there was a sorta off the dance floor there was a long corridor and the toilets – the toilets were quite exciting on their own. It wasn't ... well for me you know being that young it was sort of male and female mixed, they didn't care which one you went into [makes a face and brief puff of breath, both I think intended to indicate the oddity of non-gendered bathrooms in 1980s Belfast] so I went into one of them one of the first times I was there and saw there were things along the wall that I thought were drinking fountains [laughter]. So I sorta went over to one of them thinking how does this work and then I saw some guy beside me and thought, oh, that's what that is [laughter].[48]

Claire's continued description of Jules developed this sense of excitement and transgression. Rigid constructions of sexuality and gender both break down in this account of the club's atmosphere, with Claire 'shocked, but like pleasantly' by their dissolution. The anecdote about the unisex toilets is a nice encapsulation of the overall thrust of the narrative, capturing the unsettling of norms of respectability that Jules seems to represent for both interviewees; in terms of composure, this is a moment where Claire jokes about the naiveté of her former self not knowing what a urinal was, reinforcing her sense of the unusually benighted (and gender-segregated) culture of 1970s and 1980s Northern Ireland, but also indicating her own sense of having developed into a more knowing or sophisticated person through experience and emigration.[49] Another interviewee (who did not wish to be named or quoted directly in the book) also remembered the genderless or unisex toilets in Jules, and noted that

Gender, respectability and emigration 133

this inspired the ire of Ian Paisley and his Church; as in Hector's narrative, the figure of Paisley recurs here as an emblem of restrictive constructions of gender and sexuality in the North.

We also discussed buying clothes, which entailed a similar kind of geographical back-and-forth as the locating of Jules, although in this instance with a more explicitly temporal sense of the changing landscape of Belfast.

> Yeah ... I was trying to think about this last night because there were very small sort of very alternative outlets for clothes, there was one down Rosemary Street, I mean it's gone now but if you were going for a coffee around that time you would've gone to Delaney's and it was fantastic – they've ruined it, it's Caffè Nero now, you know the kind of style he had several pubs there would've been, but down that street if you were walking down here sort of City Hall direction down this little street you know there's some really weird old pubs down there that would've been there for ages which we wouldn't really have gone to at least one or two of them still down that little street you have to go through a little entryway to get to one of them ... [F: Pottinger's, maybe ... I know where you are anyway in town yeah] But there was a sort of, across the road from there, there was sort of, there were sometimes sort of office blocks here and there in town that some people would start selling clothes from and I can't remember the name, there was also ... Shaftesbury Square, Great Victoria Street, there was a big office block there and my mum later got very involved in feminism and she started a well women's centre and it had its offices in this big block but there were also a couple of sort of weird, mad clothing outlets there that ... we'd have got stuff from. You know I'd say Fresh Garbage as well but they sold sort of hippy stuff more, for women, they would've sold combat trousers and army surplus and stuff, we would've bought stuff from, combat trousers and stuff like that. And there was, there were little sort of outlets of shops down Old Street Arcade, but I can't remember if they were concurrent to that time but I'm sure I bought bondage trousers and stuff down there. Which I was running around in! My mum and dad thought was very amusing, but ... they never sorta said get that stuff off you, they'd just laugh at me.[50]

As at the start of the interview where we discussed Claire's sense of outsiderness as being partly parentally inculcated, she emphasises a kind of benign amusement on the part of her mum and dad, as well as a sense of intergenerational connection between her politics and those of her mother. But what mainly comes through here is a vivid sense of a kind of alternative geography of central Belfast, incorporating 'weird old pubs', a women's centre, Fresh Garbage, the Old Street Arcade. As my somewhat forlorn interjection in the middle of the quote suggests, I am not from Belfast and despite spending a fair amount of time there my sense of the streetscape and especially the names of streets is pretty hazy, which made it harder for me to play my part in the call-and-response mapping here. Despite that, Claire gives an exhilarating sense of the spatialisation of punk as a structure of feeling and how it helped to shape her engagement with the city as a teenager.

But Claire was also attentive to some of the ambivalences within the punk scene in relation to gender, sexuality, respectability and politics more widely. In part, she suggested this was a product of her own involvement in more formal political activism with Militant (a Trotskyist socialist organisation that was influential in the British Labour party in the 1980s) and with various feminist organisations.[51] Socialism offered a more convincing road map for her than the somewhat diffuse anarchism prevalent among the punks she knew. 'I sometimes thought you know it was great for them to say you know nobody rules me, because I would've agreed with that a lot, and – but some of the punks I knew were taking that a bit to mean I could do whatever I want', she observed.[52] This manifested itself in various ways, including a party where Claire's flat was trashed and her clothes and records stolen; she also discussed the hedonistic tendencies of the scene more generally in a way that recalled some of Hector's stories, although she was more explicit about the psychological and physical damage this hedonism could entail.[53] Challenges to the dominant orders of moral conservatism did not necessarily generate liberatory possibilities, in her account. Her willingness to rub against the grain of the cultural memory of punk extended to a slight criticism of the hagiographic view of Good Vibrations and Terri Hooley: 'There was Good Vibes the record shop where you could get the sort of music you wanted to listen to in but ... um ... it wasn't always the most pleasant experience [laughter].'[54]

This strand of her narrative was emphasised through the story of a brief romantic relationship with a punk: 'I'd been attracted to him cos he was very punky, and I liked that about him', she said.[55]

However, she quickly became disillusioned with the relationship, in part because of a lack of shared political and cultural interests, and in part because after leaving school and following a period of unemployment he decided to join the Ulster Defence Regiment, a locally raised branch of the British Army known for being composed almost exclusively of Protestants and for alleged collusion with loyalist paramilitary groups.[56]

> I think his parents were, he was an only child and his parents were getting at him about getting a job, so he called up – I was back at my parents for the weekend – so he called up to my parents' house in this uniform and I just thought, you know, I thought you were supposed to be this great punk. And he went over all that blether about you know he needed to sort his life out and his parents were on his back and all this stuff and I just thought, I can't really accept that. From any sort of ... political way of thinking, and as I say I was meeting, I was going out socially with another crowd.[57]

The disillusionment here – 'I thought you were supposed to be this great punk' – seems to also speak to a degree of disillusionment with the potentialities of punk as such, and certainly with its capacities to respond to the political problems of Northern Ireland. But this was mixed with a continued sense of the punk scene as a structure of feeling that offered some possibilities and some pleasures. Summarising at the end of the interview, Claire said: 'I enjoyed it, it was a bit wild sometimes, it was great fun, I loved the style, I loved the music, the colour, loved the make-up, all that sort of stuff. Loved the clothes, stuff like that. And the characters, you know. So I feel quite positive about it. And as I say ... just the sort of general feeling in a lot of aspects of life of fighting the status quo was quite good.'[58]

Conclusion

Hector and Claire suggest a further way of thinking about the structure of feeling of the punk scene, as constituting a collective and affective response to the restrictive moral universe of 1970s and 1980s Northern Ireland, particularly with regards to its prohibitions on performances of gender and sexuality. They identify different sites as the focal points of this mentality, although religion and especially Paisleyite Protestantism are recurring targets. The extent to which Northern Ireland was actually profoundly different from Britain in terms of homophobia and misogyny is hard to assess, although it is certainly true that the legislative frameworks that helped to facilitate these structures were slower to change in the North, and that religiosity as measured in terms of church attendance remained higher there than in Britain throughout this period. An important recent analysis of the struggle to achieve legal access to abortion in Northern Ireland argues that throughout the period of the conflict the North was constructed as having a special status on issues such as these.

> The region was seen as a place apart with its own conservative, deeply religious culture and values; moral issues were viewed as a matter for local resolution; local people and politicians were believed to be uniformly and unequivocally opposed to reform; and the region's distinctive position on moral issues was conceived as a kind of 'glue' that bound the community together, protecting against social and political disintegration.[59]

There are clear parallels between this 'place apart' narrative and the colonial or neo-colonial construction of Northern Ireland as primitive, atavistic and so on, and it is important to stress that the rest of the United Kingdom was also deeply enmeshed in homophobic logics in this period (as, for instance, Margaret Thatcher's Clause 28 campaign, which attempted to prevent schools, libraries and council-run institutions from 'promoting a homosexual lifestyle', makes clear).[60] Similarly, as the history of feminist activism in Britain in the 1970s and 1980s suggests, it goes without saying that institutional misogyny was a fundamental component of everyday life in the United Kingdom, not just in Ireland.[61] In other words, in listening to Hector and Claire's account of moral conservatism in Northern Ireland we should not accept a concomitant construction of the rest of Britain as a bastion of liberalism or multiculturalism. But their interviews speak to their sense of a specifically stifling atmosphere in the North.

Across both interviews, there is certainly a sense that the punk scene was able to punch a small hole in this stifling atmosphere. But there is also an unusually critical sense of the ways in which punk was complicit in elements of the socially conservative nature of Northern Irish society, or at the very least unable to escape it. Hector emphasised that the scene was as prone to outbreaks of violence as other forms of youthful sociality in the context of the Troubles; Claire described various regressive attitudes and behaviours that she perceived as being part of the scene, and critiqued its more hedonistic and apathetic tendencies, as well as the ways in which the apparent nonconformity of punk easily shifted into its own forms of micro-conformity. And with the possible exception of my conversation with Claire about Jules nightclub, none of these interviews really shifted into anything like the epiphanic mode that was mobilised in the previous two chapters to express the impact of punk on interviewees' lives and subjectivities.

This more equivocal sense of punk as a structure of feeling seemed to me to be related to a more pessimistic reading of Northern Ireland as such, and to a sense of the continued valence of the kind of conservative or moralistic structures both interviewees identified. Hector, for instance, pointed out that at the time we spoke gay marriage had not yet been made legal in the North: 'that thing about trying to get that equality going in the North, I mean how embarrassing is it now that even this fucking place [Dublin] has it'.[62] Additionally, it spoke to the importance of migration to each of the three narratives, and the way in which this trajectory can change the importance of and perspective on the past. Punk's importance in these life histories was less to do with its status as a harbinger or a precursor to political change in the North, and more to do with a sense of dislocation on the part of the interviewees that continued to be part of their lives into the present.

Hector, in an email exchange after reading a draft of the chapter, said:

> I was always very aware when talking to friends in Edinburgh, where I lived, and Dublin how odd it was to them. I can quite often see in their faces that they have no concept of what Belfast was like in those days, the normality of living with this level of violence on an everyday basis. I also notice their shock when the talk comes to friends being shot, or blown up, and that was normal too.[63]

In this context, the punk scene seems like a way of grasping a sense of outsiderness in the context of migration as well as in the context of growing up in Northern Ireland; it also seems like a way to make sense of or compose a narrative about the violence and anxiety of that period in the North. The following chapter will analyse an interview with Graeme Mullan to consider the role he understands the punk scene as having had in his life.

Notes

1. Interview with Hector Heathwood, conducted by Fearghus Roulston, 2016. He is referring here to The Jam, Paul Weller's rock band of the 1970s and 1980s, who had an ambivalent relationship to and with the punk scene but were known for their revival of 'mod' aesthetics, notably in wearing tailored suits. See Richard Weight, *Mod: A Very British Style* (London: Bodley Head, 2013).
2. HH, 2016.
3. Alex Cox, *Sid and Nancy* (London: Palace Pictures, 1986).
4. *Ibid.*
5. HH, 2016, p. 2.
6. Newby, 'Troubled Generations? (De)Constructing Narratives'.
7. Anna Sheftel, '"Monument to the International Community, from the Grateful Citizens of Sarajevo": Dark Humour as Counter-Memory in Post-Conflict Bosnia-Herzegovina', *Memory Studies* 5:2 (2011), p. 147.
8. Stéphanie Panichelli-Batalla, 'Laughter in Oral Histories of Displacement: "One Goes on a Mission to Solve Their Problems"', *Oral History Review* 47:1 (2020), pp. 73–92.
9. For an account of this kind of masculine composure in relation to memories of Australian military service, and its function in oral histories of this event, see Thomson, *Anzac Memories*, especially pp. 81–121.
10. HH, 2016, p. 2. Whether or not the IRA actually had a specific animus against punks is difficult to ascertain, although this chimes interestingly with Graeme's story in Chapter 6 about The Friendly Society and being threatened on his way home from a gig.
11. *Ibid.*
12. *Ibid.*
13. *Ibid.*
14. *Ibid.*
15. *Ibid.*
16. *Ibid.*
17. Allen Feldman, *Formations of Violence: The Narrative of the Body and Political Terror in Northern Ireland* (Chicago, IL: University of Chicago Press, 1991).

18 Sean O'Connell, 'Violence and Social Memory in Twentieth-Century Belfast: Stories of Buck Alec Robinson', *Journal of British Studies* 53:3 (2014), pp. 734–56.
19 Fidelma Ashe, 'Gendering War and Peace: Militarized Masculinities in Northern Ireland', *Men and Masculinities* 15:3 (2012), pp. 230–48.
20 HH, 2016.
21 *Ibid.*
22 Jeff Dudgeon, 'Mapping 100 Years of Belfast Gay Life', *The Vacuum* 11 (n.d.), online at: www.thevacuum.org.uk/issues/issues0120/issue11/is11arthunyea.html (accessed 20 December 2021); see also Rachel Wallace, 'Gay Life and Liberation, a Photographic Record of 1970s Belfast: Exhibiting Private Photographs and Oral Histories', *Public Historian* 41:2 (2019), pp. 144–62.
23 HH, 2016.
24 Passerini, *Fascism in Popular Memory*, p. 92.
25 Marian Duggan, *Queering Conflict: Examining Lesbian and Gay Experiences of Homophobia in Northern Ireland* (London: Routledge, 2016), pp. 54–55.
26 Steve Bruce, *Paisley: Religion and Politics in Northern Ireland* (Oxford: Oxford University Press, 2017).
27 Sean Brady, '"Save Ulster from Sodomy!" Homosexuality in Northern Ireland after 1967', *Cultural and Social History*, forthcoming.
28 *Ibid.*
29 HH, 2016, p. 1.
30 HH, 2016.
31 McCann is quoted in Diarmaid Ferriter, *Occasions of Sin: Sex and Society in Modern Ireland* (London: Profile Books, 2009), p. 487.
32 David Wilkinson, 'Ever Fallen in Love?', in Richard Cabut and Andrew Gallix (eds) *Punk is Dead: Modernity Killed Every Night*, (London: Zero Books, 2017).
33 *Ibid.*
34 Rob Kitchin and Karen Lysaght, 'Sexual Citizenship in Belfast, Northern Ireland', *Gender, Place & Culture* 11:1 (2004), p. 100.
35 Pete Hodson, 'Titanic Struggle: Memory, Heritage and Shipyard Deindustrialization in Belfast', *History Workshop Journal* 87 (2019), pp. 224–49.
36 HH, 2016.
37 Doyle, 'The Sepoys of the Pound and Sandy Row'.
38 Lee Charlesworth, *A Phenomenology of Working Class Experience* (Cambridge: Cambridge University Press, 1999); Luis Jiminez and Valerie Walkerdine, '"Shameful Work": A Psychosocial Approach to Father–Son Relations, Young Male Unemployment and Femininity in an

Ex-Steel Community', *Psychoanalysis, Culture & Society* 17:3 (2012), pp. 278–95.
39 HH, 2016.
40 See, for instance, Begoña Aretxaga, *Shattering Silence: Women, Nationalism, and Political Subjectivity in Northern Ireland* (Princeton, NJ: Princeton University Press, 1997).
41 Interview with Claire Shannon, conducted by Fearghus Roulston, 2017.
42 *Ibid.*
43 *Ibid.*
44 HH, 2016.
45 Bardon, *The Struggle for Shared Schools in Northern Ireland*.
46 CS, 2017.
47 *Ibid.*
48 *Ibid.*
49 *Ibid.*
50 *Ibid.*
51 *Ibid.*
52 *Ibid.*
53 *Ibid.*
54 *Ibid.*
55 *Ibid.*
56 Gearóid Ó Faoleán, 'The Ulster Defence Regiment and the Question of Catholic Recruitment, 1970–1972', *Terrorism and Political Violence*, 27:5 (2015), pp. 838–56.
57 CS, 2017.
58 *Ibid.*
59 Sally Sheldon et al., '"Too Much, Too Indigestible, Too Fast"? The Decades of Struggle for Abortion Law Reform in Northern Ireland', *Modern Law Review* 83:4 (2020), pp. 761–96.
60 Matt Cook, '"Archives of Feeling": The AIDS Crisis in Britain 1987', *History Workshop Journal* 83:1 (2017), pp. 51–78.
61 Margaretta Jolly, *Sisterhood and After: An Oral History of the UK Women's Liberation Movement, 1968–Present* (Oxford: Oxford University Press, 2019).
62 HH, 2016.
63 Hector Heathwood, email exchange with author, 2021.

6

Collecting, storytelling and memory

> I think it was because it definitely affected the way I look at things. I don't, you know, you don't pre-judge as much, I think, not that I ever was that bad, it's sorta hard to explain. Like there's so much creative stuff went on, not that I was in any way part of that, but all the all together it was a whole mish-mash of things coming together and the way you look at life and the way you look at things, it definitely helped my political views not to be as judgemental and you know don't judge a book by the cover, get to know someone before you brandish them, but I was already a wee bit like that anyway to be honest but it just sort of underlined it and strengthened that aspect.[1]

My interview with Graeme Mullan, or Mully, took place in his flat in south Belfast. His flat is very close to the house in which he grew up, just off the Upper Lisburn Road towards Balmoral and Musgrave Park Hospital. The first thing I noticed in his tidy, sparely furnished living room was a long glass cabinet underneath the television, packed neatly with hundreds of records; the second was a bookshelf, similarly packed with books. I recognised some of the spines, particularly the few books about punk in Northern Ireland that I was also familiar with – Terri Hooley's autobiography, the collaborative A–Z of Northern Irish punk, *It Makes You Want to Spit*, both discussed earlier in Chapter 2 – and others about punk in England. During my initial email conversation with him, Graeme had expressed doubts about his usefulness for the project, and more specifically about the historicity of his experience of the punk scene. He said that he had only been a fan, someone who attended gigs and enjoyed himself. Furthermore, he suggested that the narratives of people who played a more public role in the creation of the scene (by recording music or making fanzines, for instance) would have more innate historical value. This tendency to undervalue the historicity of one's experiences has been remarked upon as an important factor in shaping oral histories, particularly through the ways in which 'class, race and ethnicity ... create significant differences in how we remember and tell our lives'.[2]

In Graeme's case, his uncertainty led to a somewhat self-critical narrative about his young self, in which he emphasised his relative passivity as a young man caught up in the punk scene: 'It was just, yeahhh, party time, have a drink, go and watch a band, you know, and just go with the flow rather than being creative', he said of this period.[3] This part of the narrative was counterbalanced, though, by a sense of his older self's role as collector, historian and storyteller – as someone who was there, and who understands punk in Northern Ireland as part of what I have been calling a structure of feeling. What ultimately comes from the narrative is a story about immersion within a scene that allowed Graeme to make sense of his position within Northern Irish society in a new way. In this sense, the epiphanic charge of his encounter with punk is bifurcated in this interview, occurring across two timelines – firstly in his initial encounters with the scene and then later as we discuss punk retrospectively.

This chapter is divided into two sections by these two timelines. It first concentrates on Graeme's early life and his youthful engagement in the punk scene, before moving on to his account of how he relates to the punk scene now, especially as a collector of records and other memorabilia.

Community, place and school

Graeme described himself as Belfast 'born and bred', and specifically as being from the intersection of three small residential areas off the Upper Lisburn Road in the south of the city – Priory Park, Sicily Park and Locksley Park.[4] His account of this area in the early to mid-1970s intertwines questions of class and sectarianism. The houses he grew up in were terraces, with his parents' house bordered on one side by his grandparents, and on the other by his great-aunt and great-uncle. He remembered these as 'wee, as I say two-up two-down, one fireplace, poor compared to the rest of the people on the street'.[5] Despite this initial flicker of class anxiety – which will become explicit in his recounting of his school experiences – the area was nevertheless 'a wee bit of an oasis ... a little bit of an oasis of mixed community, my next-door neighbours were Catholic, you know Protestants and Catholics we had bonfires on the street and we all collected, you know we were all kids playing together'.[6] This sense of separateness and its concomitant sense of hostile outskirts which are 'sectarian, you know, hardcore, Taughmonagh, White City' serves as a narrative preparation for his baptism into the punk scene – 'there was no real sectarian upbringing for me because we had Protestant and Catholic friends, so the whole punk thing was just natural for me then, in that way'.[7] In this sense, the impact of punk is linked to his childhood experiences (as with Claire in the previous chapter, for instance, but unlike Damien and Petesy in Chapter 4), and an aversion to sectarianism is narrated as a natural, domestically inculcated attitude for Graeme, rather than an epiphanic change. But the account also works as a temporal marker within the interview for the shift that comes about through going to school, which has both negative and positive effects.

Firstly, education and getting older burst the prelapsarian bubble of childhood presented in this part of the narrative. This dynamic (a peaceful, non-sectarian pre-Troubles landscape fracturing into the animosities of the Troubles) is apparent in many autobiographical accounts of the conflict, and particularly although not exclusively in Protestant ones.[8] It serves a particular purpose in Graeme's account in stressing his sense of isolation from the violence of the period.

> It's just that I was isolated from it [the violence going on in neighbouring areas], but then it all, when it did blow up big style and we all got a bit older I mean my Catholic friends went to a Catholic school and I went to a Protestant school and you just never saw each other. I don't mean you never saw each other again, you saw each other at night and stuff, playing football in the street, but it was different then.[9]

This difference was apparent in the enforced codification of segregated education and in the increased political awareness of his adolescence, both of which contributed to the end of innocence described in Graeme's account of his early childhood.

> Whenever you were introducing friends from school to your friends from home, you felt a wee bit, well I felt a wee bit intimidated by some of their friends. And I don't know whether they felt the same but it was a peer pressure thing, you know you had to ... it's not that you had to ... again, I was too young to be in one of the Tartan gangs.[10]

Graeme returned to the question of his separateness from the early years of the conflict by mentioning having been too young to take part in the street violence of the early 1970s, synedochalised here through reference to the Tartan gangs. The Tartan gangs, or Tartans, were groups of young men named for their choice of clothing (tartan scarves and denim); they engaged in forms of territorial boundary-marking, macho posturing and petty crime, something like skinheads in England, but as the Troubles developed became implicated in the maintenance of sectarian geographies and in loyalist violence more broadly.[11] Desmond Bell, in his classic work on Protestant youth cultures in Northern Ireland, links the Tartans to parading culture and particularly non-Orange Order, 'unrespectable' parading culture. He argues that 'the cultural work of the "Blood and Thunder" bands, like that of the Tartan gangs which they have largely succeeded, is best understood as a response by the young to the material decline of Protestant working-class communality'.[12] Graeme's evocation of them here is suggestive of their folk devil status during the early years of conflict, as signifiers of the 'corruption' of young people by the violent environment; it also indicates his important sense of himself as someone from the kind of attenuated, post-industrial working-class Protestant community described by Bell, but as someone who does not conform to the sectarian elements of that community. In the moment of the interview, his separateness from the sectarian surround of his childhood in south Belfast was confirmed when he went to Methody (or Methodist College Belfast, as it is formally but not popularly named) after primary school, also making him only the second person on his street to go to a grammar school. Primary school was the site where Graeme's sense of himself as a Protestant is inculcated, through a new distance emerging between him and his childhood friends; Methody, he suggested, brought different questions of class and class identity to the fore.

Methody and feeling out of place

He said: 'Methody wouldn't be called, it wasn't a hard school by any means. But for me as you know real working-class family going into, I was a fish out of water ... Going into Methody was just a total culture shock for me.'[13] Methody is an interdenominational and co-educational school, founded in 1865. It is on the south side of the city close to Queen's University Belfast, with a leafy Edwardian campus and a prestigious reputation for both sporting and academic achievements. Graeme's sense of disorientation in this environment manifested itself through a feeling that there were a new set of codes in place that he did not understand, exemplified by the fact that rugby, rather than football, was the primary sporting activity encouraged among the students.[14]

> A wee bit of class, you know you definitely noticed that … well I felt that I was a wee bit, who are all these kids, I felt poorer than them, I felt – I didn't know rugby! – it's a big rugby school. [This is] a wee bit Americanised but it was like a jock culture … Going into there I just didn't have a clue. I really did feel like a fish out of water.[15]

A slight breakdown in syntax here indicates the difficulty of expressing the remembered experience of feeling out of place – the repetition of the verb 'felt' is suggestive of the emotional or affective impact of the move to another school. Finally, the simile that ends the account – 'a fish out of water' – recalls the idyllic description of pre-school childhood in south Belfast as a small, isolated oasis that existed outside of the sectarian flows elsewhere in the city. It also emphasises Graeme's understanding of his own passivity as a teenager, one that is contrasted in the narrative with his engagement with the history of the punk scene as an adult.

The dislocation and disorientation of being educated in a middle-class institution as a working-class person has been much discussed, although not in the specific context of Northern Ireland. A key text remains Richard Hoggart's *The Uses of Literacy*, which anatomises the experience of the 'scholarship boy', existing 'at the friction-point of two cultures' and not entirely comfortable within either.[16] Expanding on the relationship between his early school years and punk, Graeme said: 'And I just didn't click in there [Methody] either and I think that's also, that's what sort of dropped me into the punk thing. It was like the disenfranchised youth, the outsider, always felt that, you know.'[17] His description of himself as 'the disenfranchised youth, the outsider' is reminiscent of Luisa Passerini's work on the use of archetypal images in her work on fascism in Turin. Specifically, the figure of punk-as-outcast evoked by Graeme is comparable to the 'born rebel' image Passerini identifies in some of her interviewees' narratives, where they explain (for instance) their later involvement in labour struggles through their fractious childhood relationships with parental or educational authority.[18] In her work, the specifically gendered element of this image is crucial, because it serves 'as a means of expressing problems of identity in the context of a social order oppressive of women, [and] also of transmitting awareness of oppression and a sense of otherness'.[19] In Graeme's narrative, the archetype is redolent of a (mostly male) tradition of outsiders in scuffed leather jackets – from James Dean to Joe Strummer – but it also expresses a problem of identity, the complicated nexus of relations formed by class, religious background and gender in 1970s Belfast, and the structure of feeling of the punk scene as being formed by these conditions. A clear sense of how punk related to this sense of outsiderness came through across the next part of the interview, where we discussed how Graeme had become interested in the punk scene.

Graeme was sixteen when he got into punk, meaning he'd been a student at Methody for around four years. He said:

> I know a definitive moment was seeing The Stranglers on Top of the Pops. 'Go Buddy Go', and the next day the whole school was talking about it. There was a group of – by that stage you know you'd made alliances in school and again it was the outsider, you know, not the rugby playing ones.[20]

His self-identification as an outsider is repeated here, but connoted positively rather than negatively through the definitive and epiphanic moment of seeing The Stranglers play on television, and being able to form 'alliances' in school subsequent to that. These alliances were cemented through encounter with what Graeme laughingly called 'a higher echelon of society', when a friendship with another schoolboy allows him and some other schoolmates to form a punk band, albeit somewhat half-heartedly, at least in his retrospective account.[21]

> They lived in a big house that had big attic rooms, he had two brothers and each of them had an attic room, and he had an attic room – he was allowed to bring his mates in [...] We used to go get a carryout [Northern Irish slang for drinks bought from an off-licence] and go up to his bedroom and then that became all the punk pictures round it and listening to records up in there [...] I think we did try to form a band [...] so that was quite funny, we actually had a name and all as well. We called ourselves Bacteria.[22]

F: That's a good punk name!

G: Yeah, Bacteria, and the album was going to be *Bacteria Grows on You*. You know we had it all sussed out! But we never made it out of the garage, never made it out of the bedroom. So that was quite fun messing about up there drinking and getting into the music.

This account speaks to the complicated class composition of punk in Belfast, suggesting a complexity that is not apparent in, for instance, Dick Hebdige's sociological study of the scene in *The Meaning of Style*, where punk is analysed as a symbolic form of working-class resistance.[23] On a macro level, facilitators of the punk scene – like Terri Hooley in Belfast or Malcolm McLaren in London – used capital, nous and contacts to arrange gigs and help create the beginnings of a cultural infrastructure, the conditions of possibility for the scene to exist; on a micro level, bands needed money for instruments and space to practice, attic rooms or garages, and tolerant or at least helpfully absent parents. In terms of Graeme's narrative, he offers a vivid, affective sense of punk here – his discomfort with the 'higher echelon of society' that he had initially encountered at Methody is transmuted into a resonant sense of sociality engendered through shared interests, the imagining of possible, never-quite-realised bands, and the material ephemera of punk – records, zines, and pictures torn out of music magazines.

Bacteria never made it outside of the attic or the garage, but Graeme's affiliation with the punk scene was confirmed when he planned to attend a Stranglers gig at the Ulster Hall in 1977, asking his mum to help him buy some suitable clothes for the occasion – namely, drainpipe corduroy jeans. Our discussion of clothing led into another digression on the duality between school and the outside world, and the fuzzy line between those two fields.

> Talking about the way you dressed as well, because you were at a grammar school there was that bit of a, you sort of nearly had to have two, you know, I couldn't dress like a punk at school, getting detention and everything. [F: You've got to wear a blazer and that?] [Inaudible] ... college socks, but you did have your own sort of private wee, you'd put your tie straight instead of having the big [makes knotting gesture around his neck to indicate the top knot in a tie], and wearing DMs and you know...[24]

The performance of identity is not always overt or overtly confrontational – unlike the self-defeatingly rebellious young men in Paul

Willis's study of adolescent resistance *Learning to Labour* whose adherence to sartorial deviation justified their exclusion from school, Graeme attempted to keep his punkness simultaneously present and private in school, performed but in a minor key.[25] This dynamic between being in-place and out-of-place, and the way it relates to both the formal rules of school and the informal rules of punk identity, is a clear indication of the way punk functions in Graeme's narrative as something that allows him to negotiate discomfiting and unfamiliar spaces.

From favourite bands to clothes and gigs, we moved on to records, the crucial final component of sealing his position within the punk scene in Graeme's account.

> You started going into Good Vibes and they had the singles, the punk singles up and imports [...] started going in there because of second-hand records and you were seeing, excuse me, seeing the people, and then 'Big Time' was out, and it was playing in the shop, what the fuck's that, you know, Rudi, oh my god that's, ahh brilliant, you know. And then you were starting to get into the local scene, The Outcasts [...] You know you were just sort of learning these things as you went along.[26]

Graeme foregrounds the educational or didactic element of punk fandom, the way in which familiarity with the scene is developed in an apparently aleatory way through chance encounters and overheard records, 'learning these things as you went along'. Records are an important connection between the two parts of the narrative – as explained above, Graeme remains a collector of records and other documents of the punk scene, even buying back some of the albums he had originally owned but sold as a younger man. And again, he gives a vivid sense of the pleasure and excitement of this didactic process and the way in which it created relationships with other people, emphasising the collectivity of the structure of feeling in his account of hearing Rudi's record in the shop and asking what it was. This collective affect was also part of the appeal of punk gigs, as Graeme went on to explain.

His first concert (The Stranglers, fittingly, who played Belfast in September 1978 after having a planned gig in September 1977 cancelled) was another epiphanic moment in his narrative. Initially his parents were unsure about the idea, but he made a deal with his mother that he would be allowed to stay out after eleven as long as he and his friends sit in the balcony of the Ulster Hall rather than stand with the crowd in front of the stage.[27] In the event, this proves to be an ideal vantage point.

> The whole facade of the Ulster Hall was just cracking, the plaster was falling down on to the ones below, it was just so amazing, it really was, and then the stage got invaded at the end – there's a picture in [Belfast punk anthology] *It Makes You Want to Spit* of Burnel playing among all these kids. And I mean I'm looking at it thinking I'm young to be here and there's fucking wee kids up on the stage![28]

The idea of punk as claiming of space – the different relationship punk allowed young people to have with space and with the city – is vividly symbolised here in the cracking facade of the somewhat dilapidated monument to middle-class, Protestant tastefulness that is the Ulster Hall. Temporally, this anecdote makes interesting use of the photograph of the gig, seen years afterwards when the book is published in 2002, as a punctum that opens a way into thinking about age and adolescence. Several times throughout the interview, Graeme alluded to his feeling of being too young for the punk scene as a feeling that has been challenged or at least reassessed through his adult awareness of how many very young people were involved in the scene. This willingness to interrogate his former self from his adult position was one facet of his engagement in a kind of historical practice around punk. In terms of the first part of our interview and its narrative focus on his early encounters with the scene, the gig is another moment in which punk provides an exhilarating moment of disruption. Graeme emphasised that this exhilaration extended to more quotidian modes of participation in the scene, like going to the Harp Bar for a pint on the weekend.

He said:

> We used to go down [to the Harp] sometimes on a Saturday afternoon when they had a punk disco. [...] And you'd go up these stairs into this dark room, you just saw there was faces that you knew about but you didn't know to talk to them, you know? But you never felt intimidated or anything because you were all there for the music. And again the whole thing about the Protestant–Catholic thing and punk breaking all that down and music being the first interest.[29]

His embodied sense of punkness 'breaking all that down' means Graeme can walk 'up these stairs into a dark room' and not feel intimidated, with the shared structure of feeling that exists there breaking down the Protestant–Catholic dichotomy that made meeting strangers in Belfast in the 1970s particularly intimidating.

However, the vivid description of a step into the dark and the unknown being made easier by a mutual interest in the punk scene was followed by a long pause on Graeme's part, as he gathered himself for an extended analysis of the relationship between punk and sectarianism, one that did not chime perfectly with the hegemonic cultural memory of the scene as discussed in Chapter 2 and throughout the rest of the book. Although the fact of a mutual interest in punk helped to dissuade any feeling of intimidation, it did not make the possibility of intimidation, fractious conversation or disagreement disappear. Graeme's analysis here complicates the too-easy evocation of punk's role in 'breaking all that down', while still maintaining that it did do so, to an extent.

> That's probably true but you still knew by people's names, if you got talking to them ... it's not that you cared. I always felt that I liked to know in case I insulted anybody. Indirectly talked about something I shouldn't have been talking about and upset someone you know. So I just liked to know...[30]

In this account, punk in Belfast is not exactly about transgression or resistance. Instead, it is a set of practices that allow its practitioners to negotiate the boundaries of Northern Irish social life in a safe way, but largely through acts of camouflage, concealment and avoidance rather than through acts aimed at countering sectarian narratives or producing alternative narratives. Graeme added:

> That was just part of it but it didn't matter. And then those ... [deep breath] ... I don't know whether punk really opened up the city centre as such but it certainly might have been a wee trickle in the dam. Cracked it open you know. But very rarely would I, like after, at night I wouldn't have gone into the city centre at all.[31]

The 'trickle in the dam' is quickly reconsidered via Graeme's recognition of the continued salience of the conflict for him and for others – 'at night I wouldn't have gone into the city centre at all', he remembers, despite its status as a relatively space part of Belfast. This limiting gesture, though, came alongside a more expansive understanding of the friendship and sociality of punk, even if this sociality could not dislodge him from the discursive, knowledge-producing 'telling' practice that reads people as Catholic or Protestant.

> When you did go into town on an afternoon when the town was open – cos you would go down to the Smithfield Market [...] you know there definitely was, you could see people, there was always wee cliques of other punk people. And you acknowledged [one another] ... you know I never really got any people shouting, any wee women coming over ... but you definitely did feel a sort of sidestep apart from everybody else. And it felt good![32]

The sense of feeling 'a sort of sidestep apart from everybody else' is only slightly spoiled by its failure to generate a satisfying level of opprobrium from the general public – 'I never really got any people shouting, any wee women coming over'. Again, Graeme is both acknowledging the gravitational pull of the cultural memory, and the archetypal image, of the punk as outsider, and giving it a little tweak, suggesting that this outsiderness could be forged through indifference as much as through more dramatic acts of scorn or violence. He also described it as being forged in opposition to other groups perceived as being more invested in the territorial and sectarian culture of Belfast – like the Tartan gangs he mentioned earlier in the interview – although he reflected,, in a typically thoughtful aside, that these groups might also have enjoyed the same affective sense of togetherness he enjoyed in the punk scene. 'It was sort of a gang culture with them, more like an anti-gang culture with us but we were ganging together for protection. Because we were the outsiders, not the norm.'[33] These experiences of a shared outside, and the persistence of the structure of feeling attached to it, has continued to shape Graeme's subjectivity, he suggested.

> You don't pre-judge as much, I think, not that I ever was that bad, it's sorta hard to explain [...] it was a whole mishmash of things coming together and the way you look at life and the way you look at things, it definitely helped my political views not to be as judgemental and you know don't judge a book by the cover [...] I was already a wee bit like that anyway to be honest but it just sort of underlined it and strengthened that aspect.[34]

His assessment here, along narratives presented above, suggest two kinds of practices that taking part in the punk scene entailed for Graeme. These cohere around a deliberate practice of avoidance – not saying certain things, not asking certain questions, not performing one's identity in certain ways – and a deliberate practice of non-judgement that requires a repetitive, reflexive questioning of one's own political and social background.

Limits, threats and historical reflection

The usefulness of these practices was tempered throughout, however, with an understanding of their limits. This awareness foregrounds Graeme's sense of himself as adopting multiple identities and moving between different spaces as an adolescent. These limits are shown in different ways throughout the interview, including a digression on the way in which punk's semiotic content changed when transplanted from England to Northern Ireland – wearing a T-shirt copy of Jamie Reid's famous Sex Pistols album cover featuring a defaced image of the Queen, Graeme pointed out, could be read as an anti-monarchy and thus explicitly republican statement in Belfast, rather than as expressing a diffuse anti-authoritarian or anarchic politics, as it was intended to do in London. But they were most apparent in a dramatically recounted story about an encounter after a gig in 1979. The gig was at the Ulster Hall, Siouxsie and the Banshees with local support from The Outcasts, and ran much later than planned because the English band's equipment was misplaced somewhere on the journey. Graeme left before The Outcasts came on, but his friend decided to stay.

> So I was left one o'clock at night in Belfast walking up Bedford Street towards Shaftesbury Square on to the Lisburn Road, and I had parked my wee moped at his house – he lived up just past the city hospital – so I was walking up to there to pick up my bike to head on home, and these two guys were walking down the side of the street. And I mean there's nobody else about, no cars, streets are quiet and you're sort of – you're wary. And I started speeding up a wee bit and they started crossing the road. So I sped up a wee bit more and they curved to meet me. So I said when they hit the white lines in the middle of the road, I'm taking off. And I ran and they tried to catch me, I just ran and ran and ran, I ran right the way up on to the Lisburn Road up past the

Samaritans there, and stopped and looked around, there was nobody about and I was going thank god, absolutely wrecked you know, lactic acid building up, couldn't get a breath, walking along and the next thing I hear this dum-dum-dum-dum [indicating footsteps], looked round and they're running after me again. [Performatively deep intake of breath to suggest how shocked he was, or perhaps how winded he was.] And I had to take off again, I just, you know, and again it was just that fear – flight or fight and it was flight for me! I ran and they chased me all the way up to my mate's house, I got into the door and luckily his mum had left the door on the latch. So I turned round and closed it, went round the back, got onto my moped and wheeled it out, and they were waiting for me. So I just started up and tore out, then by the time I got home of course, I nearly wished they had of caught me cos my ma went through me for a shortcut.[35]

Reflecting on the event, he added: 'And then I since found out that there was sort of an offshoot of the paramilitaries called The Friendly Society that decided to beat up on punks, I'm sort of wondering were they part of that.'[36]

In the interview, this anecdote directly preceded a discussion of the divisive elements of punk culture as interpreted in a Northern Irish context, prefacing Graeme's attempt to set some limits on its potentially emancipatory capacities. The evocation of familial (or specifically maternal) authority – something that loomed large throughout Graeme's account of his adolescence – is ironically juxtaposed with the threat of street violence; this might suggest that punk, here, helps Graeme evade certain domestic concerns but is unable to extricate him from the material threat of paramilitary (or simply indiscriminate) violence, in a moment that recalls the story told by Damien McCorry in Chapter 4 about meeting a woman after a gig and being sheepishly collected from her flat by his dad. The performance of this story of atmospheric violence was especially animated on Graeme's part, as I have tried to indicate in the brackets within the text, and the vividness with which he recalled and recounted this frightening event is an important counterpart to the equal vividness with which he recounted his early encounters with punk gigs and records. At the level of narrative, it is the clearest attempt made to suggest that the punk scene's relational powers were confined to certain sites (school, gigs, certain bars, the relatively safe town centre) and not applicable to others; indeed, as his digression on a paramilitary society that targeted young punks suggests, in particular places looking and dressing like a punk could put you at risk of violence – this was also alluded to in Hector Heathwood's interview.

In an email conversation we exchanged while I was drafting the book, Graeme – having read a previous version of the chapter – told me that a recent conversation with the unnamed friend mentioned in this story had reshaped his understanding of the night's events. According to his friend, they had both left the gig early, and both been chased from Bedford Steeet up the Lisburn Road.[37] This revision put me in mind of Alessandro Portelli's account of the death of Luigi Trastulli, where many of his interviewees displace the death from when it really happened (anti-NATO protests in 1949) to another central moment in the post-war history of Terni (protests against factory closures in 1953).[38] Portelli proposes that the temporal and spatial reordering of Trastulli's death are suggestive of his role in the political imaginary of workers' struggles in the Umbrian city; as he puts it, 'even though Trastulli did not die fighting for jobs in 1953, the workers carried him along in their minds when they took to the barricades then'.[39] Similarly, the initial version of Graeme's story seems like a meaningful misremembering. Being alone for the encounter emphasies the sense of vulnerability and fear he is evoking in the story, and pushes home the point that the possibilities engendered by adopting a punk identity did not totally change your relationship to the city and to violence. Graeme's revision of this narrative through facts received after the event (from understanding it as random street violence to understanding it as potentially driven by a specific paramilitary animus against punks via The Friendly Society, as well as through the later addendum that his friend was actually chased alongside him) was also typical of his reflexive approach throughout the interview, suggesting his historicising desire to understand the past through an accretion of facts and objects as well as through his own memory. It is to this specifically historical approach that I will now turn.

'I wanna see some history' – historical practice in Graeme's interview

The start of my interview with Graeme was enlivened by an account of his meeting the lead singer of Rudi, Brian Young, who Graeme interviewed for a Stranglers fanzine and webzine that he occasionally writes for. Rudi's single 'Big Time' was the first record produced by Terri Hooley's Belfast-based Good Vibrations label, and the band's fitful success in comparison to contemporaries like Stiff Little Fingers and The Undertones have made them perennial favourites of the Belfast scene, as a band that never received the plaudits or exposure they deserved in their heyday.[40] Graeme described his excitement at meeting a former hero (and his surprise at realising they were both doing similar jobs at the time of the interview), then discussed Brian's new band, a rockabilly group called The Sabrejets. This led to a further digression on the increasing diversity of Graeme's music interests as he gets older and grows more engaged in the antecedents and offshoots of the punk scene.

> I swear to God, you know, you can sort of again it's the punk rock sort of thing, initially it was the year zero, everything else before then doesn't exist, but you sort of see as you get older and you get into music and you're sort of finding out The Damned were doing 'Ballroom Blitz' by The Sweet and when I was a kid listening to glam rock, you know, that was sort of, they're doing that, and they're doing The Beatles, 'Help', there's all these interconnections when bands are doing cover versions, you sort of then delve back and get into the nuggets stuff...[41]

As I suggested above, the epiphanic charge in Graeme's narrative is bifurcated. There is, typically for my group of interviewees, his initial encounter with punk as the impetus for the formation of a punk identity; then, more subtly, there is his current positioning as someone with an investment in and memory of the punk scene, which he contrasts with his passivity as a younger man. This theme was present throughout, but came out most clearly near the end of the interview in a discussion about *Good Vibrations*. Graeme described how he managed to get tickets to the premiere and the afterparty of the film.

> I don't want to be blowing smoke up my own arse here but I got tickets for the premiere to be shown, because there was a track on the ... a soundtrack, or a track on the soundtrack! By The Animals, called 'I'm an Outcast'. And I think it was on Facebook was probably where I got to hear about it, they needed a different format of it. And I was able to do it. Now I'm the worst technical person in the

> world but there's a lot of sort of bootleg stuff ... illegally downloaded probably [laughter] ... and I just happened to have this app I suppose you would call it that changes it from what it was to what they wanted it to be. And they said if you can forward that you'll get a ticket to the premiere so I did.[42]

His anecdote was carefully couched in self-deprecation and humour, but it suggests Graeme's sense of connection to the film, and to the history of the punk scene that the film narrates, as well as indicating the ways in which 'retro' cultural documents and moments can allow for a re-engagement with the past. In *Theatres of Memory*, Raphael Samuel argues for understanding micro-historical practices (in the context of punk, searching for bootlegged concert records or collecting records, zines and other documents could all fit into this category) as both useful ways of understanding the perceptions of the past that exist in everyday life, and as forms of historical understanding in their own right. It seems possible, in his reading, that this kind of historical work has 'prepared the way for a whole new family of alternative histories, which take as their starting point the bric-a-brac of material culture.'[43]

In Graeme's account, his near-lifelong gathering up of this musical flotsam and jetsam moves him into a different relationship with the punk scene much as his interview with Brian Young does. It also generates a space for an affectionate but authoritative critique of *Good Vibrations* as a representation of the past.

> So, um, again, it's [the film] taken on a life of its own. There's a lot of the film I really like but a lot of it is poetic licence used ... I actually went to school, went to Methody with the writer of it Glenn Patterson and went to Finaghy Primary with him as well.[44]

Patterson, a well-known Northern Irish novelist, journalist and screenwriter, was more a spectator of than a participant in the punk scene as described by Graeme, and this writerly, distanced engagement with punk is one factor in the 'poetic licence' Graeme reads into *Good Vibrations*. This does not entail dismissing the film entirely, in his account. Instead it led into a nuanced critique that emphasised the interplay between facticity, authenticity and narrative. He described several key scenes from the film – Rudi playing to a near-empty town hall in Omagh, a depiction of a particularly debauched young punk called Fangs in the film and Wee Gordy in reality – as being based on actual events and actual people. 'There's a lot of truth in it but there's also a lot of the legend, the rose-tinted glasses, the story fluffed out a wee bit to make it sound – that's my impression.'[45] Graeme does not suggest that his lived experience is more genuine, or more real, than the one proposed by the film, however.

> But again you can understand, it's a film, you know, so if you're going to – again you could talk to three different people and get three different stories about the same thing that happened, so who's to say that I'm right and that's not right, this is just my impression. I think it's a very good, a very good film, but I do think there's an awful lot of rose-tinted glasses looking back on the ... what it was like, and I'm probably adding to it by talking here! You know, the revisionist thing, as I said it's middle-aged men reliving their youth.[46]

There is a bathetic deflation at the end of this point, deflecting any sense of self-importance, but the thrust of the argument is that the film needs to be understood as one narrative within a polyphonic, multiple set of narratives, narratives that are not fixed but instead open to revision and to interpretation.

This act (of positioning his narrative as one of those that can help historicise and understand the Belfast punk scene) helps complete the transition described at the start of the chapter – that is, Graeme's transition towards understanding his own experience as historical, which is also a transition between the younger and older selves presented in the interview. He explained:

> Um and I just didn't have the, an inkling, I knew I couldn't be in a band because I wasn't good enough but I didn't even think about starting a fanzine! Didn't even think about, I could've been a Don Letts [celebrated documenter of the London punk scene as a DJ and filmmaker] but I never even thought about doing that it was just, yeahhh, party time, have a drink, go and watch a band, you know, and just go with the flow rather than being creative.[47]

This passivity is additionally countered in two ways through the older self that is being presented in the narrative. Firstly, in the performance of the narrative itself; secondly, in his role as a collector. These narrative strategies will be considered in turn.

Storytelling, collecting and local history

This sense of narrating history from experience given here is redolent of the anthropologist Henry Glassie's account of storytelling in the Fermanagh townland of Ballymenone.[48] Glassie's account suggests a way of thinking about Graeme's historical practice that extends Raphael Samuel's schema, in that Samuel focuses more on the structures that allow for an engagement with (for instance) the retro than on the ways in which what comes into the structures are actively mediated, engaged with and used (ironically, earnestly, critically, and so on).

For Glassie, the stories told at ceilidhs are irreducible to the status of objects under the lens of academic analysis, and in fact are themselves simultaneously acts of analysis and acts of performance as well as forms of historical practice. 'Stories preserve actions and quotations; their wholeness requires memory as well as skill. While existing for themselves as confections of the speaker's craft, stories connect the transitory to the immutable through the fragile self.'[49] The performance of these selves requires both skill and experience on the part of the teller: 'Books can preserve the unmemorable, but the history that owes its existence to an oral dynamic, to limited memory, and to the intricacies of the social contract, cannot be boring.'[50] The stories do not only rely on their position within this social contract, they performatively reinscribe it – they can bring groups together, although they can also underline the distinction between communities depending on their content and how, why and where they are told.[51]

There are limits to the way in which Glassie's attractively generous understanding of storytelling as a specifically folkloric practice can be extended to the practices being discussed here – both the oral history interview and the ways in which Graeme tells his story outside of the interview, either in conversation with fellow aficionados of the scene (like Brian Young) and on websites or in zines.[52] But without collapsing these into one structure – one story – it is possible to see some points of connection. Stories, for the folk historians Glassie speaks to in Ballymenone, are intimately connected to a sense of place.[53] A similar relationship between place and stories is apparent in several places in Graeme's account, where punk acts as a mediation between his sense of self and his sense of place. And the stories

Collecting, storytelling and memory 159

Glassie records are often ways of talking about, thinking about and dealing with the memory and history of violence and division in Ballymenone – as mentioned in Alison's chapter, sectarianism is just as embedded in the rural society of Fermanagh as in the urban society of Belfast, even if it is sometimes less immediately apparent.

Storytelling as a means of expressing and understanding the tensions of broader society was apparent, for instance, in Graeme's account of the Punk and New Wave Festival (notably portrayed in the finale of *Good Vibrations*, as discussed in Chapter 2).

> Definitely, and it's the whole thing, what was it Joe Strummer said about it if there's any place that punk should have been it was Northern Ireland. Because it was anarchy when you think about it, the things that were going on, and then The Damned broke up and became The Doomed, and they were playing the Pound, on that Bloody Monday – well there were bomb scares, there was bombs everywhere – and I don't know if it was actually Bloody Monday or not but whatever day it was there were bomb scares going off all over the place. And I nearly didn't get out that night because of the Troubles that were going on, mum was going 'How are you going to get home?', you know, 'Look what's been going on today' ... 'I'll be alright, I'll be with my mates' ... again we went drinking, don't remember a thing about the gig at all ... there's been so many gigs in the younger days that are like that, just don't remember. I went to the ... Terri Hooley put on the Punk and New Wave Festival, I think that was in '79 or '80. And they had The Stimulators and The Saints, who were from Australia, The Stimulators are from New York, Rudi were playing, The Outcasts were playing, Stage B were playing, two-day festival thing in the Ulster Hall. And the only thing I can remember of that whole ... well I didn't even make it to the second day. The first day the only thing I remember is hearing [a DJ playing a record by] Killing Joke.[54]

This is a troubling anecdote, although it was told with a degree of levity. It is not folklore or myth, but it captures something of what Glassie calls the 'problem vibrating without resolution' that folklore, myth and local history contain and express in his study of Ballymenone.[55] 'Bloody Monday' is generally used to refer to a 1972 bomb in Claudy, near Derry, that killed nine people, and so is unlikely to be the incident that is described here. It is possible that Graeme is thinking of 'Bloody Friday', another 1972 Irish Republican

Army bombing in Belfast, slightly before the Claudy bombing, in which nine also died. While this happened at least six or seven years before the gig being described, it looms large in the cultural memory of Belfast as one of the most violent incidents that occurred in the city centre during the conflict.[56] It is a striking transposition here and suggests the way in which the sociality of the punk scene was generated through violence and the fear of violence. Coming after the discussion about division within the punk scene, it re-enacts the community within the punk scene – a community that is generated through being both within and outside of the threat of violence. Graeme also places himself both within and outside the narrative here; he describes a failure of memory through being drunk (and, as his spoken tone if not his transcribed words make unavoidably clear, frightened), while offering up a historical memory that reads IRA bombing campaigns in Belfast through the lens of a punk gig.

In the sense that the people Glassie speaks to in Ballymenone are historians, Graeme is also practising a kind of history, and this generates a difference in the sense of self being presented when he is describing his older self.

As suggested in the Introduction, this is a public as well as a private transformation. Catherine Nash, in a perceptive 2005 essay on the practice of local history in Northern Ireland already mentioned in Chapter 2, offers an insight into the particular public affect of this practice in its specific historical and political context. Local history, she suggests, has been engaged in an attempt from the 1960s onwards to 'reimagine Northern Ireland as a region characterized by cultural diversity rather than division, as a society made up of a complex mix of multiple shared and distinctive traditions, rather than "two communities" or "two traditions"'.[57] It is in this context that Graeme's various historical practices can be placed – this is also a frame that could be widened out to include the various punk heritage activities that have taken place in Belfast in the last few years (such as concerts, DJ nights and other events aimed at bringing together both older punk and younger enthusiasts for the scene), and also to include spaces like Sean O'Neill's Spit Records website and the various Facebook pages dedicated to memorialising the Northern Irish punk scene.[58] One thing this framing does is expand the concept of local as it is used within local history.[59]

Another is to place punk heritage in conversation with the problematics of local history in Northern Ireland, which for Nash are twofold – the danger that top-down initiatives aimed at finding 'the common ground' in the past will erase memories that don't fit into that schema, and the danger that a mythologised account of the past will take preponderance over a critical, politically engaged one. These issues exist in the history of punk in Belfast just as they do for other subjects of 'local history', and are apparent at various points in Graeme's narrative. As indicated in the story above, however, there is a way of acknowledging difficulty and division while still affirming community and shared emotional structures within these histories. Nash claims: 'If one challenge for local history in Northern Ireland is how to deal with history in a context where history has been used in sectarian ways, and where distant and recent histories of conflict are deeply sensitive and contentious, another is how to affirm a version of the local that does not serve exclusive, introspective and conservative versions of community.'[60]

Reading Graeme's role here as historical, and understanding his sense of his historical role within his narrative, suggests one way to expand the local beyond the parochial. The importance of punk in affirming this is emphasised in a 2011 article written by Graeme for the *Louder Than War* webzine, where he returns to the image of the 'crack in the dam' discussed in our interview. 'Thirty plus years on and Belfast has changed beyond all recognition – a buzzing city centre with an equally vibrant nightlife. Was this due to punk? Not entirely, but I do believe that it was the early punks who cracked open the closed door, broke down the barricades and allowed a trickle to become a flood.'[61]

The second way in which Graeme counters his young self's passivity comes in the account of his interest in the development of punk music and the records, books and objects he has collected as this interest increased. Graeme started collecting albums when he was still at school, but this proved financially difficult.

> Then you were selling stuff [records] again back to them to get beer tokens. [Laughter] Cos you, like, I was still at school – as I said I come from a very poor family compared to some of the other people I was hanging about with – not that I had to, you know, keep up with the Joneses [...] And then you wanted to be drinking with them so you were selling your records, and now in my middle age I'm buying records back at exorbitant prices to get what I had when I was a kid. [Laughter] And that's another aspect of it that I really took to was the collecting of the records.[62]

This narrative describes a complicated temporal movement, where the older Graeme is able to redress the losses he experienced as younger man, while recognising the melancholic difficulty, or impossibility, of this backwards-looking restoration. Walter Benjamin, describing his feelings when unpacking his collection of books after moving to a new flat, puts it well: 'Every passion borders on the chaotic, but the collector's passion borders on the chaos of memory [...] To renew the old world – that is the collector's deepest desire when he is driven to acquire new things.'[63] This is perhaps too neat a formulation, however. Naomi Schor, describing the act of collecting postcards of Paris, suggests that the pleasure this evokes for her is related not just to the representations on the cards but to their status as historical objects – 'a fragment of past Parisian life'.[64] The pleasure they generate is the pleasure of the snapshot, a snapshot in which 'the complex and shifting reality that was Paris at the turn of the century is here reduced to a series of discrete units that can be easily manipulated and readily consumed'.[65] The appeal of collecting records for Graeme seems to fall between these two conceptions: on the one hand an attempt to make up for the records he couldn't keep as a younger man; on the other, an attempt to order and reorder the complex and shifting reality of past experience.

Collected items cannot create a window into the past, but they can be generative of memories and narratives of the past, in a similar way to the family photographs analysed by Annette Kuhn as artefacts of cultural memory.[66] Describing a 'performative viewing' of a family photograph owned by a young Chinese man that shows his mother holding him as an infant, Kuhn describes the temporal movement a discursive and conversational analysis of these images can track. 'Clearly for Jack the photograph is as much about his life now, far from where he was born and grew up, as it is about his own, his family's or his country's past; though in a way these pasts and the present are folded together in his account', she explains.[67] This also touches on the way in which collection is both a public and private act, one that both literally and figuratively involves imagined communities of other collectors, as well as particular narratives about the past that are both public and personal.

> And The Stranglers stuff, like I need to have everything, completist, so this is way post-punk but when they were bringing out 12 inches,

7 inches, CDs, cassettes, picture discs [F: and the imported stuff] ... got a couple of quite rare stuff, and then just punk records, punk books, sort of just getting into the scene of it. I think it's an OCD part of me [laughter]. Especially with The Stranglers stuff you have to be a completist. And on Facebook, because I go over and see them quite a bit in England there's sort of a social scene to these Stranglers gigs, you're seeing people, real hardcore following who all hate 'Golden Brown' [a crossover hit single for The Stranglers].[68]

In this account, then, the bifurcated epiphanies described above are resolved; Graeme's initial encounter with punk is a route into one form of community, and his later position as a historian of punk and a collector of punk memorabilia and records is a route into another.

Conclusion

Graeme's interview suggests a further facet of the punk scene as structure of feeling – as a structure of feeling that emphasised the capacity for self-work and for change, while remaining conscious of its relatively bounded status; so in the example Graeme gives of visiting the Harp Bar for the first time and maintaining a consciousness of the processes of sectarian identification while not allowing them to determine his attitude towards others, there is a sense of punk as changing his attitude towards the segregated and sectarianised spaces of the city without changing the space itself.

His engagement in the punk scene does not neutralise the sense of social realities in Graeme's narrative, but it does alter his perception of what is accessible to him and opens up 'a wee trickle in the dam' in terms of his spatial experience of segregation and sectarianism in the city.[69] It creates a lasting change in his sense of self, described by Graeme when he said:

> And you know when you're going, I went away to university and like I did a science degree, not one bit creative at all, but when I was there I took that – it was still part of me there. And when I'm going over to see The Stranglers in England ... you can take the Belfast out of the boy but you, or, you can take the boy out of Belfast but you can't take Belfast out of the boy.[70]

This is the clearest statement in the interview of the way in which the structure of feeling he described throughout the interview retains an affective and embodied capacity throughout Graeme's life – it was still part of him at university, and it is still part of him when he goes to Stranglers reunion gigs thirty years later. The initially muddled syntax of the final clause is suggestive of the deliberate muddling of self, culture and city in this account, the ways in which the material components of life in Belfast, engaged with through his identification of himself as a punk, have formed his understanding of himself as a person.

In Graeme's narrative, dislocation is produced through two factors. Firstly, through going to Methody and being made uncomfortably conscious of his working-class childhood as making him out of place in the middle-class school; secondly, through the increasing segregation and violence entailed by the emergence of the conflict in the early 1970s, because of which his 'little bit of an oasis of mixed community' in south Belfast changes in terms of atmosphere if not in terms of direct exposure to violence. Graeme's formative memories of punk suggest both his awareness of its role in generating different attitudes and behaviours, and a broader sense of punk in Belfast as a structure of feeling that made a creative playful engagement with the urban landscape possible, albeit within lasting and unavoidable limits.

Notes

1 Interview with Graeme Mullan, conducted by Fearghus Roulston, 2015.
2 Joan Sangster, 'Telling Our Stories: Feminist Debates and the Practice of Oral History', in Rob Perks and Alistair Thomson (eds), *The Oral History Reader* (London: Routledge, 2003), p. 89.
3 GM, 2015.
4 *Ibid.*
5 *Ibid.*
6 *Ibid.*
7 *Ibid.*
8 Bryson, 'Whatever You Say, Say Nothing'.
9 GM, 2015.
10 *Ibid.*
11 Gareth Mulvenna, *Tartan Gangs and Paramilitaries: The Loyalist Backlash* (Liverpool: Liverpool University Press, 2016).

12　Bell, *Acts of Union*, p. 109.
13　*Ibid.*
14　In the period Graeme is talking about rugby was a largely middle-class and Protestant sport; football was popular with both working-class Protestants and working-class Catholics.
15　*Ibid.*
16　Richard Hoggart, *The Uses of Literacy* (London: Penguin, 2009 [1957]), p. 243. For an overview of this literature see D. L. LeMahieu, '"Scholarship Boys" in Twilight: The Memoirs of Six Humanists in Post-Industrial Britain', *Journal of British Studies* 53:4 (2014), pp. 1011–31; for a Northern Irish example of the genre see John Boyd, *Out of My Class* (Belfast: Blackstaff Press, 1985).
17　GM, 2015.
18　Passerini, *Fascism in Popular Memory*, p. 25.
19　*Ibid.*, p. 26.
20　GM, 2015.
21　*Ibid.*
22　*Ibid.*
23　Dick Hebdige, *Subculture: The Meaning of Style* (London: Penguin, 1979).
24　GM, 2015.
25　Paul Willis, *Learning to Labour: How Working-Class Kids get Working-Class Jobs* (Farnham: Ashgate, 2000).
26　GM, 2015.
27　*Ibid.*
28　*Ibid.* See O'Neill and Trelford, *It Makes You Want to Spit.*
29　GM, 2015.
30　*Ibid.*
31　*Ibid.*
32　*Ibid.*
33　*Ibid.*
34　*Ibid.*
35　*Ibid.*
36　*Ibid.*
37　Email correspondence with the author, 2020.
38　Alessandro Portelli, *The Death of Luigi Trastulli and Other Stories: Form and Meaning in Oral History* (New York: State University of New York Press, 1992), p. 14.
39　*Ibid.*, p. 20.
40　See the Introduction and Chapter 2 for parts of my interview with Brian Young, Rudi's lead singer.
41　GM, 2015.
42　*Ibid.*

43 Samuel, *Theatres of Memory*, p. 114.
44 GM, 2015.
45 *Ibid.*
46 *Ibid.*
47 *Ibid.*
48 Henry Glassie, *Passing The Time in Ballymenone: Life and Art in a Northern Irish Community* (Bloomington, IN: Indiana University Press, 1998).
49 *Ibid.*, p. 48.
50 *Ibid.*, p. 109.
51 Charles Tilly, *Stories, Identity, and Political Change* (Oxford: Rowman and Littlefield, 2002, p. 10).
52 See for instance Graeme Mullan, 'Never Mind the Politics, Here's an Alternative Ulster', *Louder Than War*, 7 April 2011, online at: https://louderthanwar.com/classic-belfast-punk-top-ten/ (accessed 17 December 2021).
53 Glassie, *Passing the Time*, pp. 200–10.
54 GM, 2015.
55 Glassie, *Passing the Time*, p. 305.
56 McKittrick and McVea, *Making Sense of the Troubles*, p. 87.
57 Nash, 'Local Histories', p. 54.
58 See the first chapter for a more extended engagement with these various sources.
59 Doreen Massey, *Space, Place and Gender* (Minneapolis, MN: University of Minnesota Press, 1994), especially pp. 146–56.
60 Nash, 'Local Histories', p. 58.
61 Mullan, 'Never Mind The Politics'.
62 GM, 2015.
63 Walter Benjamin, *Illuminations* (London: Pimlico, 1999), p. 60.
64 Naomi Schor, '*Cartes Postales*: Representing Paris 1900', *Critical Inquiry* 18:2 (1992), p. 237.
65 *Ibid.*
66 Kuhn, *Family Secrets*.
67 Annette Kuhn, 'Photography and Cultural Memory: A Methodological Exploration', *Visual Studies* 22:3 (2007), p. 290.
68 GM, 2015.
69 *Ibid.*
70 *Ibid.*

Conclusion

I grew up in dour, post-industrial Ballymena in the 1990s, part-aware of the optimism occasioned by the Belfast/Good Friday Agreement in 1998, and part-aware of the difficult and intractable past that optimism was referring to and hoping to quarantine or exorcise. Before I started going to pubs and clubs in my late teens, I visited Belfast very rarely – my sense of Belfast was always a sense of startling and appealing cosmopolitanism and danger, a site of possibility and of possible anxiety or fear. I remember on one of our occasional trips to the city as a child, with my parents, walking past City Hall, an imposing neoclassical building which sits uncomfortably in the heavily redeveloped centre of town. Then and still now, the pompous solemnity of the architecture is usually offset by the people who hang out in the grassy area in front of the building, enjoying one of the few bits of public space that exist in the centre of town. In the 1990s, on the visit I remember, most of the people hanging out there were punks, and I am told by friends who grew up in Belfast that City Hall was indeed one of the places where young 'alternative' people met – not just punks but goths, skaters and so on. I remember being with my parents in my unexciting, parentally mandated jeans and T-shirt and watching, shyly, an inexplicable confusion of colour and style: piercings, leather, incredible spiked haircuts. The punks I was amazed by then were listening to Green Day, The Breeders and Hüsker Dü rather than or as well as The Clash and Rudi, and I would not say this vivid memory was the impetus for the book, exactly. As my parents have pointed out, I was also very excited to see the automatic escalator in Great Victoria Street shopping centre and I haven't written a book about that, yet. But I hope the book I have written has gone some way to capturing the pleasure, excitement and sociality I perceived in those gatherings outside City Hall, and the shared structure of feeling that my interviewees expressed.

In focusing on what I have called, via Raymond Williams, a structure of feeling, I have aimed to show something of the complicated dynamics and relations that constituted the punk scene in Belfast, and of the nuanced and affective ways in which my interviewees evoked the past in the present. Sectarianism and the sectarian structuring of the state was one of the contexts that shaped their experiences and memories, but not the only one. While I do not disagree with the consensus in the small historical literature on Northern Irish punk that it was 'non-sectarian' in the sense of generating friendly relationships between young Protestants and Catholics, I have tried throughout the book to think about the scene from a slightly different angle.[1] Focusing on the everyday lives of participants suggests both the impossibility of transcending the structures of sectarianism, and the relevance of other factors such as class and gender in the construction of the scene. It also suggests the complicated ways their memories are composed, within the cultural memory of the scene as well as wider discourses about the past in Northern Ireland and the Troubles. Ambivalence, avoidance, uncertainty and anxiety are all present in their memories, as well as happiness, hope and solidarity.

This slight shift in approach might seem banal or irrelevant – an expression of the revisionist tendency to the narcissism of small differences or of the historian's tendency for minor, punctilious disagreement. Some of that might be going on, but to conclude here I want to emphasise the importance of thinking seriously about sectarianism and about alternatives to it. The post-Belfast/Good Friday Agreement state that I grew up in is built on a political model which takes sectarian animosity as a given and which organises its politics around the reification and management of this sectarian identity. This model (called 'consociationalism' in the political science literature) is intended to prevent the domination of the state by one 'ethnic' or 'sectarian' group, such as was apparent in the fifty-year Unionist hegemony over post-partition Northern Ireland, and within those bounds it can be said to have succeeded despite a few recent wobbles. But various political crises over the last five years (the

Conclusion 169

Renewable Heat Incentive or 'cash for ash' scandal, the deadlock over the proposed Irish Language Act, the ongoing attempts of the DUP to prevent the effective legalisation of abortion in the North) and the increasing likelihood of a poll on the reunification of the island of Ireland have highlighted the failure of the post-Agreement state to function properly, even within its own narrowly liberal-democratic remit. These crises are themselves only manifestations of a deeper problem in Northern Irish (and British) capitalism, where some 110,000 children are living in poverty and nearly 80,000 food parcels were delivered by food banks across the region in 2020 and 2021, and where suicide rates in impoverished areas are more than twice the Northern Irish average.[2] The politics of consociationalism have proven to be wholly inadequate to addressing this reality. Chris Gilligan puts it neatly: 'All the parties are attempting to respond to the austerity agenda, but at present they are doing so within the given multicultural or consociational framework. No party has yet attempted to cross ethnic lines in the name of uniting to challenge austerity.'[3]

One of the stories that makes this ongoing violence possible is the story that sectarianism, rather than being a historically determined structure that emerged from colonialism and the discriminatory post-partition state, is a skein of interpersonal relations with atavistic or primitive roots, maintained by small but loud and dangerous groups of aberrant 'sectarians', who require correction or reorientation, and who stand in need of the guidance of the paternalistic state or of 'democratic' British norms. This story is effective in depoliticising events such as the April 2021 riots in working-class Protestant communities, by framing them as part of a long and confusing 'sectarian' history rather than within the deprivation of working-class communities across the city; it is also effective in setting Northern Ireland outside of the history of British imperialism and racial capitalism rather than inside of it. In thinking of the punk scene as uncomplicatedly non-sectarian, there is a danger of reproducing some elements of that story in a way that smooths off the trickier or more complicated dynamics expressed by all of my interviewees.

Segregated schools, segregated residential communities, unemployment patterns and experiences of state violence were the material preconditions for sectarianism as it was embodied and expressed at the level of youth culture. In this sense, to call the punk scene non-sectarian is to give it both too much and too little credit. On the one hand, it is to think of its participants as having primarily engaged in a liberal politics of recognition and contact, as a subcommittee to what Desmond Bell calls 'the caring agencies and committed professionals of the British welfare state', and to undersell its desire for the creation of different rhythms and different relations.[4] On the other hand, it is to think of it as capable of somehow transcending or existing outside of the formidable structures of spatialised segregation and institutionalised disadvantage that constituted and reproduced sectarianism within the Northern Irish state. What I have tried to suggest throughout my analysis of the interviews is that the interviewees themselves present a more complicated image of how sectarianism functioned in their lives and in the punk scene, and that reducing these images to the bloodless rhetoric of 'good relations' between the two communities does their depth and texture a disservice.

In her beautiful work on photography, history and blackness, the feminist theorist and historian Tina Campt reads (or 'listens to', in her formulation) a series of passport photographs stored in the Ernest Dyche Collection at Birmingham City Archives. The Dyches, she says 'were the photographers of choice for many members of the city's largely working-class Afro-Caribbean community (as well as many in the South Asian and Irish migrant communities that also settled in Birmingham)', and took thousands of pictures of members of these communities over their time as a working studio.[5] While passport photos might seem like an unpromising avenue for the traces of memory, sociality and community Campt is looking for, she finds a mode of listening that tunes into their frequencies, suggesting that 'they are archetypically quiet photos, yet they are photos that ruminate loudly on practices of diasporic refusal, fugitivity, and futurity'.[6] What she finds in this encounter is 'a quotidian practice of refusing to stay put or to stay in their designated place, and a refusal to accept the rejection of and limitations on black futurity many ultimately confronted in the United Kingdom'.[7]

I do not evoke Campt's work here to draw any direct or spurious parallel between racism as it worked against the British Afro-Carribbean communities she is writing about here and sectarianism as it functioned in Northern Ireland in the 1970s and 1980s. But I think her concept of refusal is a helpful one. Refusal, Campt says, refers to those 'nimble and strategic practices that undermine the categories of the dominant' – to not acquiescing to being called one thing or another, to not letting whatever the state sees you as determine anything about what really matters in your life and in your sense of self, to not allowing the real and material existence of structural violence to be the only thing that is legible about your history or your memory. Something of this sense of refusal and possibility seems to me to be part of the structure of feeling referred to across all of the interviews analysed here. The interviewees' memories of punk as a structure of feeling point, with their stress on the affordances, excitements and pleasures of punk, to a sociality shared between people that is perhaps inchoate but nonetheless present within their narratives. This shared sense of possibility cannot be reduced to the etiolated language of 'good relations' between Protestants and Catholics that characterises much public discourse on sectarianism in Northern Ireland now, and it is that possibility which animates their narratives and my analysis.

Notes

1 Martin McLoone, 'Punk Music in Northern Ireland'; Francis Stewart, '"Alternative Ulster": Punk Rock as a Means of Overcoming the Religious Divide in Northern Ireland', in John Wolffe (ed.), *Irish Religious Conflict in Comparative Perspective: Catholics, Protestants and Muslims* (London: Palgrave Macmillan, 2014), pp. 76–90; Timothy Heron, 'Alternative Ulster: Punk and the Construction of Everyday Life in 1970s Northern Ireland', *Popular Culture Today: Imaginaries* 19 (2015), pp. 1–17; Stuart Bailie, *Trouble Songs: Music and Conflict in Northern Ireland* (Belfast: Stuart Bailie, 2018); Timothy Heron, '"Alternative Ulster": le punk en Irlande de Nord (1976–1983)' (unpublished PhD thesis, Ecole doctorale Sciences de l'homme et de la société, 2017).
2 For the first figure see the Joseph Rowntree Foundation, *Poverty in Northern Ireland* (York: Joseph Rowntree Foundation, 2018); for the second see The Trussel Trust, online at: www.trusselltrust.org/news-and-blog/latest-stats/end-year-stats/ (accessed 17 December 2021); for the third see *Protect Life 2: A Strategy for Preventing Suicide and Self Harm in Northern Ireland 2019–2024* (Belfast: Department of Health, 2019).

3 Chris Gilligan, 'Austerity and consociational government in Northern Ireland', *Irish Studies Review* 24:1 (2018), pp. 35–48.
4 Bell, *Acts of Union*, p. 47.
5 Tina Campt, *Listening to Images* (Durham, NC: Duke University Press, 2017), p. 24.
6 *Ibid*.
7 *Ibid*., p. 43.

Appendix: Bands

The information here on Northern Irish bands is largely sourced from *It Makes You Want to Spit*, and from Sean O'Neill's unparalleled Spit Records website, which has been an invaluable resource throughout the writing of this book.[1] Any errors are my own.

The Animals – English rock band formed in Newcastle in the 1960s. Especially famous for their much-covered single 'House of the Rising Sun'.

Au Pairs – British post-punk band from Birmingham, whose 1981 debut album *Playing with a Different Sex* is notable for its caustic lyrics on sex, gender and (on 'Armagh'), the British government's use of 'interrogation techniques' in Northern Ireland.

Bacteria – The punk band formed by Graeme Mullan and his schoolmates, as discussed in Chapter 6.

The Beatles – Liverpudlian band who became one of the most famous groups in the world in the 1960s. Played at the King's Hall in Belfast in 1964.

Bucks Fizz – An English pop group from the 1980s, best-known for winning the Eurovision Song Contest in 1981 with 'Making Your Mind Up'.

The Clash – English punk band, founded in London in 1976 and, along with the Sex Pistols, probably the best-known exemplars of this wave of punk. Occasioned the 'riot of Bedford Street' in Belfast in 1977 after a planned gig at the Ulster Hall was cancelled.

Conflict – From south London, an anarcho-punk band closely associated with Crass and with Ian Bone's British anarchist network Class War.

Crass – An English anarcho-punk band and art collective formed in 1977, widely considered the apotheosis of the DIY tendency in punk. Known for their engagement in a range of political issues, including the role of the British state in Northern Ireland, they played at the A Centre in 1982 in what was a formative gig for my interviewee Petesy Burns.

The Damned – One of the earliest English bands associated with the punk scene after the release of their single, 'New Rose', in 1976. Played in Belfast in the 1970s.

Echo & the Bunnymen – The central band in Alison Farrell's account, as discussed in Chapter 3, Echo & the Bunnymen were formed in Liverpool in 1978. Known for their charismatic frontman, Ian McCulloch.

The Idiots – Formed in 1977, The Idiots featured Barry Young, Dee Wilson and Gordy Owen. Dee Wilson is working on a history of the punk scene and as part of the Alternative Ulster Historical Society recently placed a plaque on the original site of the Trident bar in Bangor, where many of the early Northern Irish punk bands played.

Killing Joke – Formed in London in 1978, their eponymous debut album was released in 1980. Part of the post-punk scene at the time, they later became an important influence within industrial music.

The Miami Showband – One of the most successful of the Irish showband groups, cabaret bands who played pop and country songs and were a major live attraction in Ireland in the 1960s and 1970s. Band members Fran O'Toole, Tony Geraghty and Brian McCoy were killed by the Ulster Volunteer Force in 1975, in an attack alleged to be planned with the collusion of the Royal Ulster Constabulary. See *The Miami Showband Massacre: A Survivor's Search* *for the Truth* for an account of former member Stephen Travers' attempts to relate the killing to British state collusion.

The Outcasts – Formed in January 1977, they picked their name after getting turned away from five nightclubs in two weeks. Their debut album, *Self-Conscious Over You*, was released on Good Vibrations in 1979. They went on to record several more albums and retain a cult following in France.

Patti Smith – American writer and singer who first came to prominence in the New York punk scene of the early to mid-1970s. Released her first album, *Horses*, with the Patti Smith Group in 1975.

Poison Girls – An anarcho-punk band from Brighton fronted by Vi Subversa and known for their feminist, anarchist politics. They played in Belfast several times.

Protex – Formed in 1978, recorded on Good Vibrations, and later moved to London to work with Polydor Records. They were recorded playing in New York in an unreleased short film by John T. Davis, *Sham Rock*.

Pulp – From Sheffield, Pulp were formed in 1978 but rose to prominence in the 1990s as slightly atypical members of the Britpop scene. See Owen Hatherley's wonderful book *Uncommon* for a consideration of their career that relates it to the post-industrial heritage of Sheffield and to working-class politics more generally.

Ramones – American punk band known for their short, catchy songs and simple lyrics. Very influential on the Northern Irish punk scene and played several gigs in the Ulster Hall in the 1970s.

Rudi – Probably the first punk band in Belfast, Rudi – formed in 1975 by Brian Young, Ronnie Matthews, Graham 'Grimmy' Marshall, Leigh Carson and Drew Brown – were influenced by glam rock and old rock 'n' roll as much as by the nascent punk scene. Their 1978 single 'Big Time' was the first and the best record released by Good Vibrations.

Ruefrex – Ruefrex, from the Shankill and the Ardoyne in north Belfast, were, along with Stiff Little Fingers, one of the few bands from the first wave of Northern Irish punk to address politics directly in their songs. Influenced by The Clash, their first album was released in 1985. The band played a benefit gig for Lagan College, Northern Ireland's first integrated school, in the mid-1980s.

The Sabrejets – Former Rudi singer Brian Young's current band, influenced by rockabilly, rock 'n' roll and the New York Dolls.

The Saints – From Brisbane in Australia, The Saints were formed in 1973 and were arguably one of the first punk bands in the world. They also played at the Punk and New Wave Festival in 1980.

Sex Pistols – Very famous, swore on television, managed by Malcolm McLaren. Only released one studio album and four singles. Formed in 1975 and split up in January 1978.

Siouxsie and the Banshees – A post-punk and goth band from London, known for their experimental instrumentation. They played in Belfast several times.

The Slits – All-woman punk band formed in England in 1977, featuring Ari Up, Palmolive, Viv Albertine and Tessa Pollit. Their first album, *Cut*, was released in 1979. Viv Albertine has played an important role in historicising the punk scene via her memoir, *Clothes, Clothes, Clothes, Music, Music, Music, Boys, Boys, Boys*.

Spider – Belfast band, signed to Good Vibrations and released a single on the 1978 Battle of the Bands EP.

Stage B – A Northern Irish punk band who made their first appearance at the Harp Bar in 1979. They were booked to support Siouxsie and the Banshees in 1979, but the gig didn't happen because the Banshees' equipment was left in England; this is the gig that Graeme attended and left, later being chased down the Lisburn Road, as discussed in Chapter 6.

Stalag 17 – Featuring Petesy Burns on bass, Stalag 17 were the mainstays of the Northern Irish anarcho-punk scene alongside

Newtownards band Toxic Waste. Formed in 1979, they were central in the formation of the Warzone Collective, bringing bands from across Europe to play in Belfast.

Stiff Little Fingers – The Stiffs are best-remembered for their debut album *Inflammable Material*, co-written with the English journalist Gordon Ogilvie. Their career is covered exhaustively in Roland Link's 2009 book, *Kicking up a Racket: The Story of Stiff Little Fingers, 1977–1983*.

The Stimulators – A punk band from New York who played at the Punk and New Wave Festival in the Ulster Hall in 1980.

The Stranglers – Emerged from the pub-rock scene of the mid-1970s to become a fixture of the punk scene and beyond, changing their style and sound several times. An important band for Graeme Mullan, interviewed in Chapter 6.

The Sweet – British glam rock band, formed in London in 1968 and best-known for their 1973 single 'The Ballroom Blitz'. Described as a precursor to punk by Graeme in Chapter 6.

Terri Hooley – Better known for his record shop and record label, Terri also recorded a single in 1979, 'Laugh at Me' – a cover of the 1966 Sonny & Cher song – on Fresh Records.

Toxic Waste – Formed in 1983, and from Ards, Toxic Waste became the fulcrum of the Northern Ireland anarcho-punk scene along with Stalag 17. Founding member Roy Wallace is now a filmmaker and historian who has made documentaries on the punk scene (*The Day the Country Died*) and on the Rathcoole Self-Help Group (*Goodbye Ballyhightown*).

Toyah – Toyah were a punk and new wave band formed by Toyah Wilcox in 1977. Their first album, *Sheep Farming in Barnet*, was released in 1979. Alison expresses her identification with Toyah in Chapter 3.

The Undertones – The Derry band are the most recognisable sound of Northern Irish punk, along with Stiff Little Fingers, and released a string of excellent singles – most notably 'Teenage Kicks', Radio 1 DJ John Peel's favourite song.

Victim – Formed in mid-1977 and gigging by 1978, Victim moved to Manchester in 1979 and became something of a feature of the punk scene in the north of England, playing at the Haçienda and rehearsing in the same space as Magazine, Joy Division and the Buzzcocks. Mike Joyce, later of the Smiths, was briefly their drummer.

Xdreamysts – Signed to Good Vibrations, Xdreamysts – from the north coast of Ireland – were more of a rock than a punk band, and went on to support, among others, Thin Lizzy.

Notes

1 O'Neill and Trelford, *It Makes You Want to Spit*; *Spit Records*, www.spitrecords.co.uk (accessed 30 September 2020).

Select bibliography

Abrams, Lynn, 'Liberating the Female Self: Epiphanies, Conflict and Coherence in the Life Stories of Post-War British Women', *Social History* 39:1 (2014), pp. 14–35.

Abrams, Lynn, *Oral History Theory* (London: Routledge, 2010).

Ahmed, Sara, 'Collective Feelings: Or, the Impressions Left by Others', *Theory, Culture & Society* 21:2 (2004), pp. 25–42.

Alfaro, Garikoitz Gómez, and Fearghus Roulston, 'Nostalgia for "HMP Divis" and "HMP Rossville": Memories of the Everyday in Northern Ireland's High-Rise Flats', *Journal of War & Culture Studies* 14:1 (2021), pp. 25–44.

Anderson, James, and Liam O'Dowd, 'Imperialism and Nationalism: The Home Rule Struggle and Border Creation in Ireland, 1885–1925', *Partition and the Reconfiguration of the Irish Border* 26:8 (2007), pp. 934–50.

Aretxaga, Begoña, *Shattering Silence: Women, Nationalism, and Political Subjectivity in Northern Ireland* (Princeton, NJ: Princeton University Press, 1997).

Ashe, Fidelma, 'Gendering War and Peace: Militarized Masculinities in Northern Ireland', *Men and Masculinities* 15:3 (2012), pp. 230–48.

Bailie, Stuart, *Trouble Songs: Music and Conflict in Northern Ireland* (Belfast: Stuart Bailie, 2018).

Baker, Stephen, 'Tribeca Belfast and the On-Screen Regeneration of Northern Ireland', *International Journal of Media and Cultural Politics* 16:1 (2020), pp. 11–26.

Bardon, Jonathan, *A History of Ulster* (Belfast: Blackstaff Press, 1992).

Bardon, Jonathan, *The Struggle for Shared Schools in Northern Ireland: The History of All Children Together* (Belfast: Ulster Historical Foundation, 2009).

Barros D'Sa, Lisa, and Glen Leyburn, *Good Vibrations* (London: Universal Pictures UK, 2012).

Bell, Desmond, *Acts of Union: Youth Culture and Sectarianism in Northern Ireland* (London: Macmillan Education, 1990).

Bell, John, *For God, Ulster, or Ireland?: Religion, Identity and Security in Northern Ireland* (Belfast: Institute for Conflict Research, 2013).

Bender, Barbara (ed.), *Landscape: Politics and Perspectives* (Oxford: Berg, 1993).

Benjamin, Walter, *Illuminations* (London: Pimlico, 1999).

Berlant, Lauren, 'Thinking about Feeling Historical', *Emotion, Space and Society* 1:1 (2008), pp. 4–9.

Bottomley, Andrew J., 'Play It Again: Rock Music Reissues and the Production of the Past for the Present', *Popular Music and Society* 39:2 (2016), pp. 151–74.

Bourke, Richard, *Peace in Ireland: The War of Ideas* (London: Pimlico, 2012).

Boyd, John, *Out of My Class* (Belfast: Blackstaff Press, 1985).

Boym, Svetlana, *Common Places: Mythologies of Everyday Life in Russia* (Cambridge, MA: Harvard University Press, 1994).

Brady, Sean, '"Save Ulster from Sodomy!" Homosexuality in Northern Ireland after 1967', *Cultural and Social History*, forthcoming.

Brewer, John, and Gareth I. Higgins, *Anti-Catholicism in Northern Ireland, 1600–1988: The Mote and the Beam* (London: Macmillan, 1998).

Brewer, John D., and Gareth I. Higgins, 'Understanding Anti-Catholicism in Northern Ireland', *Sociology* 33:2 (1999), pp. 235–55.

Bruce, Steve, *Paisley: Religion and Politics in Northern Ireland* (Oxford: Oxford University Press, 2017).

Bryson, Anna, '"Whatever You Say, Say Nothing": Researching Memory and Identity in Mid-Ulster, 1945–1969', *Oral History* 35:2 (2007), pp. 45–56.

Burke, Andrew, 'Music, Memory and Modern Life: Saint Etienne's London', *Screen* 51:2 (2010), pp. 103–17.

Burton, Frank, *The Politics of Legitimacy: Struggles in a Belfast Community* (London: Routledge & Kegan Paul, 1978).

Cabut, Richard, and Andrew Gallix (eds), *Punk is Dead: Modernity Killed Every Night* (London: Zero Books, 2017).

Cadwallader, Anne, *Lethal Allies: British Collusion in Ireland* (Cork: Mercier Press, 2013).

Cairns, David, 'The Object of Sectarianism: The Material Reality of Sectarianism in Ulster Loyalism', *Journal of the Royal Anthropological Institute* 6:3 (2000), pp. 437–52.

Cairns, Ed, *Caught in the Crossfire: Children in the Northern Ireland Conflict* (Belfast: Appletree Press, 1987).

Campt, Tina, *Listening to Images* (Durham, NC: Duke University Press, 2017).

Castro, Ingrid, and Jessica Clark (eds), *Representing Agency in Popular Culture: Children and Youth on Page, Screen and In Between* (London: Lexington Books, 2018).

Cavanaugh, Kathleen A., 'Interpretations of Political Violence in Ethnically Divided Societies', *Terrorism and Political Violence* 9:3 (1997), pp. 33–54.

Charlesworth, Lee, *A Phenomenology of Working Class Experience* (Cambridge: Cambridge University Press, 1999).

Chidgey, Red, 'Reassess Your Weapons: The Making of Feminist Memory in Young Women's Zines', *Women's History Review* 22:4 (2013), pp. 658–72.

Cleary, Joe, *Literature, Partition and the Nation-State: Culture and Conflict in Ireland, Israel and Palestine* (Cambridge: Cambridge University Press: 2004).

Coaffee, Jon, *Terrorism, Risk and the Global City: Towards Urban Resilience* (London: Routledge, 2006).

Cobain, Ian, *Anatomy of a Killing: Life and Death on a Divided Island* (London: Granta, 2020).

Cook, Matt, '"Archives of Feeling": The AIDS Crisis in Britain 1987', *History Workshop Journal* 83:1 (2017), pp. 51–78.

Cormack, R. J. (ed.), *Religion, Education and Employment* (Belfast: Appletree Press, 1983).

Corporaal, Marguérite, Christopher Cusack and Ruud van den Beuken (eds), *Irish Studies and the Dynamics of Memory: Transitions and Transformations* (Oxford: Peter Lang, 2017).

Corthorn, Paul, 'Enoch Powell, Ulster Unionism, and the British Nation', *Journal of British Studies* 51:4 (2012), pp. 967–97.

Coulter, Colin, 'Under Which Constitutional Arrangement Would You Still Prefer to Be Unemployed? Neoliberalism, the Peace Process, and the Politics of Class in Northern Ireland', *Studies in Conflict & Terrorism* 37:9 (2014), pp. 763–76.

Coulter, Colin, and Michael Murray (eds), *Northern Ireland After the Troubles: A Society in Transition* (Oxford: Oxford University Press, 2008).

Cox, Alex, *Sid and Nancy* (London: Palace Pictures, 1986).

Crenshaw, Kimberlé, 'Mapping the Margins: Intersectionality, Identity Politics, and Violence against Women of Color', *Stanford Law Review* 43:6 (1991), pp. 1241–99.

Cresswell, Tim, *In Place/Out of Place: Geography, Ideology and Transgression* (Minnesota: University of Minnesota Press, 1996).

Cresswell, Tim, *On the Move: Mobility in the Modern Western World* (London: Routledge, 2006).

Cunningham, Niall, '"The Doctrine of Vicarious Punishment": Space, Religion and the Belfast Troubles of 1920–22', *Journal of Historical Geography* 40:1 (2013), pp. 52–66.

Cunningham, Tim, 'Changing Direction: Defensive Planning in a Post-Conflict City', *City* 18:4–5 (2014), pp. 455–62.

Curtis, Jennifer, '"Profoundly Ungrateful": The Paradoxes of Thatcherism in Northern Ireland', *PoLAR: Political and Legal Anthropology Review* 33:2 (2010), pp. 201–24.

Dawson, Graham, *Making Peace with the Past? Memory, Trauma and the Irish Troubles* (Manchester: Manchester University Press, 2007).

Dawson, Graham, *Soldier Heroes: British Adventure, Empire and the Imagining of Masculinities* (London: Routledge, 1994).

Dawson, Graham, 'Trauma, Place and the Politics of Memory: Bloody Sunday, Derry, 1972–2004', *History Workshop Journal* 59:1 (2005), pp. 221–50.

Devlin, Bernadette, *The Price of My Soul* (London: Pan Books, 1969).

Donohue, Laura K., *Counter-Terrorist Law and Emergency Powers in the UK, 1922–2000* (Dublin: Irish Academic Press, 2001).

Dooley, Brian, *Black and Green: The Fight for Civil Rights in Northern Ireland and Black America* (London: Pluto Press, 1998).

Downes, Gerry (ed.), *Brits, Balconies and Bin-Lids: Residents Remember Life in Divis Flats* (Belfast: Divis Study Group, 1998).

Downes, Julia, 'The Expansion of Punk Rock: Riot Grrrl Challenges to Gender Power Relations in British Indie Music Subcultures', *Women's Studies* 41:2 (2012), pp. 204–37.

Doyle, Mark, 'The Sepoys of the Pound and Sandy Row: Empire and Identity in Mid-Victorian Belfast', *Journal of Urban History* 36:6 (2010), pp. 849–67.

Duggan, Marian, *Queering Conflict: Examining Lesbian and Gay Experiences of Homophobia in Northern Ireland* (London: Routledge, 2016).

Edensor, Tim, 'Mundane Hauntings: Commuting through the Phantasmagoric Working-Class Spaces of Manchester, England', *Cultural Geographies* 15:3 (2008), pp. 313–33.

Elliott, Marianne, *The Catholics of Ulster: A History* (London: Penguin, 2001).

Farren, Sean, 'A Lost Opportunity: Education and Community in Northern Ireland 1947–1960', *History of Education* 21:1 (1992), pp. 71–82.

Feldman, Allen, *Formations of Violence: The Narrative of the Body and Political Terror in Northern Ireland* (Chicago, IL: University of Chicago Press, 1991).

Feldman, Allen, 'Violence and Vision: The Prosthetics and Aesthetics of Terror', *Public Culture* 10:1 (1997), pp. 24–60.

Ferriter, Diarmaid, *Occasions of Sin: Sex and Society in Modern Ireland* (London: Profile Books, 2009).

Field, Sean, *Oral History, Community and Displacement: Imagining Memories in Post-Apartheid South Africa* (London: Palgrave Macmillan, 2012).

Fields, Rona, *Northern Ireland: Society Under Siege* (London: Routledge, 1980).
Finn, Daniel, *One Man's Terrorist: A Political History of the IRA* (London: Verso, 2019).
Fisher, Mark, *Capitalist Realism: Is There No Alternative?* (London: Zero Books, 2009).
Fisher, Mark, *Ghosts of My Life: Writings on Depression, Hauntology and Lost Futures* (London: Zero Books, 2014).
Fitzpatrick, Richard, 'Catholic Inheritance under the Penal Laws in Ireland', *Irish Historical Studies* 44:166 (2020), pp. 224–47.
Ford, Alan, and John McCafferty (eds), *The Origins of Sectarianism in Early Modern Ireland* (Cambridge: Cambridge University Press, 2005).
Ford, Laura Oldfield, *Savage Messiah* (London: Verso Books, 2011).
Gaffikin, Frank, Chris Karelse, Mike Morrissey, Clare Mulholland and Ken Sterret, *Making Space for Each Other: Civic Place-Making in a Divided Society* (Belfast: Queen's University Belfast, 2016).
Gaffikin, Frank, and Michael Morrissey, *Northern Ireland: The Thatcher Years* (London: Zed Books, 1990).
Gallagher, Tom, and James O'Connell (eds), *Contemporary Irish Studies* (Manchester: Manchester University Press, 1983).
Gilligan, Chris, 'Austerity and Consociational Government in Northern Ireland', *Irish Studies Review* 24:1 (2018), pp. 35–48.
Gilligan, Chris, *Northern Ireland and the Crisis of Anti-Racism: Rethinking Racism and Sectarianism* (Manchester: Manchester University Press, 2017).
Glassie, Henry, *Passing The Time in Ballymenone: Life and Art in a Northern Irish Community* (Bloomington, IN: Indiana University Press, 1998).
Graham, Brian, and Yvonne Whelan, 'The Legacies of the Dead: Commemorating the Troubles in Northern Ireland', *Environment and Planning D: Society and Space* 25:3 (2007), pp. 476–95.
Grossman, Lionel, 'Anecdote And History', *History and Theory* 42:2 (2003), pp. 143–68.
Haddad, Fanar, *Understanding 'Sectarianism': Sunni–Shi'a Relations in the Modern Arab World* (Oxford: Oxford University Press, 2020).
Hamill, Heather, *The Hoods: Crime and Punishment in Belfast* (Oxford: Princeton University Press, 2011).
Harney, Stefano, and Fred Moten, *The Undercommons: Fugitive Planning and Black Study* (Wivenhoe: Minor Compositions, 2013).
Hatherley, Owen, *Uncommon* (London: Zero Books, 2011).
Hebdige, Dick, *Subculture: The Meaning of Style* (London: Penguin, 1979).
Hennessey, Thomas, *Northern Ireland: The Origins of the Troubles* (London: Gill & Macmillan, 2005).

Heron, Timothy, '"Alternative Ulster": le punk en Irlande de Nord (1976–1983)' (unpublished PhD thesis, Ecole doctorale Sciences de l'homme et de la société, 2017).

Heron, Timothy, 'Alternative Ulster: Punk and the Construction of Everyday Life in 1970s Northern Ireland', *Popular Culture Today: Imaginaries* 19 (2015), pp. 1–17.

Heron, Timothy, '"We're Only Monsters": Punk Bodies and the Grotesque in 1970s Northern Ireland', *Etudes irlandaises* 42:1 (2017), pp. 139–54.

Hill, Christopher R., 'Nations of Peace: Nuclear Disarmament and the Making of National Identity in Scotland and Wales', *Twentieth Century British History* 27:1 (2016), pp. 26–50.

Hirsch, Shirin, *In the Shadow of Enoch Powell: Race, Locality and Resistance* (Manchester: Manchester University Press, 2018).

Hodson, Pete, 'Titanic Struggle: Memory, Heritage and Shipyard Deindustrialization in Belfast', *History Workshop Journal* 87 (2019), pp. 224–49.

Hoggart, Richard, *The Uses of Literacy* (London: Penguin, 2009 [1957]).

Hooley, Terri, and Richard Sullivan, *Hooleygan: Music, Mayhem, Good Vibrations* (Belfast: Blackstaff Press, 2010).

Hyndman, Dave, *The A Centre or The Lost Tribe of Long Lane* (Belfast: Northern Visions TV, 1981).

Jackson, Alvin, *Home Rule: An Irish History, 1800–2000* (Oxford: Oxford University Press, 2003).

James, Daniel, *Doña María's Story: Life History, Memory and Political Identity* (Durham, NC: Duke University Press, 2001).

Jiminez, Luis, and Valerie Walkerdine, '"Shameful Work": A Psychosocial Approach to Father–Son Relations, Young Male Unemployment and Femininity in an Ex-Steel Community', *Psychoanalysis, Culture & Society* 17:3 (2012), pp. 278–95.

Jolly, Margaretta, *Sisterhood and After: An Oral History of the UK Women's Liberation Movement, 1968–present* (Oxford: Oxford University Press, 2019).

Keenan-Thomson, Tara, 'From Co-op to Co-opt: Gender and Class in the Early Civil Rights Movement', *The Sixties* 2:2 (2009), pp. 207–25.

Kelleher, William, *The Troubles in Ballybogoin: Memory and Identity in Northern Ireland* (Ann Arbour, MI: University of Michigan Press, 2003).

Kelly, Aaron, 'Geopolitical Eclipse', *Third Text* 19:5 (2005), pp. 545–53.

Kirkland, Richard, 'Visualising Peace: Northern Irish Post-Conflict Cinema and the Politics of Reconciliation', *Review of Irish Studies in Europe* 1:2 (2017), pp. 12–25.

Kitchin, Rob, and Karen Lysaght, 'Sexual Citizenship in Belfast, Northern Ireland', *Gender, Place & Culture* 11:1 (2004), pp. 83–103.

Kuhn, Annette, *Family Secrets: Acts of Memory and Imagination* (London: Verso, 2002).
Kuhn, Annette, 'Memory Texts and Memory Work: Performances of Memory in and with Visual Media', *Memory Studies* 3:4 (2010), pp. 298–313.
Kuhn, Annette, 'Photography and Cultural Memory: A Methodological Exploration', *Visual Studies* 22:3 (2007), pp. 283–92.
Lane, Karen, '"Not-The-Troubles": An Anthropological Analysis of Stories of Quotidian Life in Belfast' (unpublished PhD thesis, University of St Andrews, April 2017).
Laucht, Christoph, and Martin Johnes, 'Resist and Survive: Welsh Protests and the British Nuclear State in the 1980s', *Contemporary British History* 33:2 (2019), pp. 226–45.
Leary, Peter, *Unapproved Routes: Histories of the Irish Border, 1922–1972* (Oxford: Oxford University Press, 2016).
Legg, George, *Northern Ireland and the Politics of Boredom: Conflict, Capital and Culture* (Manchester: Manchester University Press, 2018).
LeMahieu, D. L., '"Scholarship Boys" in Twilight: The Memoirs of Six Humanists in Post-Industrial Britain', *Journal of British Studies* 53:4 (2014), pp. 1011–31.
Magennis, Caroline, '"Bubbles of Joy": Moments of Pleasure in Recent Northern Irish Culture', *Etudes irlandaises* 42:1 (2017), pp. 155–68.
Maillot, Agnès, 'Punk on Celluloid: John Davis' Shellshock Rock (1979)', *Historical Journal of Film, Radio and Television* 20:3 (2000), pp. 375–83.
Massey, Doreen, *Space, Place and Gender* (Minneapolis, MN: University of Minnesota Press, 1994).
McAtackney, Laura, 'Peace Maintenance and Political Messages: The Significance of Walls During and After the Northern Irish "Troubles"', *Journal of Social Archaeology* 11:1 (2011), pp. 77–98.
McAuley, James W., and Jonathan Tonge, '"For God and for the Crown": Contemporary Political and Social Attitudes among Orange Order Members in Northern Ireland', *Political Psychology* 28:1 (2007), pp. 33–52.
McCleery, Martin Joseph, 'The Creation of the "New City" of Craigavon: A Case Study of Politics, Planning and Modernisation in Northern Ireland in the Early 1960s', *Irish Political Studies* 27:1 (2012), pp. 89–109.
McDermott, Jim, *Northern Divisions: The Old IRA and the Belfast Pogroms 1920–22* (Belfast: Beyond the Pale, 2001).
McDonald, Henry, *Colours: Ireland from Bombs to Boom* (Edinburgh: Mainstream Publishing, 2004).
McDonald, Henry, *Two Souls* (Newbridge: Merrion Press, 2019).
McGovern, Mark, *Counterinsurgency and Collusion in Northern Ireland* (London: Pluto Press, 2019).

McGovern, Mark, '"See No Evil": Collusion in Northern Ireland', *Race & Class* 58:3 (2017), pp. 46–63.

McGovern, Mark, '"The 'Craic' Market": Irish Theme Bars and the Commodification of Irishness in Contemporary Britain', *Irish Journal of Sociology* 11:2 (2002), pp. 77–98.

McKay, George, *Senseless Acts of Beauty: Cultures of Resistance Since the Sixties* (London: Verso, 1996).

McKittrick, David, and David McVea, *Making Sense of the Troubles: A History of the Northern Ireland Conflict* (Chicago, IL: New Amsterdam Books, 2002).

McLoone, Martin, 'Punk Music in Northern Ireland: The Political Power of "What Might Have Been"', *Irish Studies Review* 12:1 (2004), pp. 29–38.

McManus, Carla, and Clare Carruthers, 'Cultural Quarters and Urban Regeneration – the Case of Cathedral Quarter Belfast', *International Journal of Cultural Policy* 20:1 (2014), pp. 78–98.

McVeigh, Robbie, *It's Part of Life Here: The Security Forces and Harassment in Northern Ireland* (Belfast: Committee on the Administration of Justice, 1994).

McVeigh, Robbie, *Sectarianism in Northern Ireland: Towards a Definition in Law* (Belfast: Equality Coalition, 2014).

McVeigh, Robbie, 'The Undertheorisation of Sectarianism', *Canadian Journal of Irish Studies* 16:2 (1990), pp. 119–22.

McVeigh, Robbie, and Bill Rolston, 'From Good Friday to Good Relations: Sectarianism, Racism and the Northern Ireland State', *Race & Class* 48:4 (2007), pp. 1–23.

Mieszkowski, Jan, 'Who's Afraid of Anacoluthon?', *MLN* 124:3 (2009), pp 648–65.

Mills, Helena, 'Using the Personal to Critique the Popular: Women's Memories of 1960s Youth', *Contemporary British History* 30:4 (2016), pp. 463–83.

Mitchell, Claire, *Religion, Identity and Politics in Northern Ireland: Boundaries of Belonging and Belief* (London: Routledge, 2017).

Montgomery, Nick, and carla bergman, *Joyful Militancy: Building Thriving Resistance in Toxic Times* (Stirling: AK Press, 2017).

Muldoon, Orla T., 'Children of the Troubles: The Impact of Political Violence in Northern Ireland', *Journal of Social Issues* 60:3 (2004), pp. 453–68.

Mulholland, Marc, *Northern Ireland at the Crossroads: Ulster Unionism in the O'Neill Years, 1960-9* (London: St Martin's Press, 2000).

Mulvenna, Gareth, *Tartan Gangs and Paramilitaries: The Loyalist Backlash* (Liverpool: Liverpool University Press, 2016).

Munck, Ronnie, and Bill Rolston, *Belfast in the Thirties: An Oral History* (Belfast: Blackstaff Press, 1987).

Murphy, Oonagh, and Laura Aguiar, 'When a 1981 Diary Meets Twitter: Reclaiming a Teenage Girl's Ordinary Experience of the Northern

Irish Troubles', *British Journal for Military History* 5:1 (2019), pp. 49–70.

Murtagh, Brendan, *Community and Conflict in Rural Ulster* (Coleraine: University of Ulster, 1999).

Nash, Catherine, 'Local Histories in Northern Ireland', *History Workshop Journal* 60:1 (2005), pp. 45–68.

Nash, Catherine, and Bryonie Reid, 'Border Crossings: New Approaches to the Irish Border', *Irish Studies Review* 18:3 (2010), pp. 265–84.

Newby, Lucy, 'Troubled Generations? An Oral History of Youth Experience of the Conflict in Belfast, 1969–1998' (unpublished PhD thesis, University of Brighton).

Newby, Lucy, 'Troubled Generations? (De)Constructing Narratives of Youth Experience in the Northern Ireland Conflict', *Journal of War & Cultural Studies* 14:1 (2021), pp. 6–24.

Northern Ireland Housing Executive, *More Than Bricks: 40 Years of the Housing Executive* (Belfast: Northern Ireland Housing Executive, 2011).

Ó Faoleán, Gearóid, 'The Ulster Defence Regiment and the Question of Catholic Recruitment, 1970–1972', *Terrorism and Political Violence* 27:5 (2015), pp. 838–56.

O'Brien, Harvey, 'Somewhere to Come Back to: The Filmic Journeys of John T. Davis', *Irish Studies Review* 9:2 (2001), pp. 167–77.

O'Connell, Sean, 'Violence and Social Memory in Twentieth-Century Belfast: Stories of Buck Alec Robinson', *Journal of British Studies* 53:3 (2014), pp. 734–56.

O'Leary, Brendan, *A Treatise on Northern Ireland Volume 2: Control – The Second Protestant Ascendancy and the Irish State* (Oxford: Oxford University Press, 2019).

O'Neill, Sean, and Guy Trelford (eds), *It Makes You Want to Spit: The Definitive Guide to Punk in Northern Ireland* (Dublin: Reekus Music, 2003).

Panichelli-Batalla, Stéphanie, 'Laughter in Oral Histories of Displacement: "One Goes on a Mission to Solve Their Problems"', *Oral History Review* 47:1 (2020), pp. 73–92.

Parkhill, Trevor, 'Emigration & The Great Famine: The Ulster Experience', *Folk Life* 37:1 (1998), pp. 80–91.

Parkinson, Alan, *Belfast's Unholy War: The Troubles of the 1920s* (Dublin: Four Courts Press, 2004).

Parkinson, Alan, *Friends in High Places: Ulster's Resistance to Irish Home Rule, 1912–14* (Belfast: Ulster Historical Foundation, 2012).

Passerini, Luisa, *Fascism in Popular Memory: The Cultural Experience of the Turin Working Class*, trans. Robert Lumley and Jude Bloomfield (Cambridge: Cambridge University Press, 2010 [1984]).

Pelaschiar, Laura, *Writing The North: The Contemporary Novel in Northern Ireland* (Trieste: Edizioni Parnaso, 1998).
Perks, Rob, and Alistair Thomson (eds), *The Oral History Reader* (London: Routledge, 2003).
Portelli, Alessandro, *The Battle of Valle Guilia: Oral History and the Art of Dialogue* (Madison, WI: University of Wisconsin Press, 1997).
Portelli, Alessandro, *The Death of Luigi Trastulli and Other Stories: Form and Meaning in Oral History* (New York: State University of New York Press, 1992).
Portelli, Alessandro, *The Order has Been Carried Out: History, Memory and Meaning of a Nazi Massacre in Rome* (Basingstoke: Palgrave MacMillan, 2003).
Prince, Simon, 'The Global Revolt of 1968 and Northern Ireland', *Historical Journal* 49:3 (2006), pp. 851–75.
Protect Life 2: A Strategy for Preventing Suicide and Self Harm in Northern Ireland 2019–2024 (Belfast: Department of Health, 2019).
Pyzik, Agata, *Poor But Sexy: Culture Clashes in Europe, East and West* (London: Zero Books, 2014).
Quinn, James, *A Life of Thomas Russell, 1767–1803: A Soul on Fire* (Dublin: Irish Academic Press, 2001).
Ramsey, Phil, '"A Pleasingly Blank Canvas": Urban Regeneration in Northern Ireland and the Case of Titanic Quarter', *Space and Polity* 17:2 (2013), pp. 164–79.
Reynolds, Simon, *Rip it Up and Start Again: Post-Punk 1978–1984* (London: Faber & Faber, 2005).
Robinson, Lucy, 'Exhibition Review Punk's 40th Anniversary – An Itchy Sort of Heritage', *Twentieth Century British History* 39:2 (2017), pp. 309–17.
Rolston, Bill, 'Ambushed by Memory: Post-Conflict Popular Memorialisation in Northern Ireland', *International Journal of Transitional Justice* 14:2 (2020), pp. 320–39.
Rolston, Bill, *Children of the Revolution: The Lives of Sons and Daughters of Activists in Northern Ireland* (Derry: Guildhall Press, 2011).
Roper, Michael, 'Re-Remembering the Soldier Hero: The Psychic and Social Construction of Memory in Personal Narratives of the Great War', *History Workshop Journal* 50:1 (2000), pp. 181–204.
Roulston, Stephen, and Ulf Hansson, 'Kicking the Can down the Road? Educational Solutions to the Challenges of Divided Societies: A Northern Ireland Case Study', *Discourse: Studies in the Cultural Politics of Education* 42:2 (2021), pp. 170–83.
Samuel, Raphael, *Theatres of Memory: Past and Present in Contemporary Culture* (London: Verso, 2012).
Schor, Naomi, '*Cartes Postales*: Representing Paris 1900', *Critical Inquiry* 18:2 (1992), pp. 188–244.

Schrader, Stuart, 'Rank-and-File Antiracism: Historicizing Punk and Rock Against Racism', *Radical History Review* 138 (2020), pp. 131–43.

Scott, David, 'The Temporality of Generations: Dialogue, Tradition, Criticism', *New Literary History* 45:2 (2014), pp. 157–81.

Shagan, Ethan Howard, 'Constructing Discord: Ideology, Propaganda, and English Responses to the Irish Rebellion of 1641', *Journal of British Studies* 36:1 (1997), pp. 4–34.

Sheftel, Anna, '"Monument to the International Community, from the Grateful Citizens of Sarajevo": Dark Humour as Counter-Memory in Post-Conflict Bosnia–Herzegovina', *Memory Studies* 5:2 (2011), pp. 145–64.

Sheldon, Sally, *et al.*, '"Too Much, Too Indigestible, Too Fast"? The Decades of Struggle for Abortion Law Reform in Northern Ireland', *Modern Law Review* 83:4 (2020), pp. 761–96.

Shirlow, Peter, 'Ethno–Sectarianism and the Reproduction of Fear in Belfast', *Capital & Class* 27:2 (2003), pp. 77–93.

Sivanandan, Ambalavaner, *Catching History on the Wing: Race, Culture and Globalisation* (London: Pluto Press, 2008).

Spit Records, www.spitrecords.co.uk (accessed 30 September 2020).

Stapleton, Karyn, and John Wilson, 'Conflicting Categories? Women, Conflict and Identity in Northern Ireland', *Ethnic and Racial Studies* 37:11 (2014), pp. 2071–91.

Street, John, Matthew Worley and David Wilkinson, '"Does It Threaten the Status Quo?" Elite Responses to British Punk, 1976–1978', *Popular Music* 37:2 (2018), pp. 271–89.

Sullivan, Richard, and Terri Hooley, *Hooleygan: Music, Mayhem, Good Vibrations* (Belfast: Blackstaff Press, 2010).

Summerfield, Penny, 'Culture and Composure: Creating Narratives of the Gendered Self in Oral History Interviews', *Cultural and Social History* 1:1 (2004), pp. 65–93.

Summerfield, Penny, *Reconstructing Women's Wartime Lives: Discourse and Subjectivity in Oral Histories of the Second World War* (Manchester: Manchester University Press, 1998).

The Joseph Rowntree Foundation, *Poverty in Northern Ireland* (York: Joseph Rowntree Foundation, 2018).

Thomson, Alistair, *Anzac Memories: Living With the Legend* (Oxford: Oxford University Press, 1994).

Tilly, Charles, *Stories, Identity, and Political Change* (Oxford: Rowman and Littlefield, 2002).

Todd, Selina, 'Class, Experience and Britain's Twentieth Century', *Social History* 39:4 (2014), pp. 489–508.

Tonge, Jonathan, and Jocelyn Evans, 'Northern Ireland: Double Triumph for the Democratic Unionist Party', *Parliamentary Affairs* 71:1 (2018), pp. 139–54.

Tonkiss, Fran, 'The Ethics of Indifference: Community and Solitude in the City', *International Journal of Cultural Studies* 6:3 (2003), pp. 297–311.

Travers, Stephen, and Neil Fetherstonhaugh, *The Miami Showband Massacre: A Survivor's Search for the Truth* (London: Hodder Headline, 2007).

Ultach, *Orange Terror: The Partition of Ireland* (Dublin: The Capuchin Annual, 1943).

Wallace, Rachel, 'Gay Life and Liberation, a Photographic Record of 1970s Belfast: Exhibiting Private Photographs and Oral Histories', *Public Historian* 41:2 (2019), pp. 144–62.

Weight, Richard, *Mod: A Very British Style* (London: Bodley Head, 2013).

Wetherall, Sam, *Foundations: How the Built Environment Made Twentieth-Century Britain* (Princeton, NJ: Princeton University Press, 2020).

Wiedenhoft Murphy, Wendy Ann, 'Touring the Troubles in West Belfast: Building Peace or Reproducing Conflict?', *Peace & Change* 35:4 (2010), pp. 537–60.

Wiener, Ron, *The Rape and Plunder of the Shankill – Community Action: The Belfast experience* (Belfast: Farset Co-operative Press, 1980).

Wilkinson, David, *Post-Punk, Politics and Pleasure in Britain* (Basingstoke: Palgrave Macmillan, 2016).

Wilkinson, David, Matthew Worley and John Street, '"I Wanna See Some History": Recent Writing on British Punk', *Contemporary European History* 26:2 (2017), pp. 397–411.

Williams, Raymond, *Marxism and Literature* (Oxford: Oxford University Press, 1977).

Williams, Raymond, *The Long Revolution* (London: Pelican, 1965).

Willis, Paul, *Learning to Labour: How Working-Class Kids get Working-Class Jobs* (Farnham: Ashgate, 2000).

Withers, Deborah, 'Re-Enacting Process: Temporality, Historicity and the Women's Liberation Music Archive', *International Journal of Heritage Studies* 20:7–8 (2014), pp. 688–701.

Wolffe, John (ed.), *Irish Religious Conflict in Comparative Perspective: Catholics, Protestants and Muslims* (London: Palgrave Macmillan, 2014).

Worley, Matt, *No Future: Punk, Politics and British Youth Culture, 1976–84* (Cambridge: Cambridge University Press, 2017).

Young, Hilary, 'Hard Man, New Man: Re/Composing Masculinities in Glasgow, *c.*1950–2000', *Oral History* 35:1 (2007), pp. 71–81.

Ziggy, 'The Story So Far', *Alternative Ulster* (34) (Belfast: Just Books, 1977).

Index

Abrams, Lynn 67–69
  See also epiphanic moments
A Centre, the 6, 95–96
Affect 81, 91–2, 98, 122, 132
  see also structures of feeling
Ahmed, Sara 98
Alternative Ulster (zine) 5, 12, 20, 27
anecdote 76–8, 108, 116–19, 153–54

Bell, Desmond 21, 144, 170
Benjamin, Walter 162
Burntollet Bridge incident 19
Burton, Frank 22

Campt, Tina 170–71
Cleary, Joe 15
composure 8, 56–57, 68–69, 73, 80, 94, 100, 122, 132
  and discomposure 85, 123
Coon, Caroline 3–4
Cunningham, Tim 24

Davis, John T. 6
  Shellshock Rock (film) 39–41
Dawson, Graham 8, 56–57
Democratic Unionist Party, the 36–37, 125, 169
Dungannon 66, 76

education 23, 26–27, 68–70, 129–30, 143–48
  see also segregation

Elliot, Marianne 14, 20
epiphanic moments 67–70, 78, 85, 94, 97–99, 131, 142, 148–49, 155

fashion and clothing 4, 71–75, 83, 133–35, 116, 147
Fields, Rona 46
Ford, Laura Oldfield 52

gender 73–4, 118, 122–29, 132
Giro's
  See Warzone Collective, the
Glassie, Henry 158–60
Good Vibrations (film) 43–47, 54, 84, 121, 148, 155–58
Good Vibrations (record shop and label) 5–6, 95, 134, 155
  see also Terri Hooley

Harp Bar, the 6, 11, 53–54, 93, 119–20, 149–501
Hebidge, Dick 147
Hooley, Terri 36–37, 120, 134
  Hooleygan 48–49
Hoggart, Richard 145

intersubjectivity 7, 119, 121–22, 131–34
It Makes You Want To Spit 40–43, 141, 149

James, Daniel 78
  see also anecdote

Jules Nightclub 132–33
Just Books 5, 96

Kelly, Aaron 52
Khun, Annette 162
Kirkland, Richard 44, 47

Lagan College 130
   see also education

Magennis, Caroline 47
McCann, Eamonn 111
McCloone, Martin 47, 49
McDonald, Henry 40, 49–52
McGovern, Mark 53, 70
memory 2, 8, 65, 37–38, 43–44,
   73–75, 55–57, 106–8, 154,
   156–57
   intergenerational connections
   83–86, 121–22, 134, 162
Miami Showband Massacre, the
   84–87
migration 137–38
Mitchell, Claire 22

Nash, Catherine 42, 160–61
neoliberalism 36–37, 101–2
nostalgia 38, 103

O'Connell, Sean 122
O'Neill, Terence 17–18

Paisley, Ian 66, 125–26, 133
partition 14–15
Passerini, Luisa 57, 106, 145–46
Peel, John 4, 54, 82
Popular Memory Group, the 29,
   55–57
Portelli, Alessandro 1, 7–8, 57,
   154
Pound, the 6, 96
Powell, Enoch 112
Provision Irish Republican Army,
   the 119, 160

Robinson, Lucy 37
Rock Against Racism 104–5
Royal Ulster Constabulary, the 4,
   80–81, 117–18

Samuel, Raphael 156
sectarianism 4, 8, 11, 15, 21, 47,
   105–6, 143–44, 150–52,
   168–70
   discrimination 16, 66
segregation 12, 17–18, 25, 70–72,
   76–77, 119–20, 143–44
sexuality 70–72, 85–86, 106–8,
   124–27
sociality 67, 146–47, 149–50,
   163–64
structures of feeling 27–8, 67,
   83–86, 106, 109, 137,
   163–64, 171
Summerfield, Penny 43

Tartan Gangs 143–44
temporality 38, 51–52, 83–85,
   102–3, 128, 149, 162–63
Thomson, Alistair 43
transgression 69–70, 73–75, 78,
   81, 106–108
Trident, the 117, 126

Ulster Defence Association, the
   108
Ulster Defence Regiment, the 135
Ulster Hall, the 147, 149, 152–53
   Battle of Bedford Street 2–3, 75
urban redevelopment 24–26,
   51–55
   see also neoliberalism

Warzone Collective, the 6, 99–102
Wilkinson, David 28–29, 101,
   126
Williams, Raymond 9
   See also structures of feeling
Worley, Matt 28–29

EU authorised representative for GPSR:
Easy Access System Europe, Mustamäe tee 50,
10621 Tallinn, Estonia
gpsr.requests@easproject.com

www.ingramcontent.com/pod-product-compliance
Lightning Source LLC
Chambersburg PA
CBHW070357240426
43671CB00013BA/2537